How I Saw It

Analysis and Commentary on
Environmental Finance
(1999–2005)

How I Saw It

Analysis and Commentary on
Environmental Finance
(1999–2005)

Richard L. Sandor

Environmental Financial Products, LLC, USA
& University of Chicago Law School, USA

World Scientific

NEW JERSEY · LONDON · SINGAPORE · BEIJING · SHANGHAI · HONG KONG · TAIPEI · CHENNAI · TOKYO

Published by

World Scientific Publishing Co. Pte. Ltd.

5 Toh Tuck Link, Singapore 596224

USA office: 27 Warren Street, Suite 401-402, Hackensack, NJ 07601

UK office: 57 Shelton Street, Covent Garden, London WC2H 9HE

Library of Congress Cataloging-in-Publication Data

Names: Sandor, Richard L., author.

Title: How i saw it : analysis and commentary on environmental finance (1999–2005) /
   Richard L Sandor, Environmental Financial Products, LLC, USA &
   University of Chicago Law School, USA.

Description: New Jersey : World Scientific, [2016] | Includes bibliographical references and index.

Identifiers: LCCN 2016047376 | ISBN 9789813202641 (hardback : alk. paper)

Subjects: LCSH: Finance--Environmental aspects. | Environmental economics.

Classification: LCC HG101 .S26 2016 | DDC 333.7--dc23

LC record available at https://lccn.loc.gov/2016047376

British Library Cataloguing-in-Publication Data

A catalogue record for this book is available from the British Library.

Desk Editor: Philly Lim

Typeset by Stallion Press
Email: enquiries@stallionpress.com

Printed in Singapore

Dedication

This book is dedicated to my wife Ellen, my children Julie (and her husband Jack Ludden) and Penya (and her husband Eric Taub), and my grandchildren Caleb Sandor Taub, Oscar Sandor Taub, Elijah Sandor Ludden and Justine Sandor Ludden for their support throughout this journey.

To my friends and mentors Les Rosenthal and T. Bruce Birkenhead.

To my friends and mentors who are no longer with us: Jacob Schmookler, David Alhadeff, Charlie O. Finley and Ronald Coase.

In memory of friends and mentors who were recently lost: Jon Goldstein and Maurice Strong.

Praises for *How I Saw It*

This book is a must-read for all who want to understand the history of environmental finance. Richard Sandor is a true champion for the planet whose provocative thought catalyzed the development of carbon markets across the world and has played an invaluable role in addressing the biggest challenges facing humanity today.

Dr. Andrew Steer, President and CEO, World Resources Institute

Richard Sandor is both a visionary and a pioneer in inventing and effectively implementing pragmatic and efficient mechanisms that have proven to enable to address one of the world most pressing issue: capturing externalities to lead to decouple growth and the use of our natural resources. This is how we will reconcile the economy and our natural capital.

Laurent Auguste, Senior EVP, Innovation & Markets, Veolia

From his experience at center stage of early environmental markets, Richard Sandor presents a living history of an important era of innovation. He played a central role in jump starting the US acid rain market's auctions, and he built the largest exchange for Europe's carbon market. These essays offer a valuable chronical of an entrepreneur's response to the enabling policies and market challenges of the time. Aspiring entrepreneurs will find his optimism and entrepreneurial zeal infectious.

Dirk Forrister, President and Chief Executive Officer, International Emissions Trading Association

Foreword

How often can you glimpse into the mind of a person who makes history? The book you are holding now is a snapshot of a decade in which Richard Sandor transformed environmental action from advocacy to finance. Advocacy matters, and Richard has done a lot of it, as the chapters here show. But finance is the lifeblood of the institutions driving climate change. Richard helped create the movement now seeking to move trillions from harm to healing.

Richard Sandor is one of the smartest men I know. Also one of the most creative. He tackles some of the gnarliest challenges facing humanity using such improbable tools as business, markets, and financial innovation. In the process, he recruits unlikely armies like Wall St traders to solve problems, makes lots of money and have a great time doing it. Recognized by the City of Chicago as "the Father of Financial Futures", he has also been honored by *TIME* magazine as a "Hero of the Planet", for creating the concept of making a market in pollution that is not emitted.

Environmentalists historically litigated, lobbied, and legislated. And the modern environmental movement is responsible for saving wild areas, species, and some semblance of quality of life. But the biggest challenges facing humanity are worsening. Left unchecked, climate change could end life as we know it on earth.

In 1997, the nations of the world gathered in Kyoto for the third of what have become endless meetings of the Conference of Parties to the global agreement to limit carbon emissions. Yes, as early as 1992 when UN member states framed the agreement, we knew that excessive releases of CO_2 and other greenhouse gases were threatening the climate. (Actually we knew it a long time before, but had then gotten around to doing something about it.) In Kyoto many of us argued for using the trading approach that Richard had created back in the 1980s to help solve acid rain. Written into the 1990 Clean Air Act, it has been cutting sulfur emissions cheaply and effectively ever since. We knew it could do the same for greenhouse gases. After days of wrangling, delegates finally agreed, and the Kyoto Protocol called for the creation of a carbon emission trading regime.

I remember partying on the plane flying home: many of the world's greatest climate scientists, government officials, environmentalists were jubilant: We'd done it! We'd achieved an international agreement to implement the mechanism that would let companies smarter about cutting their emissions win twice: to save on the energy they didn't have to buy and burn, and to sell these reductions to companies stupider, slower, less innovative — which in turn incentivizes those companies to start cutting their emissions.

Then the US Senate said "NO".

Damn. What's it gonna take?

Richard wasted no time. He said, "wait a minute, governments don't make markets, traders do. I'm a trader, let's create a market". And Chicago Climate Exchange (CCX) was born. Richard and his team signed up companies, dozens of them, to commit to cut their carbon emissions at least 2% a year. If they cut even more, they created tradable emissions reduction credits that they could then sell to offset emissions caused by people like me, who, because we fly all over everywhere, are responsible for global warming we can't eliminate by efficiency, alone. My little nongovernmental organization (NGO), Natural Capitalism Solutions, as one of CCX's first members, was able to offset all of our emissions. Yes, I'd fixed up our 100-year-old farmhouse office, installed more efficient lightbulbs, a more efficient boiler, bought a Leaf, installed solar on my ranch — all the measures we should all do. But I was proud to be a member and to be a small part of the success profiled in this book.

Richard used CCX to innovate. I was giving a speech on climate protection in 2003 in southern Iowa. A representative of the Iowa Farm Bureau stood up and admitted that he wasn't all that sure that climate change was real, but his farmers were now getting paid to switch to organic agriculture by this "Climate Exchange" up in Chicago, so he was all in favor of getting involved in what I was saying. And that matters: as the recent Rodale Institute report, "Regenerative Organic Agriculture and Climate Change: A Down-to-Earth Solution to Global Warming", shows "We could sequester more than 100% of current annual CO_2 emissions with a switch to widely available and inexpensive organic management practices, which we term "regenerative organic agriculture". CCX was the first group to give carbon credits to farmers switching to organic agriculture. CCX was also the first carbon market to create protocols for regenerative grazing, which may turn out to be the approach to taking carbon from the air and returning it to the soil that saves humanity from climate chaos.

This book ends in 2005, but both time and Richard march on. A few years ago the phone rang. It was Richard. "I'm going to China", he chortled. "Think about it. . .". And hung up.

Huh? What?! Why would Richard go to China. . .?

Ah, it dawned on me: he's creating a carbon market in China.

China now has seven pilot markets, which when they combine in 2017 will be the world's largest effort to curtail one of the worst threats to human survival.

This is the story of how it all began.

Hunter Lovins
June 2016

Acknowledgments

Many thanks to Graham Cooper for the invitation to share our thoughts with the readers of *Environmental Finance* magazine.

The six years of writing the *Environmental Finance* column corresponded to the formative years of the Chicago Climate Exchange (CCX). The help of the CCX staff during these busy times was critical. They acted as reviewers, honest critics and provided valued intellectual input. Special thanks to Michael J. Walsh, Murali Kanakasabai, Claire Jahns, and Rafael Marques for their ongoing assistance with the articles.

We also owe a big debt of gratitude to all the members and advisors of the Chicago Climate Exchange who supported us throughout the creation and launch of this market. Special mention to the Board of Directors of CCX (Maurice Strong, Les Rosenthal, Clayton Yeutter, Warren Batts, Gov. Christine Todd Whitman, Gov. James R. Thompson, Dale Heydlauff, Bruce Braine, Carlton Charles, Martin Zimmerman, Sue Cischke) and Climate Exchange plc (Neil Eckert, the Hon. Carole Brookins, Sir Brian Williamson, Sir Laurie Magnus, Klaus Gierstner and Matthew Whittell) for their guidance and support. Many thanks also to Ken Raisler of Sullivan & Cromwell for his early involvement with CCX.

Several individuals from business, NGOs and academia provided their time and expertise to many of the articles. To all of them mentioned in these pages, my sincere appreciation.

Our joint venture with the China National Petroleum Corporation to establish the Tianjin Climate Exchange (TCX) would not have been possible with the vision and leadership of Dr. Dai Xiansheng. To him, my sincere appreciation.

My deep gratitude to Paula DiPerna and Jeff Huang. In her role as Head of International Outreach and Public Policy for CCX, Paula made the China project a reality. Jeff Huang, the local CCX representative, was critical to process and guided us all through the establishment of TCX.

Thank you to Hunter Lovins, for agreeing to write the foreword. She was an early believer in our ideas, and we value her support and input.

Special mention to John Lothian and Jim Kharouf. Just like Environmental Finance magazine, they were early proponents of an electronic newsletter to cover the convergence of environment and finance. The newsletter is still going and successful.

World Scientific's editorial staff — Max Phua, Philly Lim, and their staff — were terrific. We very much appreciate their hard work and attention to detail. Meaghan Lidd was critical to the process. She provided enormous help with the design, layout and review of the manuscript.

About the Author

Richard L. Sandor (PhD) is Chairman and CEO of the American Financial Exchange, an electronic marketplace for small and mid-sized banks to lend and borrow short-term funds. He is also the CEO of Environmental Financial Products (EFP), which specializes in inventing, designing and developing new financial markets. EFP was established in 1998 and was the predecessor company and incubator to the Chicago Climate Exchange (CCX), the European Climate Exchange (ECX), the Chicago Climate Futures Exchange (CCFE) and the Tianjin Climate Exchange (TCX). Dr. Sandor is currently the Aaron Director Lecturer in Law and Economics at the University of Chicago Law School and a Visiting Fellow with the Smith School of Enterprise and the Environment at Oxford University. He was honored by the City of Chicago for his universal recognition as the "father of financial futures". In 2002, he was named by TIME Magazine a "Hero of the Planet"; and in 2007 as one of the magazine's "Heroes of the Environment" for his work as the "Father of Carbon Trading." In October 2013, Dr. Sandor was awarded the title of Chevalier dans l'ordre de la Légion d'Honneur (Knight in the French National Order of the

Legion of Honor), for his accomplishments in the field of environmental finance and carbon trading. He holds an honorary degree of Doctor of Science, honoris causa, from the Swiss Federal Institute of Technology (ETH). Dr. Sandor is a Member of the Advisory Board of the Center for Financial Stability and the Smithsonian Tropical Research Institute; and a Senior Fellow of the Milken Institute. He served on the board of directors of leading commodity and futures exchanges in the United States and Europe. Dr Sandor is the author of "Good Derivatives: A Story of Financial and Environmental Innovation," also published in Chinese by People's Oriental Press; and the lead author of "Sustainable Investing and Environmental Markets: Opportunities in a New Asset Class" (published by World Scientific).

Contents

Introduction

Paris, the "City of Lights", is known for an endless list of things — art, culture, food, philosophy, fashion, and science to name a few.

However, in the environmental world it has achieved a new renown. It was the birthplace in 2015 of the Paris Agreement — an international agreement in which 197 nations achieved a consensus on the next steps to fight climate change. This was the greatest milestone since the Kyoto Protocol in 1997.

A lot of other significant events took place during those 18 years. In 2003, the Europeans chose to use a market-based mechanism (known as "cap-and-trade") as a means to achieve the goals set out in the Kyoto Protocol. After a short pilot program, the European Union emissions trading system (EU ETS) was launched in 2008. In the United States, the northeastern states formed the Regional Greenhouse Gas Initiative (RGGI) and California launched their own emissions trading program. China launched seven pilot emissions trading programs. But preceding the establishment of these markets, less visible actions have to take place. One of those is educating professionals. This is about one of those lesser events.

From 1999 to 2005, I had the privilege of writing a monthly column for *Environmental Finance* magazine. I was invited to contribute and was thrilled to do so. The title of the publication also had special meaning to me. It was the same title of the course I taught at Columbia University's Graduate School of Business in 1991.

The publisher had the vision to start the publication at a time when environmental markets were still in their infancy. The only established "cap-and-trade" program in the world was the United

States Acid Rain program, which was administered by the Environmental Protection Agency. That program was about to complete its first decade since the Clean Air Act (which enabled it) was passed. Despite the fact there was price information coming from the auctions, there was still much doubt if it could effectively lower acid rain pollution in the United States. And there was also much disbelief that such a regional program could ever be expanded to include carbon, much less applied in other parts of the world. There were some bright spots in some emerging fields such as the link between sustainability and finance, but in general, environmental finance was still viewed with skepticism.

As an academic and financial innovator, I firmly believe you have to educate continuously. New markets need education in various levels — academic, trading, accounting, legal, to name a few — so that market institutions can be built and human capital can be created. The press plays a critical role and it was important to get the message out through the columns.

In these six years of writing for the magazine, I felt that we had to cover three main areas. One was to showcase what was going well in environmental markets. The other was to make predictions about what markets were coming next (water quality and quantity) and what trends to look out for; finally, to narrate our progress with the development of the Chicago Climate Exchange (CCX).

In the first area, we covered the development of the Dow Jones Sustainability Index (DJSI). The index was a novel way to look at sustainability. It helped prove the concept that environmental stewardship and stock performance could be connected. It proved a boost for ways to better measure sustainable performance. It spun imitators and led to greater transparency in the tools that investors, shareholders, and the public had to track the environmental performance of companies.

We also wrote several article on the progress of the Acid Rain program in the United States. It was important to that the readers had knowledge of how this program was evolving and what the auctions were telling us in terms of price information, market maturity, and environmental improvements. The success of the program is renowned. -Lower emissions of sulfur dioxide achieved at a fraction of the predicted costs, with the virtual disappearance of the acid rain problem in the Unites States. This is still to this date the most successful cap-and-trade program in the world.

The next set of articles deals with the theme of policy predictions. In the case of the Acid Rain program, we didn't envision that 10 years later, the US government would create such policy uncertainty that brought this successful cap-and-trade program to a halt. In an ironical twist, the United States has virtually been forgotten as the birthplace of emissions trading.

We were very positive about Europe. As policymakers contemplated the establishment of a cap-and-trade program for the European Union, we used our column to show our support for this new market. It was important to encourage this effort, and to show that initial setbacks should not be a deterrent. Markets take time to evolve, and they require patience.

In the immediate aftermath of the signing of the Kyoto Protocol, we also predicted that the world would not see an instant multilateral trading system for carbon. Quite the contrary, we took the view that such a system would take decades to evolve, and for many years to come it would most likely take the form of a "plurilateral" system, centered in a few regions and countries clustered around North America, Europe, and Asia. In Asia, we were always a strong a believer that both China and India would take earlier steps to implement national "cap-and-trade" systems, but most people dismissed our predictions. In 2017, China has announced that it intends to start a national program.

The column was also a space to advocate measures that could lower transaction costs and facilitate trading. One example was our support for offsets was a big belief of ours. We pushed for greater use of agricultural soil sequestration and forests in trading program worldwide. To us, there was no reason why policymakers shouldn't make widespread use of as many tools as were available with the intention of reducing emissions.

Finally, we kept our readers informed on the progress and challenges of designing and launching CCX. The concept of creating a voluntary exchange for reducing and trading emissions was new and the education of potential participants and policymakers was critical. CCX also showcased all of the things we discussed so far — the importance of starting simple and prove the concept; the ability to replicate the model; our belief in a "bottom-up" approach of developing markets (educating participants and creating the institutions needed for the market to develop); and to utilize as many tools as possible that could assist in tackling this important social issue.

We hope that almost 20 years from when it first started, this collection of articles could prove useful to the same group of readers — students of markets, policy makers, and those interested in using markets to address pressing environmental and health issues. The challenges and "to do lists" continue to be the same — only the problems or the locations might have changed. When we first started writing the column, many people believe that it was not feasible to implement a carbon market. Today, China is about to start one and carbon markets have become a reality in many places. As a matter of fact, more people tend to think that markets, if properly designed and regulated, can play a critical role in solving environmental issues. In some cases, some of the progress we had anticipated was slower to take place than we thought. In others, we believe that in some small fashion we helped to set the stage for changes that are still taking place. We hope that that the reader finds enough of a roadmap in these pages.

Richard L. Sandor
July 2016

Chapter 1

Environmental Finance Introductory Remarks

October 1999

We are delighted to introduce the first of a monthly series of articles by Richard Sandor exploring the growing use of capital markets products to solve environmental problems. Few people are better placed to comment on this important trend. Best known as "the Father of Financial Futures" for his pioneering work on interest rate futures contracts, Dr. Sandor is currently chairman and chief executive of Environmental Financial Products, a Chicago-based company which designs novel risk management tools for the environmental, financial, and commodity markets. He is also a senior advisor to PricewaterhouseCoopers on greenhouse gas emissions trading; an expert advisor to the United Nations Conference on Trade and Development on tradeable permits for greenhouse gases; a director of Zurich-based investment and risk management company Sustainable Performance Group; a principal of SAM Sustainability Group and a member of the board of Dow Jones Sustainability Group Indexes GmbH. During several years' work with the Chicago Board of Trade, he was instrumental in developing the exchange's annual auction of sulfur dioxide allowances and its options and futures contracts for catastrophe insurance.

1

Chapter 2

The Convergence of Environmental and Capital Markets

October 1999

Two facets of the convergence of environmental and capital markets became visible in September 1999 as final preparations were being made for the Conference of Parties (COP) 5 climate change meetings in Bonn.

The early news from the markets is good. The cost of reducing greenhouse gases is less than early forecasts and corporations that are sustainable yield superior value to shareholders.

In London, British Petroleum reported on the success of its pilot program in greenhouse gas emissions trading and announced its plan to expand to group-wide emissions trading in January 2000.

In Zurich and Chicago, Dow Jones and the Sustainable Asset Management (SAM) Sustainability Group announced the launch of a family of comprehensive stock indexes — the Dow Jones Sustainability Group Index (DJSGI) — that track the share prices of the leading companies that have a proven record of being financially, socially, and environmentally sustainable. The selected companies represented in the new indexes demonstrate a real commitment to reducing pollution and safeguarding human and natural resources.

In 1998 British Petroleum — a component of DJSGI — announced that it would voluntarily reduce its greenhouse gas emissions to 10% below 1990 levels by the year 2010. It began a

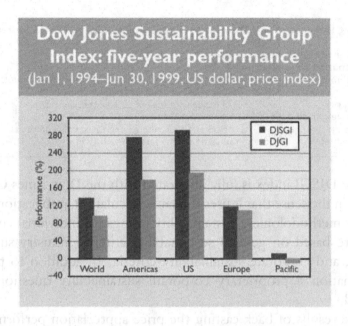

pilot emissions trading program to accomplish this objective in the most cost effective way. Twelve business units initially participated. The cost of reducing a ton of carbon emissions in early trades was approximately $63–$70 ($17–$20/ton CO_2). Although the initial prices should be viewed cautiously, they are significantly below some early forecasts of $200/ton. Furthermore, the expansion to group wide emissions trading and the inclusion of credit-based trading (e.g., net emission reductions associated with external investments in energy efficiency and carbon sequestration) should witness a further reduction in costs associated with meeting the corporate targets. It is important to emphasize that British Petroleum extended its commitment when it acquired two US companies, Amoco and Arco.

The comprehensive sustainable stock index family includes an index with global coverage, the DJSGI World, as well as regional indexes focused on companies in Europe, North America, Asia-Pacific, and a country index — DJSGI USA.

The table shows salient features of the global DJSGI index.

Salient features of the Dow Jones Sustainability Group World Index	
Number of companies:	229
Total market capitalisation:	$4.3 trillion
Selection criteria:	Dow Jones Global Index companies scoring in the top 10% of SAM sustainability index
Coverage:	73 major industries in 22 countries, best-of-class selection
Share weighting process:	market capitalisation
Currency:	prices and total returns expressed in US dollars and euros
Base value:	set at 1,000 on December 31, 1998

The DJSGI index is fully integrated with the Dow Jones Global Index in the sense that it uses the same calculation, publication, and review methodologies. Sustainability ratings for individual companies are based on general sustainability criteria, industry sustainability, and corporate sustainability criteria. In addition to public information a proprietary corporate sustainability questionnaire is used.

The results of back casting the price appreciation performance of the indexes are very instructive. As shown in the chart, in all instances the sustainable indexes outperformed the standard Dow Jones index. Furthermore, these superior returns were realized with minimal increases in volatility (risk) relative to comparable indexes. Evidence from the markets shows that sustainability and maximization of shareholder value are entirely compatible.

Both these examples of the convergence of the environmental and financial markets provide interesting price signals. The cost of reducing greenhouse gas emissions appears to be lower than many predicted and corporations that cut pollution and manage for sustainability will increase value to their shareholders.

Special thanks to Dr. Alois Flatz, Dr. Michael Walsh, and Rafael Marques for their valuable input.

Chapter 3

Voluntary Carbon Deals Break Records

November 1999

Since the 1997 Kyoto Protocol to the Rio Climate Convention, Washington legislators have spoken about global warming and its policy cousin emissions trading — like old soldiers vaguely remembering a defeated enemy in a long-passed military conflict.

However, this month in the capital markets and in a few cities in North America, the dialogue has become vivid and more animated, with the completion of two of the largest greenhouse gas emission trades in history.

Currently, there is no central market for greenhouse gas emissions, and historical trades have not disclosed all of the transaction details.[1] It appears that since the 1992 Rio Earth Summit, there have been almost 20 trades involving over 10 million tons of carbon dioxide (CO_2)-equivalent emission reductions. It should be noted that many of these transactions involved options for future purchase of reductions rather than a full-fledged spot or future sale.

---

[1] Emission "credits" are generally earned for reductions below a reference emissions level or rate. An emission "allowance", as in the case of the US sulfur dioxide trading program, refers to the officially sanctioned permission to emit a unit of the regulated pollutant. The regulator distributes allowances for use in compliance and trading. The term "CO_2 emission offsets" is generally used to describe reductions or sequestration that occur outside of the polluting entity. In particular, this often refers to carbon sequestered in biomass or soils. The terms "emissions" and "emission reductions" are used to describe the transactions of the emerging market for greenhouse gas emissions because greenhouse gases are not yet regulated.

The transaction volume in November 1999 reached a total of more than 5 million tons of CO_2 equivalent reductions, equal to the emissions of 1 million cars for 1 year. This volume of trading is small relative to the capital markets and is based on voluntary commitments. Nonetheless, these two transactions are sending a strong signal that the private sector is building the required infrastructure for full-blown markets. An examination of one of the transactions can help demystify the mechanics of an environmental derivatives trade as well as the motivations of the participants.

On 26 October 1999, the Wall Street Journal reported that Ontario Power Generation had purchased emissions reductions of 2.5 million tons of CO_2-equivalent from Zahren Alternative Power Corporation (ZAPCO), a developer of landfill methane collection systems. The reductions were, or will be, generated in the years 1998, 1999, and 2000.

The trade is significant for several reasons:

- It is the largest spot greenhouse gas emissions trade in history.
- The participants are a Canadian buyer and a US seller, thereby making it international.
- The reductions have and will be registered by the US Department of Energy under the Energy Policy Act of 1992 and will also be recorded by the Canadian government under its Pilot Emission Reduction Trading Program.
- The emission reductions will be monitored twice — by ZAPCO and by the buyer of the methane gas — and independently attested to by PricewaterhouseCoopers.
- The reductions achieved were carefully selected to ensure that they are surplus to any regulatory requirements in the United States and that the transfer is legally incontestable.

Ontario Power Generation has set a voluntary, corporate target of stabilizing its greenhouse gas emissions at 1990 levels of 26 million tons of CO_2-equivalent from the year 2000 forward. The company's goal is to expand into new electricity markets while operating in a safe, open, and environmentally responsible manner. It is also committed to meeting environmental goals at the lowest cost to its customers.

Ontario Power's greenhouse gas emissions reduction pledge will be achieved through a portfolio of activities. Internal energy efficiency measures will produce a significant amount of the reductions. Alternatively, some portion of the reductions can be achieved by purchasing offsets (reductions achieved by others), where this is financially desirable and serves the purpose of stimulating this new market.

After a considerable search, ZAPCO was identified as a natural counterparty. The company's principal business is to drill wells in solid waste landfills, extract methane, and sell the methane for energy use, primarily to generate electricity. Methane is a natural byproduct of landfill waste. As a greenhouse gas, it is also chemically 21 times more potent than CO_2 in contributing to global warming. If not collected from the landfill and destroyed (burned), it will seep into the atmosphere. In this particular example, without ZAPCO's intervention, 2.5 million tons of CO_2-equivalent would have seeped into the atmosphere. This would have had the same impact on global warming as 500,000 cars operating for a year.

ZAPCO's incentive for trading is easy to understand. The sale of the emissions reductions provides a new revenue stream for its production of sustainable energy. As a result, its "return on investment" increases. ZAPCO can expand its operations, thereby cleaning additional landfills.

This trade also provides additional resources to monitor, verify, and independently attest to emissions reductions. Through these processes, we will take another critical step in the development of environmental derivatives. Defining and accurately measuring emissions reductions are prerequisites for creating a "homogenous" commodity and an effective trading system. Product standardization is essential for all of us to fully realize the gains from market-based solutions to environmental problems.

The carbon market is here – significant deals

- Niagara Mohawk-Arizona P.S. SO_2 for CO_2 Swap (1997)
- Norway purchase of carbon offsets from Costa Rica's rainforests (1997)
- Costa Rica sale of carbon offsets to Environmental Financial (1998)
- Suncor buys GHG options from Niagara Mohawk (1998)
- Waste Management sold GHG credits as options to Japanese buyer (1999)
- IGF sells soil sequestration credits to Canadian energy consortium (1999)
- Ontario Power Generation purchase of GHG emission credits from Zahren Alternative Power Corporation (1999) [arranged by Environmental Financial Products]

I would like to thank Dr. Michael Walsh, Alice LeBlanc, and Rafael Marques for their assistance in the preparation of this article.

Chapter 4

Seeing the Wood for the Trees

December 1999/January 2000

Scroll through most summaries of the Kyoto Protocol and you will notice that they all seem the same. There are discussions on the impact of climate change on weather, reports on the danger of continued reliance on fossil fuels and articles on the impact of rainforest destruction and the need to reforest our planet.

The careful student of the Protocol will quickly notice the difference between the quantitatively specified emission reductions by country and the ambiguous role of forests and soils in meeting these requirements.

For example, the treaty clearly specifies in article 3.1 that developed countries such as Japan, Germany, and the United States must achieve reductions from the 1990 baseline of 6%, 8%, and 7%, respectively during the budget period of 2008–2012. Specific gases to be controlled are identified, and the exchange rates across those gases are set.

Contrast the clarity of article 3.1 with articles 3.3 and 3.4, which deal with forestry and land use change. Article 3.3 states that "the net changes in greenhouse gas emissions by sources and removals by sinks resulting from direct human-induced land use change and forestry activities, limited to afforestation, reforestation, and deforestation since 1990, measured as verifiable changes in carbon stocks in each commitment period, shall be used to meet the commitments under this article of each party". This seems to imply that reforestation and soil sequestration could be counted in meeting the quantified mitigation objectives. However, article 3.4 states that the meeting of the parties to the Kyoto Protocol shall "decide on which additional human induced activities (besides afforestation, reforestation, and deforestation) related to changes in greenhouse gas emissions and removals by sinks in the agricultural soil and land use change and forestry categories shall be added to, or subtracted from, the assigned amount for parties included in annex 1".

There has been no clarity added by the Conference of the Parties meetings in Buenos Aires in 1998 or Bonn in 1999. All indications suggest that the special Intergovernmental Panel on Climate Change report on carbon sinks, due in May 2000, will not provide the detailed answers needed to operationalize trading in credits earned by sink enhancement. Feasible paths forward have not yet been illuminated by individual national efforts or by voluntary private sector action.

However, there is reason to believe that subsequent meetings of the Parties and other sovereign and private sector efforts will provide more structure in the next 2 years. There are four specific reasons for this optimism. First, the importance of reforestation is clear. In this case, two pictures are more valuable than a 1000 words. Maps 1 and 2 clearly indicate the potential for reforestation in both the northern and southern hemispheres. Second, just as with the reduction of emissions, it is now widely recognized that the actions that increase forest and soil carbon storage also provide a multitude of local and regional environmental benefits in addition to their climate protection benefits. Third, the Clean Development Mechanism, which allows industrialized countries to undertake mitigation projects in developing countries, is scheduled to apply to signatories in the year 2000. Therefore, individual states that establish targets for greenhouse gas emissions and specify flexible mechanisms in the next few years will need to clarify the role of forests and soil sequestration. Furthermore, voluntary activities by the private sector will

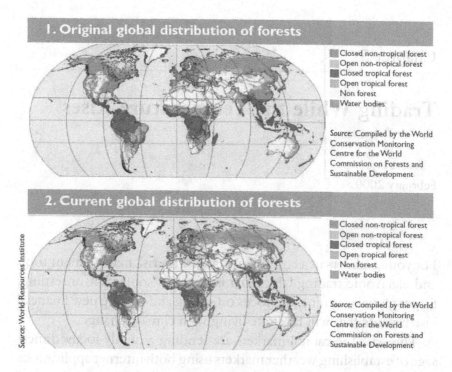

1. Original global distribution of forests

Closed non-tropical forest
Open non-tropical forest
Closed tropical forest
Open tropical forest
Non forest
Water bodies

Source: Compiled by the World Conservation Monitoring Centre for the World Commission on Forests and Sustainable Development

2. Current global distribution of forests

Closed non-tropical forest
Open non-tropical forest
Closed tropical forest
Open tropical forest
Non forest
Water bodies

Source: Compiled by the World Conservation Monitoring Centre for the World Commission on Forests and Sustainable Development

Source: World Resources Institute

cause a series of market-generated standards. The final reason for optimism is that the outcome of the international debate will ultimately be influenced by the benefits accruing to the private sector. For example, in the United States, increased carbon sequestration in forests and soils, primarily on private lands, has the potential to capture 200 million tons carbon per year, or up to one-third of the Kyoto emissions gap.

Now is the time to undertake pilot trades, incorporate sinks into voluntary trading programs, and enlist the capabilities of recognized third-party verification professionals. The historical experience with a host of other physical commodities has shown that there is no realistic alternative to the learning-by-doing approach. Governments and regulators cannot achieve their goals without guidance from real world practitioners.

Chapter 5

Trading While the Temperature Rises

February 2000

For young traders in a culture saturated with risk management tools and electronic trading, the pitch is easy but somewhat unsettling: forget global warming and focus on selling and trading new financial instruments that will facilitate living with climate change.

This year the capital markets are sending a highly focused message of establishing weather markets using both internet applications and traditional exchanges.

Weather has an impact on a wide variety of businesses around the world — from transport, agriculture, and utilities to construction and hospitality. Its inherent unpredictability and volatility drives the demand for weather risk management. Although their roots lie in agriculture and catastrophic events (such as hurricanes), weather derivatives achieved a separate identity about 3 years ago. Since their inception in 1997, the growth has been exceptional. Market participants estimate that transactions in 1999 alone were worth notional $2–3 billion.

On the organized market run by the Chicago Mercantile Exchange, 341 contracts have been traded since its launch in September last year, with the single largest trade being 50 contracts based on heating degree days (HDDs) in Atlanta. The existence of both over-the-counter and listed markets may provide an arbitrage opportunity, thereby potentially enhancing the liquidity of both.

What are weather derivatives and how are they used? Simply stated, they are risk management tools based on a variety of metrics such as temperature or precipitation. Among the most frequently used metrics are HDDs and cooling degree days (CDDs). HDDs are a measure of a day's coolness and are calculated by subtracting a day's average temperature from 65°F. For example, an average temperature of 45°F during a single day would result in a HDD of 20 (65 − 45 = 20). If the average temperature is above 65° the HDD would be zero. A CDD is a measure of a day's warmth. It is calculated by subtracting 65 from the average temperature during a day.

In the first quarter of this year alone, two online exchanges are being launched: Tradeweather and I-WeX. These will allow companies to post both bids and offers in a wide variety of derivatives including puts, calls, and collars for both HDDs and CDDs which are location specific. The site then matches the buyer with the seller. Similar transactions could obviously occur using other weather metrics such as rainfall or snowfall. In addition, the Chicago Mercantile Exchange is planning to launch additional contracts for both HDDs and CDDs in 10 US cities (Atlanta, New York, Cincinnati, Chicago, Philadelphia, Dallas, Des Moines, Las Vegas, Portland, and Tucson). It already lists some HDD contracts for Atlanta, Chicago, Cincinnati, and New York (see table).

Salient features of HDD futures	
Contract grade:	HDD for one month in Atlanta, Chicago, Cincinatti or New York
Contract size:	(HDD index) × $100
Tick size:	1.0 index points each having a value of $100.00
Contract settlement:	Cash settled to the index
Trading months:	Spot month and 11 consecutive months thereafter

How are weather derivatives used? Global warming may have totally different impacts on farmers and utilities. Farmers in the US southeast that experience extended periods of high temperatures may lose a significant portion of their crops. Agricultural futures and options and/or crop insurance may be inappropriate or unavailable for transferring all their risk. Electric utilities, on the other hand, may benefit from hot summers, which increase the demand for air conditioning. A weather derivative might provide a win-win situation for both counterparties.

Pricing associated with weather events may require a historical database as well as the ability to run simulations. But the recent string of record warm temperatures experienced in many locations reminds us that excessive reliance on historical weather data may cause mispricing of these novel instruments. Global warming may already be changing the nature of this important new market.

A number of analytical services have already emerged to service this new market.

A final measure of the maturity of the weather derivatives market was the issuance of a weather-linked bond by Koch Industries (Environmental Finance, November 1999). Goldman Sachs underwrote the $50 million issuance of a bond, for which interest and principal

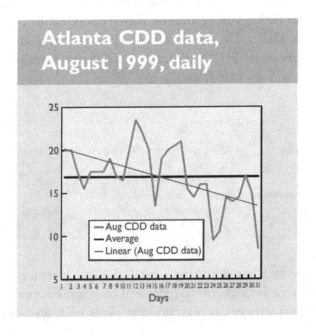

Atlanta CDD data, August 1999, daily

is dependent on a portfolio of 28 separate weather risks. The securitization of this market follows the pattern established by insurance derivatives. A repeat of that experience suggests that securitization could grow into a market in excess of $10 billion outstanding within a reasonable period of time.

Capital markets are providing new risk management tools, which provide temporary hedges in the face of climate change. The spirit of innovation will help economic entities to temporarily hedge against adverse movements in price and profits associated with global warming. But it is important to emphasize that these tools only minimize collateral damage of global warming in the short run. They are not long-range solutions for the environment.

I would like to thank Dr. Michael Walsh, Cody Burke, and Tradeweather.com for their assistance in the preparation of this article.

Chapter 6

DaimlerChrysler, Ford Change Lanes

March 2000

Bolstering a trend that would have been unbelievable in the pre-Kyoto era, both Ford and DaimlerChrysler have recently announced their decision to leave the Global Climate Coalition. This coalition is a group of companies that believes that the science of global warming is uncertain and opposes international agreements to reduce emissions of greenhouse gases (GHGs). Ford, one of the largest and most powerful multinational corporations, became the first American car maker to announce its controversial departure (see Chapter 4 "Seeing the Wood for the Trees", December 1999/January 2000). This followed the earlier departure of a group of other large companies including American Electric Power, Dow Chemical, and Royal Dutch/Shell.

It is important to emphasize that Ford will continue to support "voluntary" efforts to deal with climate change. Its opinions will almost certainly be part of the debate that is likely to emerge when Bob Smith (Republican — New Hampshire), chairman of the Senate Environment and Public Works Committee, reintroduces legislation to create incentives for companies that voluntarily reduce GHG emissions. It is also likely that the debate will continue at the state level if Senator Byron Sher (Democrat — Palo Alto) of the California legislature introduces a bill that would limit statewide GHG emissions.

Two obvious questions emerge:

- Why are the departures of Ford and DaimlerChrysler important?
- What is the role of state and national legislation in promoting voluntary actions in the debate surrounding global climate change?

These departures could serve as a precursor to Ford and Daimler-Chrysler executing individual trades in GHG credits, making investments in forestry sequestration similar to those of Toyota, General Motors and Peugeot, and establishing internal trading systems similar to those of BP Amoco and Shell. State level legislation that sets ceilings on GHG emissions or national legislation providing credit for voluntary activities might serve as a precursor to the evolution of national GHG markets similar to those proposed in Canada, the UK, and Australia.

Scorecard 1 (March 2000): summary of greenhouse gas emissions trading activity

International agency initiatives	Emerging plurilateral trading groups	Initiatives for national GHG trading schemes or the CDM	Provincial, state, local programmes	Corporate initiatives and exchange activity	Examples of trading activity
World Bank Carbon Fund UNCTAD Global Policy Forum OECD Workshops & Research International Energy Agency UNEP UNDP UNIDO European Commission Nordic Council EBRD	*Umbrella Group* Japan, US, Canada, Australia, New Zealand, Iceland, Norway, Russia, Ukraine *European Union* *Scandinavia*	United States United Kingdom Canada Australia Norway Denmark Netherlands New Zealand Russia Brazil Costa Rica Central America Slovakia 32 host countries with CDM/AIJ offices or projects	*United States:* Oregon, New Jersey, California *Statement of US mayors:* Denver, Washington, DC, San Francisco, Atlanta, Chicago *Australia:* NSW, Western Australia *Canada:* PERT (Ontario) GERT (BC) Canadian Federation of Municipalities *International:* International Council of Local Environmental Initiatives	BP Amoco, Royal Dutch/Shell, Dupont, Ford Motor Co, Ontario Power, TransAlta, Suncor Energy, AES Environmental Financial Products Dutch Electricity Board (FACE Foundation) Edison Electric Institute (Utilitree) Pew (21 corporate members) World Resources Institute (3 corporate members) 180 companies report in USDoE voluntary reduction database International Climate Change Partnership International Petroleum Exchange Sydney Futures Exchange Winnipeg Commodities Exchange Chicago Board of Trade Paris Bourse Insurance Industry (Climate Pledge) Canada's Voluntary Challenge and Registry	Environmental Financial–Costa Rica Ontario Power–Zahren Alternative Power GEMCO-IGF Insurance BP Amoco–Nature Conservancy Arizona Public Service–Niagara Mohawk Suncor Energy–Niagara Mohawk Sumitomo–United Energy Systems (Russia) Pacific Power Australia–NSW Forests Tesco–Uganda forests Waste Management Inc– Enron American Electric Power–The Nature Conservancy Central & Southwest–The Nature Conservancy Illinova–US Reforestation Consorcio Noruego–Costa Rica Toyota–New South Wales Tokyo Electric Power–NSW Forests

We also believe that individual sovereign efforts will result in a voluntary plurilateral trading regime[1] in advance of the ratification

---

[1] A "plurilateral" regime refers to a framework for GHG emissions trading involving a medium-sized set of countries (e.g., 5–20). The concept was first introduced by Environmental Financial Products at the first UNCTAD GHG Emissions Trading Policy Forum in Chicago in June 1997. I would like to thank James Perkaus for first introducing this concept into the discussions while acting as a consultant to Environmental Financial Products in 1997.

of any international treaty. Markets are often the response to public opinion and potential legislation. A set of market rules and regulations are then developed in the private sector and ultimately ratified by legislation. This is the way markets have emerged in the past and will emerge in the future.

These recent developments are an unmistakable sign that market-based solutions to global warming are now emerging worldwide prior to the implementation of the Kyoto Protocol. We hope to give our readers an occasional scorecard of progress on GHG emissions trading. The first one is on the following page.

Further updates will surely include many more developments motivated by the recent declaration of hundreds of business and government leaders from around the world at the World Economic Forum's Annual Meeting in Davos, Switzerland, stating that climate change is the greatest challenge facing the business world at the beginning of the century.

I would like to thank Dr. Michael Walsh and Rafael Marques for their assistance in preparing this article.

Chapter 7

The CDM: Opportunities and Challenges

April 2000

> "Teach us to delight in the simple things"
> —Rudyard Kipling

In a stunning financial innovation that may radically alter the way developing countries and industrialized nations deal with issues of climate change, participants in the Kyoto debate crafted a project-based carbon crediting system termed the Clean Development Mechanism (CDM).

This mechanism may be critical to jumpstarting the carbon emissions markets. It also provides a vehicle for forging political consensus between the industrialized and developing countries, thereby expanding the comprehensiveness of the Kyoto Protocol. While it is still too early to assess the likely impact of the CDM, its early effective date (this year) provides an opportunity to design functional market architecture for the mechanism specifically and for emissions trading in general.

What is the CDM? Simply stated, it is a mechanism whereby developing and industrialized economies can both benefit from projects that mitigate greenhouse emissions in developing countries. "Certified emission reductions" (CERs) are created when a project causes emissions to be lower than they might have been. The projects must contribute to environmentally sustainable economic development. Emission sources in industrialized countries can use the emission reduction credits arising from those

1. Salient features of the Clean Development Mechanism	
Participation	Transactions between industrialised (Annex I) and developing countries
Timing	Certified emission reductions can be accumulated starting in 2000 for use in 2008–2012
National emission budgets	Acquisition of CERs raises the "assigned amount" (emissions budget) of the buyer
Recognised projects	Emission reduction projects; treatment of carbon sinks not yet clear
Fees	To be levied to cover CDM administrative costs and to contribute to the adaptation and assistance fund for developing countries vulnerable to climate change damage
Project approval, monitoring and verification	Participation by any country is voluntary. Monitoring protocols, and independent auditing and verification procedures are to be developed
Reporting of transfers	Registries to be established; likely to include both international and national systems

2. Summary of estimates of the potential size of the CDM			
CDM share of overall carbon market (%)	*Total CDM volume (million tons carbon)*	*Assumed market price ($/t of carbon)*	*CDM market value ($bn)*
19–57	144–723	13–37	5.2–21

Source: adapted from Grubb, Michael and Vrolijk, Christiaan, "The Potential size of the CDM", Greenhouse Gas Emissions Trader, Issue 6, February 1999

investments toward meeting their own greenhouse gas emission caps. There is increasing momentum to ensure that credits for reforestation projects are included in the CDM and it is important to emphasize that the use of the credits is not dependent on either country having developed its own emissions trading program.

The salient features of the CDM, and the associated references to the treaty, are summarized in Table 1.

Although we cannot unambiguously determine the likely size of the CDM portion of the carbon market, academics and governments have attempted to forecast its importance. Most analysts use the assumption that 1 billion tons of annual carbon mitigation will be required worldwide during the period 2008–2012. Michael Grubb and Christiaan Vrolijk of the Royal Institute of International Affairs have summarized various estimates of the possible size of the CDM (see Table 2). A model developed by Grubb and Vrolijk yields

Article 12 of the Kyoto Protocol (extracts)

"The purpose of the clean development mechanism shall be to assist Parties not included in Annex I in achieving sustainable development and in contributing to the ultimate objective of the Convention, and to assist Parties included in Annex I in achieving compliance with their quantified emission limitation and reduction commitments under Article 3.

Under the clean development mechanism:

(a) Parties not included in Annex I will benefit from project activities resulting in certified emission reductions; and

(b) Parties included in Annex I may use the certified emission reductions accruing from such project activities to contribute to compliance with part of their quantified emission limitation and reduction commitments"

estimates that are consistent with the lower end of these estimates. In summary, it appears that the CDM might generate capital flows of approximately $10 billion per year. This is a significant figure for developing countries.

The CDM is a creative financial innovation that has the potential to make a significant impact on industrialized and developing countries. However, Article 12 of the Kyoto Protocol, in which the mechanism is defined, only provides a framework for implementation. Carbon market participants now face the same challenges summarized by the quote of the day in the internet community — execution is everything — and Goethe's famous thought — the genius is in the details. It's all about execution and details.

Fees, major regulatory uncertainties and significant transaction costs could undermine this potentially powerful mechanism. It's our view that we must develop a simplified CDM process. The widespread use of a rule-based system will enhance sustainable development. We plan to share some simple market architecture with you in the coming months. Our hope is that policy makers will hear this clarion call for simplicity.

I would like to thank Dr. Michael Walsh and Rafael Marques for their assistance in preparing this article.

Chapter 8

SO$_2$ Market Exceeds Expectations

May 2000

On 28 March this year, an economist from the Chicago Board of Trade sent a fax to the hotel I was staying at in California describing the results of the US Environmental Protection Agency (EPA) annual auction of sulfur dioxide (SO$_2$) emission allowances. I was properly advised of the need for confidentiality until our press conference at 10:00 a.m. central time the next day.

The seven pages of results methodically provided an answer to a question that has been hotly debated during the past decade.

The 1990 Amendments to the Clean Air Act provided the enabling legislation for a two phase "cap and trade" program designed to curtail US emissions of pollutants that cause acid rain in the United States and Canada. The first phase began in 1995. Following instructions established by Congress, the EPA allocated emission allowances to the 110 highest emitting power plants, affecting 263 combustion units. Each year the plants were required to cut aggregate emissions to conform to steadily declining quantified emissions limits. The second phase of the program began in January 2000. Phase II extended the limits to include another 2100 units and the national emissions cap was set at approximately 9 million tons. This represents a 50% reduction from the 1980s.

Table 1. Pre-1992 forecasts of Phase I SO_2 allowance prices	
Source	Phase I forecast ($/ton)
United Mine Workers	981
Ohio Coal Office	785
Electric Power Research Institute	688
Sierra Club	446
American Electric Power	392
Resource Data International	309
Source: Hahn and May, The Electricity Journal, March 1994	

It is well documented that sulfur emissions fell faster than required, and the evidence of economic success is also overwhelming.

The passage of the legislation depended on the hotly debated forecasts of the price of allowances. Table 1 presents a sample of some of the forecasts of Phase I prices.

It is important to emphasize that while the optimistic projections of Phase I prices were at, or just below, $300 many predicted that allowance prices would double by Phase II. In 1992, the press reported that early Phase I trades occurred at $300. The results of the first EPA annual SO_2 allowance auction, conducted by the Chicago Board of Trade in 1993, had a spot market clearing price of $131. The results for the next five auctions further confirmed that early forecasts were significantly higher than observed prices. The apologists continued to assert that the early forecasts for Phase I were incorrect, and that they would ultimately be proven right when we entered Phase II. In fact, allowance prices in 1999 reached $207 (see Fig. 1).

The hotly debated question of the price of allowances for Phase II was answered in that seven-page fax. In fact, the spot price (for allowances usable in 2000 or later) averaged $130.69 which was below the average price from the auctions held from 1993 through 1999 (Table 2 shows the first page of that fax). Even more persuasive were the results of the "forward" market auction of allowances usable in years 2007 or later. The average price paid

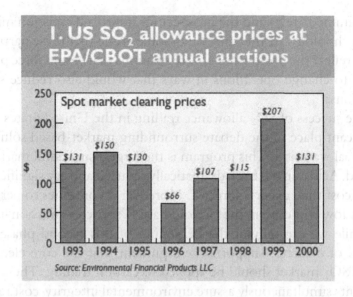

I. US SO₂ allowance prices at EPA/CBOT annual auctions

Spot market clearing prices

Source: Environmental Financial Products LLC

Table 2. 2000 acid rain allowance auction results

I. ALLOWANCES AVAILABLE FOR AUCTION

Origin	Spot auction	7-year advance auction
EPA	125,000	125,000
Privately offered	5,388	2,500
Total	130,388	127,500

II. SPOT AUCTION RESULTS

Allowances	Number of bids	Number of bidders	Bid price
Bid for: 318,509	Successful: 51	Successful: 23	Highest: $250.00
Sold: 128,388	Unsuccessful: 34	Unsuccessful: 13	**Clearing: $126.00**
	Total: 85	Total: 36	Lowest: $80.05
			Weighted av: $130.69

III. 7-YEAR ADVANCE AUCTION RESULTS

Allowances	Number of bids	Number of bidders	Bid price
Bid For: 210,224	Successful: 21	Successful: 6	Highest: $200.00
Sold: 125,000	Unsuccessful: 3	Unsuccessful: 2	**Clearing: $55.27**
	Total: 24	Total: 8	Lowest: $40.57
			Weighted av: $68.32

Source: US Environmental Protection Agency, Chicago Board of Trade

for those allowances was $68.32![1] Forward prices naturally reflect the time value of money (payment for these allowances must be

---

[1] It should be noted that most market participants focus on the auction "clearing" price, the price at which the last available allowances are sold. By definition this price is lower than the average auction price.

made immediately) and the prospect for improved emission mitigation technology. At the same time, some argue that these particular prices reflect the prospect of new regulations that would force power plants to change operations in ways that would also reduce sulfur emissions.

The success of SO_2 allowance trading in the United States has a significant place in the debate surrounding market-based solutions to global warming. This program is the largest successful market of its kind. Acid rain has been dramatically reduced and at a significantly lower cost than experts forecast. Moreover it continues to perform at very low cost even in the face of Phase II's stricter emission limits.

While we are only at the beginning of this second phase, the weight of evidence supports the argument that the core elements of the SO_2 market should be applied to carbon trading. These core elements simultaneously assure environmental integrity, cost reduction, efficient trading, and valid price discovery. They include: clear rules on emission monitoring and noncompliance penalties; unimpeded trading; fully fungible trading instruments; public-private partnerships to achieve transparent prices. We hope those who are now working to set guidelines for carbon trading take a close look at these critical success factors.

I would like to thank Dr. Michael Walsh for his assistance in the preparation of this article.

Chapter 9

US Carbon Trading Project Wins Funding

June 2000

It is commonly accepted in industrialized nations around the world that efforts to create a market-based solution for mitigating greenhouse (GHG) gas emissions have totally stalled in the United States, but commonly accepted knowledge doesn't apply in the Midwest.

Last month, the Midwest-based Joyce Foundation announced a one-year grant to the Kellogg Graduate School of Management at Northwestern University. Under this grant Environmental Financial Products will carry out the design phase of a voluntary GHG emissions trading system based in the Midwest.

Emissions trading has been advocated as the most efficient means of reducing GHG emissions. It uses the private marketplace by creating financial incentives for pollution reduction, rather than imposing more costly "command and control" regulation. The design phase of the program will begin a real-world test of the hypothesis that GHG emissions trading is a feasible and least-cost solution to the problem of climate change. If the design phase is successful, a second phase would establish the market.

There are several important reasons to implement a pilot GHG emissions trading program in the Great Lakes region. Such a project would demonstrate the concept on a relatively small scale. Lessons for the design of a larger system could be drawn from a pilot.

27

The Great Lakes region has a diversity of potential participants — electric utilities, agricultural producers, forestry companies, large landowners, refineries, steel plants, other heavy industry, and several of the world's largest car makers. Numerous companies based in the Midwest, or with a major presence in the region, have been proactive on the climate change issue. Some have already traded carbon emissions reductions and/or have internal trading systems or self-imposed caps on GHG emissions.

Faculty from universities in the region offer world-class expertise in soil science and forestry that will prove valuable in specifying procedures for verifying carbon sequestration. Furthermore, experts in relevant areas of law and economics are affiliated with Midwestern universities. PricewaterhouseCoopers, through its regional, national, and international professionals, provides an enormous resource in both market architecture and accounting protocols. Finally, the Midwest is home to world-class financial and market institutions such as the Chicago Board of Trade.

The underlying premise of the research is that market creation begins with a voluntary private sector initiative. It is hoped that the customs and practices that are developed in the pilot program will be incorporated in any subsequent trading efforts initiated by national, state, and local governments.

The research will follow a 12-stage process that includes the steps that are necessary and sufficient to build a market. These stages were developed by the principal researchers involved in the pilot program design, based on their prior experience and research. Simply stated, they are

   (i) clearly define the commodity;
  (ii) establish market oversight;
 (iii) define baselines;
 (iv) set emission targets, allocate permits, and monitor emissions;
  (v) establish uniform and nonsegmented allowances;
 (vi) develop an allowance clearing house;
(vii) employ existing exchanges and trading systems;

(viii) develop auctions;
 (ix) refine and develop trade documentation practices;
  (x) foster harmonization with other research and markets;
 (xi) develop appropriate accounting principles; and
(xii) launch an international effort to ensure that participants in other markets can trade in the pilot program as soon as is feasible.

The core goals of the market are real environmental progress, a functional market with price discovery, learning and business advantage for the participants, and international linkages. The research will start by adapting the model of sulfur dioxide (SO_2) trading, which began 5 years ago under the terms of the Clean Air Act, to GHGs. It is important to note that this voluntary regional pilot program will be much more complex than the current SO_2 program, which primarily involves electric utilities. Participants will be more diverse, since GHGs are emitted or sequestered by most sectors of the economy, not just the electric utility industry.

Major design issues for a Midwest-based GHG emissions trading system include decisions on who should participate in the system and its structure. For example:

- To what extent should entities that actually emit GHGs (e.g., electric utilities or "downstream" sources) be the targeted participants as opposed to producers of fuel or manufactured goods that use energy ("upstream" sources)?
- How should the system be structured to obtain the greatest coverage of emissions and to prevent "leakage" if not all sectors are included?
- What is the best way to provide coverage for emissions from motor vehicles and airplanes?
- How can forestry and agriculture, with their potential for increased carbon sequestration, as well as methane sources, be integrated into the system?
- How will this domestic regional trading system interface with national and international emissions trading among developed

countries and with emission reduction credits generated in developing countries under the Clean Development Mechanism of the Kyoto Protocol?

We expect that the pilot GHG emissions trading program will give the participants a head start in both reducing emissions and building critical trading skills. This would enable them to take part in early reduction crediting programs and establish them as global leaders in implementing cost-effective solutions to climate change. Both customers and shareholders should gain from this competitive edge.

I want to thank Michael Walsh, Alice LeBlanc, and Rafael Marques for their contributions to both this article and the entire efforts of Environmental Financial Products.

Based in Chicago with assets of approximately $1 billion, the Joyce Foundation supports efforts to strengthen public policies in ways that improve the quality of life in the Great Lakes region (Illinois, Indiana, Iowa, Michigan, Minnesota, Ohio, and Wisconsin). The grant for development of the carbon-trading pilot market was developed by Joyce Environment Program officer Margaret O'Dell.

Chapter 10

The Case for a Simplified CDM

July–August 2000

It seems as if two different scenarios will be played out in the next 5 months as 160 nations begin to formulate rules to implement the Clean Development Mechanism (CDM) of the Kyoto Protocol.

In one scenario, signatories to the Protocol will be developing the elements of rules governing the creation of certified emission reductions (CERs) from CDM projects. These rules cannot become "official" until sanctioned by parties to a ratified Kyoto Protocol, which could be several years in the future. In another scenario, the private sector, driven by custom and practice in the capital and commodity markets, will begin experimenting with CDM architecture designed to minimize transaction costs and promote transparency.

However, there is a fervent hope that the private sector design process will also guide policy-makers charged with developing rules and regulations associated with the origination of CERs.

Efficiency in the capital markets relies on both standardization of a financial instrument or commodity as well as market architecture that minimizes transaction costs and provides transparency. For example, successful spot and futures trading of commodities like wheat depends on uniform warehouse receipts specifying the quality of the underlying commodity.

It is self-evident to market participants that the greater the ambiguity in this process and in the definition of the CERs the higher the transaction costs will be. It is in this spirit that we strongly advocate a streamlined CDM origination process which results in Simplified Emission Reduction Credits (SERCSM). Participation would be voluntary. This new financial instrument would in many cases provide a lower cost, fast track alternative to the project-by-project analysis required to generate conventional CERs.

What is a SERCSM? Simply stated, it is an emission reduction credit that is measured by the difference between a predetermined reference emission rate (RER) and the implemented emissions rate (IER) associated with new or modified facilities. Measurement of the IERs would be conducted on a standardized basis.

As a hypothetical example of the SERC calculation process, assume the RER for electric power generation reflects a conventional gas-fired plant (0.55 tons of carbon dioxide [CO_2] per megawatt hour [MWh]). A newly installed zero-emission solar or wind plant producing 1000 MWh in a year would therefore earn 550 tons CO_2 worth of SERCs. Independent monitoring and verification would only involve an on-site visit to determine the existence of the facility and subsequent documentation of its production rate. Baselines and additionality would have already been addressed through the use of a predetermined RER and the IER.

Simply summarized:

$$
\begin{aligned}
SERCSM &= (RER - IER) \times Production \\
&= (0.55 - 0) \text{ tons } CO_2/MWh \times 1000 \text{ MWh/year} \\
&= 550 \text{ tons } CO_2/year
\end{aligned}
$$

The table below gives a numerical example of a real 50 kilowatt solar facility in Amazonas, Brazil, and illustrates four possible baselines that it could face. It also shows the value of SERCs under a further simplifying assumption that the initial certification is for 10 years.

Applying the SERC methodology, the project proponent would use a common global RER. This would vastly reduce uncertainties and CDM processing costs, while guaranteeing that renewable

Alternative credit calculations and value of credits for a 50kW power plant* in Amazonas, Brazil

Possible emission baselines	Baseline CO₂ per MWh	Total tons credited per year (CO₂)	Value of credits at $5/ton CO₂	Value of credits at $10/ton CO₂
Coal	0.9 tons	105	Annual: $525 DPV: $3,226	Annual: $1,050 DPV: $6,452
Gas	0.55 tons	64	Annual: $320 DPV: $1,966	Annual: $1,966 DPV: $3,932
Gas combined cycle	0.37 tons	43	Annual: $215 DPV: $1,321	Annual: $430 DPV: $2,642
Hydro	~0 tons	0	0	0

* Estimated production: 117MWh/yr. DPV = present value of a flat 10-year revenue stream discounted at 10%. The solar plant is assumed to run 365 days/year, at 80% of rated capacity for 8 hours/day

energy projects receive credits. Without this SERC one could imagine lengthy debates over project-level details among administrators of the host country government, staff of the climate secretariat, the CDM executive board, certifying agencies, nongovernmental organizations (NGOs) and others. Without an agreed-upon standard, the debate could be endless.

The solar facility cited above could cost between $70,000 and $100,000. However, at a price of $5 per ton of CO_2, this project would yield carbon credits that are worth $1,300–$3,200 (discounted present value over 10 years) depending on the RER. A project 50 times the size of this one would yield SERCs with a value of $65,000–160,000.

Why is this important? Numerous studies of the activities implemented jointly (AIJ) pilot phase conclude that establishing emission baselines and project additionality on a nonstandardized, project-by-project basis causes high transaction costs and uncertainty regarding the carbon benefits produced. Initial estimates indicate that the process of defining a CDM project, establishing the case-specific emission baseline, documenting additionality and conducting all required certification, government approvals and registration would cost at least $40,000 for the simplest project types. This does not include the costs of selling these credits in the capital markets. Additional fees for legal, accounting, and underwriting might still be required. We will be calling for simplicity in these parts of the process as well. All of this suggests that solar projects that cost as much as $5 million might derive little or no net economic benefit under the conventional CDM process. This is hardly a recipe for success for this important financial innovation.

Once again, we hope that policymakers will hear this clarion call for simplicity.

The research on a Simplified CDM was supported in part by Ontario Power Generation. The proposal was presented at Conference of the Parties (COP) 5 in Bonn, in October 1999. Michael Walsh and Alice LeBlanc were the presenters and research team leaders. The research benefited from the input of Brian Jantzi and Corinne Boone.

The viewpoints presented here are solely those of Environmental Financial Products LLC. I would like to thank Michael Walsh, Alice LeBlanc, Scott Baron, and Rafael Marques for their assistance in the preparation of this article.

Chapter 11

The US and EU: Closer than You Think

September 2000

Two widely held beliefs continue to play a role in the political debate preceding Conference of the Parties (COP) 6, the November meeting of the UN's Climate Change Convention in The Hague. They are

- that the unwillingness of US legislators to ratify the Kyoto Protocol is partly predicated on a booming economy and the concomitant growth of greenhouse gas (GHG) emissions; and
- that the willingness of governments in the European Union (EU) to ratify the Protocol is based on the efficacy of current efforts to reduce GHG emissions. A corollary of the latter is that emissions trading is of limited importance.

Neither of these beliefs is true. Economic growth in the United States has been largely decoupled from increases in GHG emissions. During the period 1990–1999, gross domestic product (GDP) rose by 27% (in inflation-adjusted terms) whereas GHG emissions grew by only 12% (see Fig. 1). The growth rates have been even more dramatically different in the past 2 years. In 1998, carbon dioxide (CO_2) emissions grew by about 0.4% whereas GDP grew by 4%. In 1999, CO_2 emissions grew by about 1% whereas the economy grew by 4.2%.

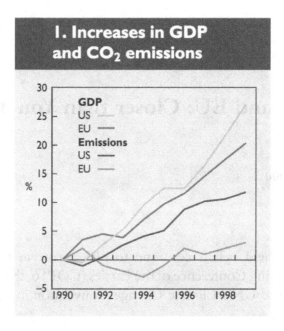

What explains this phenomenon? The "new economy" and the rapid growth of information technology have both increased economic growth and flattened emissions growth. In his paper, *The Internet Economy and Global Warming*,[1] author Joe Romm cites research by the Environmental Protection Agency and Argonne National Laboratory suggesting "one third of the recent improvements in energy intensity are structural". The low-emitting service sectors of the economy have grown rapidly and now represent 46% of US GDP whereas manufacturing has fallen from 22% to 18% since 1990. The remaining two-thirds improvement in energy efficiency comes from economy-wide improvements: better technology and smarter energy use throughout the economy.

Explicit action to cut GHG emissions also contributes to the improvements. Major corporations, such as IBM and Johnson & Johnson, have recently announced voluntary commitments to

---

[1] Joseph Romm, Arthur Rosenfeld, and Susan Herrmann, "The Internet Economy and Global Warming — A Scenario of the Impact of E-commerce on Energy and the Environment," *The Center for Energy and Climate Solutions,* December 1, 1999, www.cool-companies.org.

reduce CO_2 emissions. Renewable energy sources represent a small but rapidly growing share of the energy system. The great majority of newly installed electric power plants use less GHG-intensive fuels, such as natural gas.

It is important to emphasize that the numbers cited here represent a gross change in CO_2 emissions and do not reflect increases in soil or biomass carbon sequestration as a result of changes in tillage practices or land use (such as reforestation).

Within the EU, absolute GHG emissions declined during the early 1990s. However, the belief that public policies have brought the EU closer to its goal of a reduction from 1990 levels is not accurate. Similar to the US experience, these gains are largely (but not exclusively) the fortuitous byproduct of other developments (e.g., fuel switching at UK power stations, economic decline, and retooling of the former East Germany). Although economic growth in the EU has been less dramatic than in the United States, there has been an even more pronounced decoupling of economic growth and GHG emissions, as shown in Fig. 1.

Because emissions and economic growth are not yet fully decoupled, acceleration of economic growth in Europe is likely to keep GHG emissions above 1990 levels in the next few years in the absence of more aggressive policy measures.

Figure 2 shows a long-term trend toward convergence in the emissions per unit of GDP for the United States, EU, and Japan.

We are witnessing not only a convergence in emission trends, but also one in philosophy. Emissions trading is becoming more widely accepted throughout the EU. The United Kingdom is leading the effort and plans to implement a scheme in 2001. Denmark launched a capped GHG emissions trading system for its electricity sector in January 2000. The Netherlands and Norway are contemplating or implementing cap-and-trade schemes. Germany's Green party has recently advocated use of a trading system for controlling emissions. The EU intends setting up a market by 2005.

Two important facts put the United States and EU on common ground as we move toward COP 6. Contrary to popular conception,

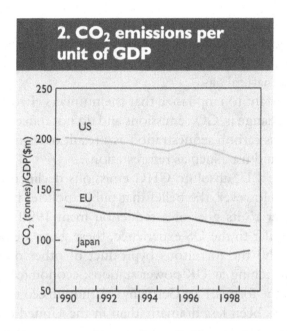

2. CO$_2$ emissions per unit of GDP

Source: US Department of Energy, Energy Information Agency, OECD

both have benefited from unplanned reductions in GHG intensity, but both are realizing rapid economic growth and rising absolute emissions. Despite the decline in emissions intensity, for the foreseeable future economic growth will raise absolute emissions, enhancing the importance of trading as the path to cost efficiency in reducing emissions.

While there may be significant differences of opinion among the parties at COP 6 regarding implementation, the macro trends in declining emissions per unit of GDP, along with the more prevalent view that trading is a desirable policy tool, should help the final negotiations. Growing adoption of emissions trading around the world will reduce the global cost of cutting GHG emissions: the vision of a broad-based international market — with its attendant efficiencies — appears more attainable every day.

I would like to thank Michael Walsh, Alice LeBlanc, Rafael Marques, and Scott Baron for their assistance in the preparation of this article.

Chapter 12

CDM — Simplicity is the Key

October 2000
Environmental Finance Supplement

> The Clean Development Mechanism (CDM) is a major
> financial innovation that may radically alter the way devel-
> oping countries and industrialized nations deal with issues
> of climate change. Richard Sandor explains its importance
> and recommends a simplified CDM process.

The CDM may be critical to jump-starting the carbon emissions
markets. It also provides a vehicle for forging political consensus between the industrialized and developing countries, thereby
expanding the comprehensiveness of the Kyoto Protocol.

Simply stated, the CDM is a mechanism whereby developing and
industrialized economies can both benefit from projects that mitigate emissions of greenhouse gases (GHGs) in developing countries. "Certified emission reductions" (CERs) are created when a
project causes emissions to be lower than they might otherwise
have been. The projects must also contribute to environmentally
sustainable economic development. Emission sources in industrialized countries can use the emission reduction credits arising from
those investments toward meeting their own GHG emissions caps.
There is also increasing momentum to ensure that credits for reforestation projects are included in the CDM.

It is important to emphasize that the use of these credits is not dependent on either country having developed its own emissions trading programme. The salient features of the CDM and the associated references to the treaty are presented in summary form in Table 1. Many of the details are expected to be finalized during the Conference of the Parties (COP) 6 meeting in The Hague, in November.

Although we cannot precisely determine the likely size of the CDM portion of the carbon market, academics and governments have attempted forecast its importance. Most analysts use the assumption that 1 billion tons of annual carbon mitigation will be required worldwide during the period 2008–2012, the first period when Kyoto's binding targets are measured. As a result, it appears that the CDM might generate capital flows of approximately $10 billion per year (see Table 2).

1. Salient features of the Clean Development Mechanism

Participation	Transactions between industrialised (Annex I) and developing countries
Timing	Certified emission reductions can be accumulated starting in 2000 for use in 2008–2012
National emission budgets	Acquisition of CERs raises the "assigned amount" (emissions budget) of the buyer
Recognised projects	Emission reduction projects; treatment of carbon sinks not yet clear
Fees	To be levied to cover CDM administrative costs and to contribute to the adaptation and assistance fund for developing countries vulnerable to climate change damage
Project approval, monitoring and verification	Participation by any country is voluntary. Monitoring protocols and independent auditing and verification procedures are to be developed
Reporting of transfers	Registries to be established; likely to include both international and national systems

2. Summary of estimates of the potential size of the CDM

CDM share of overall carbon market (%)	Total CDM volume (million tons carbon)	Assumed market price ($/t of carbon)	CDM market value ($bn)
19–57	144–723	13–37	5.2–21

Source: adapted from Grubb, Michael and Vrolijk, Christiaan, "The Potential size of the CDM", Greenhouse Gas Emissions Trader, Issue 6, February 1999

The CDM, therefore, has the potential to make a significant impact on industrialized and developing countries. However, Article 12 of the Kyoto Protocol, which defines the CDM, only provides a framework for implementation. Carbon market participants now face the same challenges summarized by the quote of the day in the internet community — execution is everything — and Goethe's famous thought — the genius is in the details. It's all about execution and details.

Fees, regulatory uncertainties, and transaction costs could undermine this potentially powerful mechanism. It's our view that we must develop a simplified CDM process. The widespread use of a rule-based system will enhance sustainable development. We hope that as the private sector begins experimenting with the CDM, its design approach, driven by lessons from the capital and commodity markets, will guide policy makers charged with developing rules and regulations associated with the origination of CERs.

Simplified Emission Reduction Credits

Efficiency in the capital markets relies on both standardization of a financial instrument or commodity as well as a market architecture that minimizes transaction costs and provides transparency. For example, successful spot and futures trading of commodities, like wheat, depends on uniform warehouse receipts specifying the quality of the underlying commodity. At the Chicago Board of Trade, criteria, such as eligible grain types and grain moisture content, provide standards defining commodity grades acceptable for delivery.

It is self-evident to market participants that a greater degree of ambiguity in this process and in the definition of CERs implies higher transaction costs. It is in this spirit that we strongly advocate a streamlined CDM origination process, which results in Simplified Emission Reduction Credits (SERCs). Participation would be voluntary.

This new financial instrument would in many cases provide a lower cost, fast track alternative to the project-by-project analysis required to generate conventional CERs. A rules-based system also provides transparency and uniformity that allows all projects to be treated equally and reduces the potential for favoritism and corruption.

What is a SERC? Simply stated, it is an emission-reduction credit that is measured by the difference between a predetermined reference emissions rate (RER) and the implemented emissions rate (IER) associated with new or modified facilities. Measurement of the IERs would be conducted on a standardized basis. As a hypothetical example of the SERC calculation process, assume the RER for electric power generation reflects a conventional gas-fired plant (0.55 tons of carbon dioxide [CO_2] per MWh). A newly installed zero-emission solar or wind plant producing 1000 MWh in a year would earn 550 tons CO_2 worth of SERCs. Independent monitoring and verification would involve only an onsite visit to determine the existence of the facility and subsequent documentation of its production rate. Baselines and additionality would have already been addressed through the use of a predetermined RER and the IER.

Simply summarized:

$$SERC = (RER - IER) \times Production$$
$$= (0.55 - 0) \text{ tons } CO_2/MWh \times 1000 \text{ MWh/year}$$
$$= 550 \text{ tons } CO_2/year$$

Table 3 shows a numerical example of a real 50 kW solar facility in Amazonas, Brazil, illustrating four possible baselines that the

3. Alternative emissions reduction credit calculations and value of credits for a 50 kW electric power generating plant[1] in Amazonas, Brazil

Possible emission baselines	Baseline CO_2/MWh (tons)	Total tons credited/year (CO_2)	Value of credits			
			$5/ton CO_2		$10/ton CO_2	
			Annual	DPV	Annual	DPV
Coal	0.9m	105	525	3,226	1,050	6,452
Gas	0.55	64	320	1,966	640	3,932
Gas combined-cycle	0.37	43	215	1,321	430	2,642
Hydro	~0	0	0	0	0	0

1 Estimated production: 117 MWh/year; DPV = present value of a flat 10-year revenue stream discounted at 10%. Based on actual experience, the solar plant is assumed to run 365 days/year, at 80% of rated capacity for 8 hours/day

new facility could face. It also shows the value of SERCs under a further simplifying assumption that the initial certification is for a 10-year period.

Applying the SERC methodology, a project proponent would use a common global RER. This would vastly reduce uncertainties and CDM processing costs, while guaranteeing that renewable energy projects receive credits. Without this SERC, one could imagine lengthy debates over project-level details among administrators of the host country government, staff of the climate secretariat, the CDM executive board, certifying agencies, nongovernmental organizations (NGOs) and others. Without an agreed-upon standard, the debate could be endless.

Why is this important? Numerous studies of the activities implemented jointly (AIJ) pilot phase conclude that establishing emission baselines and project additionality on a nonstandardized, project-by-project basis causes high transaction costs and uncertainty regarding the carbon benefits produced. Initial estimates indicate that the process of defining a CDM project, establishing the case specific emissions baseline, documenting additionality and conducting all required certification, government approvals and registration would cost at least $40,000 for the simplest project types. This does not include the costs of selling these credits in the capital markets. Additional fees for legal, accounting, and underwriting might still be required. We will be calling for simplicity in these parts of the process as well.

At realistic CO_2 prices, we estimate that solar power projects that cost as much as $5 million might derive little or no net economic benefit under the conventional CDM process. This is hardly a recipe for success for this important financial innovation.

The Role of Forestry and Agriculture in a Simplified CDM

It is important to note that there is a difference between the quantitatively specified national emissions reduction targets and the unresolved role of forests and soils in meeting these requirements.

For example, the Kyoto treaty clearly specifies in Article 3.1 that Japan, Germany, and the United States must achieve reductions from the 1990 baseline of 6%, 8%, and 7%, respectively, during the budget period 2008–2012. Specific gases to be controlled are identified and the exchange rates across those gases are set.

Contrast the clarity of Article 3.1 with Articles 3.3 and 3.4, which deal with forestry and land-use change. Article 3.3 states that the "net changes in greenhouse gas emissions by sources and removals by sinks resulting from direct human-induced land use change and forestry activities, limited to afforestation, reforestation and deforestation since 1990, measured as verifiable changes in carbon stocks in each commitment period, shall be used to meet the commitments under this Article of each party".

This seems to imply that sequestration of carbon due to reforestation could be counted in meeting the quantified mitigation objectives. However, Article 3.4 leaves open the treatment of issues such as soil carbon sequestration and modified management of existing forests. It states that the meeting of the parties to the Kyoto Protocol shall: "decide on which additional human induced activities (besides afforestation, reforestation, and deforestation) related to changes in greenhouse gas emissions and removals by sinks in the agricultural soil and land use change and forestry categories shall be added to, or subtracted from, the assigned amount for parties included in Annex I".

In order to illustrate a simplified approach to carbon sinks, we will assume that ambiguities associated with forestry and agriculture will be resolved at COP 6. Furthermore, we will assume the parties will recognize assisted and natural regeneration of forests and a switch to no-till agriculture as desirable policies. These activities virtually define sustainability as they allow for economic utilization of natural resources while simultaneously reducing soil erosion, improving water quality, and fostering biodiversity.

It is in this spirit that we assume there will be three guiding principles associated with emission offsets (EOs):

1. Natural and assisted regeneration projects and changes in tillage practices that cause an increase in carbon stored in forests and soils initiated by legal entities in non-Annex B countries after December 10 1997 can earn EOs. The amount of EOs issued to such projects is equal to the net removals of CO_2-equivalent emissions caused by such projects minus any net emissions in non-Annex B countries resulting from land-use changes on other lands controlled by that entity or a financially affiliated entity.
2. EOs shall be earned by any non- Annex B Parties in an amount reflecting the demonstrated net increase in carbon stocks within the country, measured as verifiable changes in carbon stocks occurring after 1 January 2000 minus the quantity of EOs earned by legal entities from projects based in the territory of the Party as in 1.
3. The quantity of EOs earned under 1 and 2 shall reflect the scientifically accepted and validated methods for estimating carbon stocks, adjusted to reflect the statistical variance of the estimation technique, such that the calculation produces a conservative high-confidence estimate of net carbon stock increases. Validated methods can include statistical inference, remote sensing, or other methods for assessing overall carbon stocks held in biomass and soils.

These rules allow projects that cause the enhancement of forest-based sinks to be credited, provided they cause a net increase in carbon stored on all lands in non-annex B countries controlled by the project proponent or affiliated entities. They furthermore provide that EOs can be earned by national governments provided that there is a nationwide net increment in carbon storage. They also avoid double counting.

Because the cost of precisely monitoring and verifying carbon sinks suggests that the process could be prohibitively expensive, the adoption of conservative reference sequestration rates would allow for increased participation in these environmentally desirable activities.

It is for this reason that we propose a simplified emission offset (SEO) as a complement to the SERCs defined above.

As indicated in Table 4, inspection of a small handful of countries indicates that a staggering amount of pasture land is available for reforestation. Even if only a portion of this were to be reforested, the local benefits realized by renewing a sustainable source of food, medicines, and employment, not to mention enhancement of water quality and biodiversity, would constitute a major win-win opportunity for both local and global good. Table 5 reports the amount of land now planted in soybeans in selected countries.

Even for a single crop, widespread adoption of no-till practices could cause major increases in soil and moisture retention (in

4. Land in pasture in selected countries	
Country	Hectares
United States	239,250,000
Brazil	185,000,000
China	400,000,000
Argentina	142,000,000
India	11,100,000
Source: UN Food and Agriculture Organisation 1999 Database	

5. Land planted with soybeans	
Country	Hectares
Argentina	7,509,000
Brazil	13,011,341
China	8,200,670
India	6,450,000
Source: UN Food and Agriculture Organisation 1999 Database	

addition to lowering fuel consumption) while increasing the amount of carbon stored in the soil.

What is a SEO in forestry? For assisted or natural regenerated forests it is, simply stated, the lowest predetermined rate of sequestration determined for a given set of standard reforestation practices in a specified geographic location. For example, sequestration rates for the Atlantic Brazilian rainforests might have the following ranges: 2–3.50 tons of carbon per hectare per year for the first 10 years; 2–2.75 tons for years 11–20; and 1.0–1.5 tons for years 21–60.

In order to be confident that the number of SEOs issued does not overstate the amount of carbon absorbed by the sink enhancement project, a simplified SEO system would grant offsets equal to 80% of the lower end of the applicable reference sequestration rate. Reference sequestration rates would be established for various defined practices (such as natural forest regeneration or assisted regeneration) for specified regions by agricultural ministries or by independent organizations such as Winrock or SGS. Verification would simply involve an independent attestation by an accounting firm that the required activity was occurring. If the project owner wanted instead to be credited for the actual amount of carbon sequestered, then actual monitoring and verification could be undertaken at his expense.

What is a SEO in agriculture? It is essentially the amount of carbon sequestered at a predetermined rate when there is a shift from heavy till to no-till farming within a particular geographic location. For example, soil carbon sequestration rates in the Brazilian soybean belt might be 0.4 to 0.6 tons of carbon per hectare per year.[1] Once again, a simplified SEO would provide for 80% of the lower value (i.e., 0.32 tons of carbon per hectare per year). These rates would be determined by an appropriate government agency or

---

[1] Conversion to no-till may result in either a significant reduction in net farm-wide emissions or may cause a farm to be a net carbon sequesterer. For purposes of the simplified CDM this distinction is irrelevant.

independent consulting firm. Third party independent attestation would simply verify that the switch to no-till had occurred. If the landowner wanted to claim more than the predetermined rate, then actual monitoring and verification would have to take place.

It is important to emphasize that these numbers are only hypothetical and are meant to illustrate the predetermined nature of sequestration rates. The use of the simplified process should also extend to other offsets such as landfill gases. We are so convinced of the need to use simplified formulas for crediting mitigation projects that we will propose their widespread usage in the Midwest US pilot market we are now designing.

To borrow a phrase from the capital markets, the reader should consider our ideas for standardization to be "indicative" terms. The objective is to start a dialogue that advances the development of a workable system that can enlist the maximum possible adoption of climate friendly practices.

We are convinced that a rules-based system will enhance sustainable development. Our hope is that policy makers at The Hague will hear this clarion call for simplicity.

I would like to thank Michael Walsh, Alice LeBlanc, Rafael Marques, and Scott Baron for their assistance in the preparation of this article.

Chapter 13

Dow Jones Sustainability Group Index: One Year On

November 2000

> "The City and investment community is beginning to recognize the new commercial and environmental realities, and to make money out of them. The return on equity of the new Dow Jones Sustainability Group Index averaged 15%, compared to 8% for the regular index for the first half of this year"
>
> —UK Prime Minister Tony Blair, 24 October 2000

On 8 September 1999, the Dow Jones Sustainability Group Index — a stock index that tracks the performance of the top 10% of the leading sustainable companies in the Dow Jones Global Index — changed the asset management business in Europe. The index includes companies on the basis of best-in-class sustainability in terms of financial, environmental, and social performance. In the inaugural issue of environmental finance, this column described the launch of that new index. This is the promised update.

In the first 12 months, 16 licenses to use the index have been issued to a wide variety of financial institutions in seven different countries (see Table 1).

These licensees have created numerous financial products, including active and passive funds, equity baskets and certificates. Assets totaling approximately €1.5 billion ($1.3 billion) are managed directly by this index or use it as a portfolio performance benchmark. A simple analysis of performance charts give us some

Table 1. Institutions licensed to offer products based on DJSGI	
Institution/country	**Product offered**
SPP/Swe	Index fund
Skandinaviska Enskilda Bank/Swe	Index fund
Banque Gen de Luxembourg/Lux	Index fund
Südwestdeutsche Genossenschafts-Zentralbank/Ger	Equity linked note
Folksam Sak/Swe	Index fund
Robeco/Neth	Index fund
Rothschild & Cie Gestion/Fr	Index fund
Bayerische Hypo-Vereinsbank/Ger	Warrant
Cordius Asset Management/Bel	Index fund
Fürst Fugger Privatbank/Ger	Index fund
Oppenheim KAG/Ger	Index fund
Baloise Insurance/Switz	Index fund
DWS/Ger	Index fund
Credit Suisse First Boston/Switz	Index fund
ING Fund Management/Neth	Index fund
Sustainable Performance Gp/Switz	Investment co

insight into the reasons for the success of this index. From 1 January 1999 to September 2000, the index generated a rate of return (in euros) of 59.2%. We appear to be witnessing the beginning of a movement from qualitatively driven socially responsible investing to quantitatively driven sustainable investing.

On 6 September 2000, Dow Jones Sustainability Group Indexes announced the results of its first annual review. Effective 6 October 2000, the index includes 236 companies from 61 industries in 36 countries. The leading sustainability companies in each of the 10 market sectors are presented in Table 2.

A significant change occurred during the annual review: all components of the index are now made public (see Table 3 and also www.sustainability-index.com). Portfolio managers can, therefore, now use the sustainability ranking of individual companies as a decision tool as they modify their stock holdings. Managers seeking the better performance associated with sustainable companies can now more easily identify the best companies in a wide variety of sectors. In addition, hedge funds can more readily employ a "pairs" stock trading strategy by, for example, going long an energy company

Table 2. Sustainability leaders

Market sector leaders

BMW	Consumer, cyclical
BG Group	Energy
Bristol-Myers Squibb	Healthcare
UBS	Financial
Deutsche Telekom	Telecommunications
Dofasco	Basic Materials
Fujitsu	Technology
Procter & Gamble	Consumer, non-cyclical
Sulzer	Industrial
Thames Water	Utilities

Selected industry group leaders

Baxter International	Medical products
Dow Chemical	Chemicals
ING Group	Insurance
ST Microelectronics	Semiconductors
Teijin	Textiles and apparel
Unilever	Food product makers

with a high sustainability rating while shorting a company with a low sustainability rating in the same sector.

Public listing of the index components also provides the basis for the possible launch of exchange-traded products (ETPs), securities designed to provide a single value for the aggregate performance of the components of an index. The most actively traded securities on the American Stock Exchange are ETPs based on indices such as the S&P 500, the NASDAQ 100, and the Dow Jones Industrials Average. Public listing of the components will also allow futures and options contracts to emerge. These derivative products will provide a hedging and price discovery mechanism for sustainable investors. Derivatives trading would provide the liquidity that can foster active trading strategies focused on sustainable companies. This should give additional impetus for further change in asset management in Europe in the years to come.

The opinions expressed in this article are those of the author only. He would like to thank Michael Walsh, Rafael Marques, and Scott Baron for their assistance in the preparation of this article.

Table 3. Components of DJSGI

Australia Australian Gas Light; Broken Hill Proprietary; Cable & Wireless; Optus; Goodman Fielder; James Hardie Industries; Lend Lease Corp; Normandy Mining; Orica; Pacific Dunlop; Pasminco; Westpac; WMC (Western Mining)

Austria Bank Austria; VA Technologie

Belgium Barco; Dexia France; Electrabel; Union Minière

Brazil Banco Itaú; Cia Energetica Minas Gerais (CEMIG)

Canada Alcan Aluminum; Ballard Power System; Cameco; Canadian Imperial Bank of Commerce; Cognos; Dofasco; Domtar; Noranda; Nortel Networks; Nova Chemical; Placer Dome; Rio Algom; Royal Bank of Canada; Suncor; Transalta; Westcoast Energy

Chile Banco de A Edwards; Cervecerias Unidas

Denmark Coloplast; International Service System; Novo-Nordisk

Finland Metso; Nokia; Outokumpu; Stora Enso

France Danone; Groupe GTM; Lafarge; Lafarge Corp; Legrand; Société Générale; ST Microlectronics

Germany Adidas-Salomon; Bayer; Bayerische Hypo-und Vereinsbank; BMW; Continental; Daimler Chrysler; Degussa-Huls; Deutsche Bank; Lufthansa; Deutsche Telecom; Henkel; Karstadt; Metro; MG Technologies; RWE; SAP; Schering; Siemens; Volkswagen

Greece Altec; Athens Medical Centre; Titan Cement

Hong Kong Cable & Wireless HKT; China Telecom; Kowloon Motor Bus Holdings (KMB Holdings); New World Development

Ireland Allied Irish Banks

Italy Benetton; Telecom Italia Mobile; Telecom Italia; UniCredito Italiano

Japan Asahi Breweries; Asahi Glass; Canon; Daiwa Securities; Denso; East Japan Railway; Ebara; Fuji Photo; Fujitsu; Hachijuni Bank; Hitachi Chemical; Ito-Yokado; Komatsu; Marubeni Corp; Mitsubishi Estate; Mori Seiki; Rohm; Sony; Teijin; Tokyo Electric Power; Tokyo Gas; Tokyu Corp; Toshiba Corp; Yasuda Fire & Marine Insurance

Malaysia Malaysian International Shipping Corp; Nestle (Malaysia); YTL Power International

Netherlands ABN-AMRO; Aegon; Ahold; ING; Royal Dutch Petroleum; Philips Electronics; Unilever

Norway Norsk Hydro; Storebrand; Tomra Systems

Portugal Telecel

South Africa Sasol; Standard Bank Investment Corp; Tongaat-Hulett Group

South Korea Mirae Corp

Spain Amadeus Global Travel Distribution; Banco Bilbao Vizcaya Argentaria; Banco Santander Central Hispano; Iberdrola

Sweden Assi Doman; Atlas Copco; Electrolux; ForeningsSparbanken; Gambro; SKF; Skandia Forsakrings; Skanska; Svenska Cellulosa; Svenska Handelsbanken; Volvo

Switzerland ABB; Ciba Specialty Chemicals; Credit Suisse Group; Nestle; Novartis; Sulzer; Swiss Re; UBS Group; Valora; Zurich Financial Services

Thailand Siam Cement

UK Allied Domecq; Allied Zurich; Anglian Water; BAA; Barclays; BG Group; Boots; BP Amoco; British Airways; British Telecommunications; Cable & Wireless; Capital Shopping Centres; Diageo; EMI Group; Glaxo Wellcome; Granada Compass Group; Hammerson; J Sainsbury; Johnson Matthey; Lloyds TSB Group; Pearson; Powergen; Reuters; Severn Trent; Shanks; Shell Transport & Trading; Stagecoach Holdings; Thames Water; Unilever; WPP

US Alexander & Baldwin; America Online; Baxter International; BD Beckman Coulter; Bethlehem Steel; Bristol-Myers Squibb; Compaq; Computer Associates International; Conoco; Dell Computer; Dow Chemical; Dow Jones & Co; EMC Corp; Du Pont; Ensco International; Equity Office Properties Trust; Fannie Mae; FDX Corp; FPL Group; Gap; Global Marine; HJ Heinz; Halliburton; Harrah's Entertainment; Home Depot; Host Marriott; Intel; International Game Technology; ITT Industries; JDS Uniphase; Johnson & Johnson; Kmart; Lear; Mattel; 3M; Nicor; Nike; Pfizer; PPG Industries; Procter & Gamble; Public Service Enterprise Group; Sonoco Products; Temple Inland; Texaco; TXU; United Healthcare; United Technologies; USG; Walt Disney; Weyerhaeuser

Chapter 14

A Post-Hague Compromise on Reforestation

December 2000–January 2001

The deadlock result from The Hague, in November, is a textbook example of A.W. Tucker's 1950 treatise on games and decision theory.[1] In the "prisoner's dilemma", two players are kept apart and, acting rationally — but without knowing the other's strategy — make decisions that leave both worse off. With open communication, the players might jointly prepare a strategy that leaves them both better off. There is an analogy in the debate over the inclusion of forests in Kyoto's Clean Development Mechanism (CDM). And there is a win-win strategy that advances the interests of developing countries and the goals of the climate convention.

Society cannot get on the path to environmental sustainability if we don't improve our management of forests and soils worldwide. Effective management means we must start moving toward a system of comprehensive accounting and recognition of climate impacts from all land-use decisions. These scientific and economic facts were unambiguously recognized in the UN Framework Convention on Climate Change. Numerous other global conventions — on biodiversity, desertification, wetlands, and others — point in the same

---

[1]See, for example, R. C. Lewontin, "Evolution and the Theory of Games," *Journal of Theoretical Biology* 1 (1961): 382–403.

direction. Unlike Kyoto, these other conventions lack the capacity to steer massive capital flows to support better land management. Because emissions trading and crediting for carbon sink enhancements are core implementation tools in the Kyoto Protocol, we now have a powerful mechanism that can provide serious financing for reforestation.

However, the terms and conditions under which land use, land-use change and forestry (LULUCF) in both developed and developing countries are credited were not settled at the Conference of the Parties (COP) 6 meeting in The Hague. We now have the chance to open communications on how best to seize this rare chance to elevate environmentally sound land management to a valuable global asset that deserves large-scale financial support.

Forest destruction accounts for 20% of global greenhouse emissions. Forest destruction and degradation impoverishes local people, pollutes water, kills endangered species, and spreads deserts. Environmentally sound reforestation can reverse all these. Because forests are of overriding importance to climate and sustainability, we don't have the luxury of postponing the development of effective methods for including them in the global solution. We can't find the best way to steer serious financing to forests until we start immediately to try good approaches to carbon crediting. Despite the rhetoric, we now have these at hand.

A workable first step is to recognize inclusion of the less controversial reforestation/afforestation projects in the CDM. A specified schedule for developing technical terms and conditions should be set, with signature at COP 7 in Marrakesh in November 2001, being the goal. A negotiated agreement on standards for avoided deforestation has not yet been found because this important activity introduces unique (but solvable) questions. Once workable standards for these projects are found, they too can be recognized for inclusion.

The in-field experience of solid programs by nongovernmental organizations, governments, and private organizations based in Argentina, Brazil, Malaysia, India, the UK, Norway, Tanzania, Switzerland, South Africa, Costa Rica, The Netherlands, Germany, the United States, Canada, New Zealand, Russia, Australia, and elsewhere reminds us that good reforestation project standards can be defined and put into place now. The positive results from many of these early projects have proven that this strategy can be a win-win option for all involved.

Many of the technical questions regarding crediting of forestry projects are also faced by fossil fuel emissions reduction projects. For both categories, we know enough to act: superior solutions for both can only be found through direct experience. Good standards, combined with transparency and the right of developing countries to approve projects, will help assure quality. Finally, experience to date shows that forestry projects face long-run failure if they don't effectively engage local communities.

Estimates suggest that even a limited role in the CDM could trigger the reforestation of 3 million hectares (8.5 million acres) of land per year.[2] Reforestation is just a part of the solution to climate change. It appears that even the most aggressive global reforestation program under the CDM would account for no more than 15% of the emissions reductions required under Kyoto. But we cannot afford to wait: it will take decades to perfect the tools needed to finance all the solutions.

It's ironic that the generalization of the "prisoner's

---

[2] Michael Walsh, "Maximizing financial support for biodiversity in the emerging Kyoto Protocol markets," *The Science of the Total Environment*, 240 (1999).

dilemma" to more than two participants results in "The Tragedy of the Commons"[3]: we all follow the path to overconsumption of the planet's scarce resources. We now have the chance, in both the context of game theory and the environment, to listen to one another, find good and ratifiable solutions, and simultaneously advance both climate protection and reforestation worldwide.

I would like to thank Israel Klabin for his help in developing the ideas expressed in this paper. I would also like to thank Eric Bettelheim, Michael Walsh, Alice LeBlanc, Scott Baron, and Rafael Marques.

---

[3] Ibid.

Chapter 15

California Utilities: The S&L Crisis Revisited

February 2001

In the months leading up to the power crisis in California, pundits listed a number of factors contributing to the situation. Rolling blackouts and the potential bankruptcy of the two largest utilities in the state required an explanation.

Some focused on the demand picture. California had restructured its economy during the 1990s with high technology leading the way. According to *The Economist*,[1] statewide consumption of electricity grew by an astonishing 25% during the 1990s, mostly led by Silicon Valley. At current prices, the capacity increase needed to meet demand growth probably exceeds this figure.

Others have focused on the supply picture. There has been virtually no addition to generating capacity in the last decade. Some are eager to blame this on stringent environmental regulations. Current reserve margins are below recommended levels, and widespread interruptions indicate supply is now far short of demand. Political considerations, which led to regulators imposing a freeze on electricity prices to individual consumers, have also been offered as an explanation of limited supply growth.

---

[1] "A State of Gloom," *The Economist*, January 19, 2001.

Deregulation has also been cited as the culprit. We argue that faulty deregulation is the problem and a study of financial institutions reveals this. Experts say they see no pattern in the process that caused the problems and no historical precedent. That simply doesn't seem to be the case. The savings and loans (S&L) crisis of the 1980s is clearly analogous to the current power crisis. With the phasing out of Regulation Q, intended to allow S&Ls to raise interest payments to compete with money market funds for deposits, S&Ls found themselves subject to a mismatch of liabilities and assets. In effect, their costs became variable and their revenues were fixed — a recipe for disaster.

In an article in *The Economist* in 1982,[2] the S&L situation was succinctly summarized. Substituting the bracketed phrases would aptly describe the current situation for electric utilities in California: "Their plight has been induced by their need to pay higher rates of interest to their depositors [higher prices for natural gas and wholesale power] then they receive on their mortgages [retail electricity prices]. Forbidden by law to increase their rates of existing mortgages [prices of retail electricity]... their net worth has fallen and with it their ratio of net worth to liabilities".

The bottom line is that there is a lack of risk management: utilities sell at fixed prices but buy at variable wholesale prices. Various factors have discouraged hedging in the wholesale power market, exposing them to market risk. For example, tax and accounting considerations can cause profits from hedging to flow to consumers while losses are borne by equity holders.

S&Ls welcomed the lifting of Regulation Q and assumed that risk management would not be an issue. Ironically, electric utilities in California also welcomed deregulation, under the assumption that wholesale electricity prices would be less than retail prices.

The S&L crisis resulted in a government bailout that cost the taxpayers over $200 billion. How does this compare to the current situation in California? The holding companies of Southern

---

[2]"In a Pinch," *The Economist*, April 24, 1982.

Parallels between S&L crisis and the California energy crisis

Issue	S&L	California
Flaw in design	*Regulated:* Resolution Q mandated a ceiling on interest rates paid out (5.5%); S&Ls earn income from fixed-rate long-term mortgage loans	*Regulated:* Cost-based pricing; prices set at fixed levels approved by the regulator
	Deregulated: Short-term interest rates were allowed to fluctuate; people could move money to higher-yielding money market funds but S&Ls kept long-term fixed investments	*Deregulated:* Utilities buy power from the spot market from wholesale electricity generators. Variable market prices sometimes rise to levels 10 times the regulated level of retail prices
Deregulation context	High inflation, high short-term interest rates; high oil prices	High natural gas and oil prices; stagnant electricity supply; high demand
Risk management approach	Exposure to floating short-term rates went unhedged; use of futures market, variable-rate mortgages emerged	Hedging wholesale electricity prices has been discouraged; block forward market is now emerging
Outcome	Costly bailout	Utility bankruptcy? Power outages?
Lessons	● Utilities must use modern risk management tools ● Costs of their inputs must be tied to the price of their output if there is no hedging ● Factor in environmental goods that carry negative values (ie, SO_2, NOx, CO_2)	

The utility of the future

Utility is an asset-liability manager ● Variable price input (ie, fuel) ● Variable price outputs – positive and negative (ie, power and emissions) ● Negative price outputs (ie, SO_2 CO_2, NOx, Mercury, PM)

California Edison and Pacific Gas and Electric have accumulated $20 billion in outstanding debt that has just been downgraded to below investment grade (junk bonds). Some of the unsecured paper traded as low as 50 cents on the dollar and secured paper traded at 80 cents on the dollar. Furthermore, there is another $12 billion in short-term unsecured debt to banks and suppliers. In the middle of January, the Los Angeles County Economic Development Corporation announced that, in the 3rd week of the month, the direct cost of the crisis on sales, wages, and so on, was $1.7 billion. And there is no end in sight.

Temporary remedies are already being sought. Deteriorating credit is likely limiting the amount of available credit to purchase wholesale electricity and natural gas. The governor of the state has agreed to credit enhance the utilities by buying power directly from marketers. The first tranche was $400 million. This can't continue with the state and/or the utilities losing $600,000 an hour at current wholesale prices for electricity. Price caps on wholesale power have been tried and/or are actively being considered. Municipalities, such as the city of San Francisco, are considering starting their own utilities. Some are even calling for a total return to a fully regulated market.

However, some players are already developing financial innovations that will move toward a market-based solution to the problem. EOG Resources, an independent oil and gas producer, recently agreed to sell natural gas to Calpine, a large independent power producer, based on the price it receives for electricity — as opposed to a fixed reference price.[3] A block forward market is also taking shape. The further development of solutions should be guided by the experience with the S&L crisis. The lesson to be learned from the S&L crisis and the debacle in the California market is that utilities must actively manage risk and should be incentivized to do so. Their hedging strategies should also include environmental outputs that have negative values (i.e., emissions of sulfur dioxide, nitrogen oxides, and carbon dioxide).

California has a case of the DDDs — dysfunctional deregulatory disorder. Deregulation must be designed so that utilities can segue into free markets. Many of the solutions to the S&L crisis came from California; let's hope that similar thinking is employed for the current power situation.

I would like to thank Dr. Michael Walsh, Scott Baron, and Rafael Marques for their assistance in the preparation of this article.

---

[3] "California Dreaming", *Barron's*, January 22, 2001.

Chapter 16

The Case for Coal

March 2001

Discussions of coal, as a viable energy source of the future, usually end with cries of concern about its environmental impact. However, these discussions take a different tack when a generating company of the 21st century considers the many factors that affect the cost of producing power. These include the choice of fuel, changes in technology that alter emissions, and the costs of offsetting carbon dioxide (CO_2), sulfur dioxide (SO_2), and other pollutants. Those in the power business who make informed investment decisions and are environmentally concerned should question the premise that, under all conditions, coal is dead.

Many have long considered coal the least desirable fossil fuel because of its environmental impact. It causes acid rain and contributes to global warming. Some concluded that nothing could improve its status. Then came the US Clean Air Act Amendments of 1990. Emissions trading and the economic viability of low sulfur coal, sulfur scrubbing, and nitrogen oxide (NOx) controls have altered the belief that the only way to eliminate acid rain is to reject coal as an energy source. But, this offered only a temporary respite in the belief that coal was dead. Low gas prices bolstered the argument that there was a clean and cost-effective alternative to coal.

After an extended bull market in gas prices, however, and an energy crisis in California, things are changing. Power plant investment decisions are far more complex today and must account for the costs associated with environmental compliance.

Under what conditions might coal-fired generation remain attractive in the face of strict environmental constraints? To answer this question, we examined the economics of new power plant construction in a manner that creates a special new class of hypothetical power plants: the emission-neutral plant. We assume a new power plant must fully offset its emissions of SO_2, NOx, and CO_2 via assumed cap-and-trade systems. Analysis of the emission-neutral plant reveals some interesting and surprising conclusions about fuel choice and environmental costs.

For example, assume a utility must choose among the following alternative investments for a new power plant: coal, gas combined cycle (CC), gas combustion turbine (CT), wind, and solar. Assume the features of each plant reflect the most efficient and clean technologies that are commercially available.[1] The coal and CC plants are run as baseload units (i.e., they produce 85% and 80% of potential annual production, respectively). The gas turbine (GT) plant runs at peak demand with a low capacity factor (15%). The wind and solar plants are smaller in capacity and are assumed to operate at 30% of capacity.

We assume a natural gas cost of \$4.00/million BTU and a coal cost of \$1.21/million BTU (today's prices). Table 1 presents the assumed prices for emission allowances.

Table 1. Environmental compliance cost (\$/ton)

Commodity	Price
CO_2	\$5, \$10
SO_2	\$160
NOx	\$1,500

SO_2 and NOx figures reflect market prices. CO_2 price based on projections and early trading experience

---

[1] Analyzing Electric Power Generation under the CAAA, Office of Air and Radiation; US EPA, March 1998.

Table 2. Emission rates of newly built power plants (lbs/MMBtu)

Plant type	CO_2	SO_2	NOx
Coal	207	0.08	0.1
Gas	117	0	0.024
Wind/solar	0	0	0

Source: Clean Coal Technology Compendium, EPA, DOE

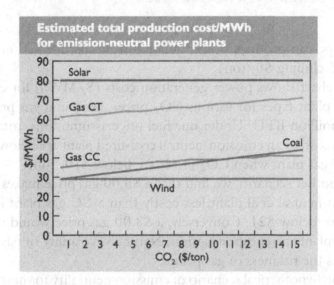

Estimated total production cost/MWh for emission-neutral power plants

The emission rates for each plant type (presented in Table 2) reflect a coal plant that uses low-NOx burners and selective catalytic reduction technologies to control NOx (and mercury), and has wet limestone SO_2 scrubbing (95% effectiveness). The CC gas plant also uses low-NOx burners and selective catalytic reduction technologies to control NOx, whereas the CT plant uses steam injection.

Table 3 presents the capital and operating/maintenance costs reported in the March 1998 Environmental Protection Agency (EPA) study cited in Footnote 1. Capital costs are spread evenly over 20 years. The fifth column shows the total cost per megawatt hour of electricity produced by each emission neutral plant assuming a CO_2 price of $5/ton. The last three columns indicate which

Table 3. Cost estimates for emission-neutral power plants ($/MWh)

Plant type	Levelised capital cost: over 20 yrs ($/MWh)	O&M costs (variable and fixed) ($/MWh)	Total fuel price ($/MWh)*	Total cost† ($/MWh) ($CO_2$ = $5)	Rank 1 (CO_2 = $0)	Rank 2 (CO_2 = $5)	Rank 3‡ (CO_2 = $10)
Wind (50MW)	19	10	–	29	2	1	1
Coal (400MW)	9	7	11	34	1	2	2
Gas CC (400MW)	4	4	27	37	3	3	2
Gas CT (80MW)	14	2	44	64	4	4	3
Solar (5MW)	77	3	–	80	5	5	4

* Coal price = $1.21/million BTU (about $25/short ton), gas price = $4/million BTU; † Includes CO_2, SO_2, NOx costs (see table 2)
‡ The costs for operating a coal unit and a CC are approximately equal at $10/ton CO_2

plant type can produce power at the lowest cost for various CO_2 prices (including $0/ton).

The chart shows power generation costs ($/MWh) for each of the five plant types for various CO_2 prices, assuming gas prices of $4.00/million BTU. Under our fuel price assumptions, total production costs at an emission-neutral coal-fired plant are below those of a CC gas plant when CO_2 prices are below $10/ton.

In another scenario, we find that a $5.00 gas price makes a new emission-neutral coal plant less costly than a CC gas plant if CO_2 prices are below $21. Conversely, a $3.00 gas price would make a CC gas plant the cheapest option. Naturally, volatility of gas prices increases the riskiness of gas plants.

In the hypothetical scenario of emission neutrality for new fossil-fuelled power plants, wind power is the least-cost option. But, while new technologies are making wind power cost competitive, even without comprehensive emission offset requirements for fossil plants, it may not be feasible to meet demand growth exclusively with wind facilities. Their production is inherently variable and they are not feasible in all locations. At the best sites, however, wind plants can be expected to achieve a capacity factor of over 30%, which reduces the cost per hour of generation.[2]

In essence, power generators in the 21st century face indifference curves when choosing to build new power plants. Various combinations of fuel prices, emissions prices (and rules), and technologies

---

[2] American Wind Energy Association.

will yield identical costs of production. A clean-burning gas plant facing high gas prices may have no cost advantage over a coal plant that faces low fuel costs but high environmental costs. Fully offset coal plants can be the least-cost option in locations such as the western United States (e.g., Montana), where power plants can be built right on top of abundant coal reserves.

New coal-fired plants are a viable option under some circumstances, even when their emissions are fully offset. It is also clear that the choice among alternative plant types is quite complex. For example, our model assumes technology is constant and does not include emissions associated with coal extraction.

With US public policy encouraging reliance on domestic energy and sophisticated private sector investment decisions, we may see more coal-fired power plants in the near future.

Chapter 17

SO$_2$ Auction Shows Power of Markets

April 2001

They don't have trading pits in Chicago for sulfur dioxide (SO$_2$) or vast arcades for environmental derivatives. The talk on the floor centers around the potential impact of foot-and-mouth disease on grain and animal prices, or whether the Dow Jones Industrial Average has bottomed.

But at a press conference in the boardroom at the Chicago Board of Trade (CBOT) and by teleconference in Washington, DC and Atlanta, Georgia, there's a genuine interest in the outcome of the ninth annual auction of SO$_2$ allowances conducted by CBOT on behalf of the Environmental Protection Agency (EPA).

The 1990 Amendments to the Clean Air Act provided the enabling legislation for the "cap and trade" program designed to curtail US emissions of pollutants that cause acid rain in the United States and Canada. Title IV of the Amendments provided the basis for two separate phases of implementation. The first began in 1995. Following instructions established by Congress, the EPA allocated emissions allowances to the 110 highest emitting power plants, affecting 263 combustion units. Each year the plants are required to cut aggregate emissions to conform to steadily declining quantified emission limits. The second phase of the program began in January 2000. It extended the limits to include another 2,100 units and the national emission cap was set at approximately 9 million tons. This represented a 50% reduction from the 1980s.

It is well documented that sulfur emissions fell faster than required and positive conclusions from early scientific impact reports have recently been confirmed. Importantly, the evidence of economic success is also overwhelming.

The passage of the legislation depended on the hotly debated forecasts of the price of allowances. Table 1 presents a sample of some of the forecasts of Phase I prices.

It is important to emphasize that while the optimistic projections of Phase I prices were at or just below $300, many predicted that allowance prices would double by Phase II. Yet the results of the first EPA annual SO_2 allowance auction, conducted by the CBOT in 1993, had a spot market clearing price of just $131. The results for the next five auctions further confirmed that early forecasts were significantly higher than observed prices (see Table 2). The apologists continued to assert that the early forecasts for Phase I were correct, and that they would ultimately be proven right when we entered Phase II. In fact, allowance prices in the 1999 auction reached $207. The chart shows the history of spot and 7-year advance market clearing prices in the annual auctions.

While the spot market clearing prices from the auction have remained consistent with prices in the private market, the advanced "forward" auctions have revealed an interesting shift in recent years. Between 1993 and 1998, the average spread between the spot

Table 1. Pre-1992 forecasts of Phase I SO₂ allowance prices

Source	Price forecast ($/ton)
United Mine Workers	981
Ohio Coal Office	785
Electric Power Research Institute	688
Sierra Club	446
American Electric Power	392
Resource Data International	309

Source: Hahn and May, The Electricity Journal, March 1994

market price and the forward market price has been tight at around $6. However, in the past three years, this differential has risen significantly to $57 on average. A low forward price for allowances may be due to uncertainty concerning regulation or a forecast that mitigation will be cheaper later in Phase II.

The success of the SO_2 program supports the argument that its core elements should be applied to carbon trading. Clear rules on emissions monitoring and penalties for noncompliance, unimpeded trading, fully fungible trading instruments, and transparent public-private partnerships are fundamental in the creation of a carbon market.

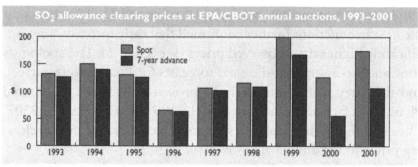

SO_2 allowance clearing prices at EPA/CBOT annual auctions, 1993–2001

Table 2. 2001 acid rain allowance auction results

I. Allowances available for auction

Origin of allowances	Spot auction	7-year advance auction
EPA	125,000	125,000
Privately offered	2,788	2,388
Total	127,788	127,388

II. Spot auction results

Allowances	Number of bids	Number of bidders	Bid price ($)
Bids for: 480,995	Successful: 14	Successful: 12	Highest: 225.00
Sold: 127,788	Unsuccessful: 71	Unsuccessful: 15	Clearing: 173.57
	Total: 85	Total: 27	Lowest: 105.00
			Average (weighted): 174.97

III. Seven-year advance auction results

Allowances	Number of bids	Number of bidders	Bid price ($)
Bids for: 355,500	Successful: 6	Successful: 1	Highest: 115.07
Sold: 127,388	Unsuccessful: 14	Unsuccessful: 4	Clearing: 105.72
	Total: 20	Total: 5	Lowest: 30.00
			Average (weighted): 110.75

Source: US Environmental Protection Agency, Chicago Board of Trade

Already, voluntary initiatives such as the Chicago Climate Exchange are harnessing the successes of the SO$_2$ program in the design of a carbon dioxide (CO$_2$) trading program. This is further supported by recently proposed cap-and-trade and carbon biomass sequestration legislation introduced by both Republicans and Democrats in the US House and Senate, as well as domestic trading programs in Europe.

These efforts are just precursors to a regulated CO$_2$ trading program. The SO$_2$ program has demonstrated the success of emissions trading in the United States. A CO$_2$ trading program can bring similar success on a global scale.

I would like to thank Dr. Michael Walsh, Alice LeBlanc, Rafael Marques, and Scott Baron for their assistance in the preparation of this article.

Chapter 18

"It Ain't Over Till It's Over"

Yogi Berra, Catcher, New York Yankees

May 2001

Efforts to address climate change are quietly continuing in the United States. In the second half of March, Christie Todd Whitman, administrator of the Environmental Protection Agency, said that President Bush's letter to Senate Republicans rejecting caps on carbon dioxide (CO_2) emissions from the electricity sector was not intended to "preclude all action on CO_2". In fact, there have recently been a considerable number of proposals in the United States to deal with climate change.

On 29 March, Richard Lugar (R-IN), chairman of the Senate Agriculture Committee, held hearings on emissions trading and carbon sinks. On 23 April, Massachusetts became the first state to announce regulations that call for significant reductions in CO_2. Three days later, Alcoa announced a plan to reduce its emissions of greenhouse gases (GHGs) by 25% (and possibly 50%) from 1990 levels by 2010. Many companies in the Semiconductor Industry Association have also agreed to make GHG reductions. Today's international debate tends to dismiss these signs. Instead, it focuses on the notion that the United States has dropped out of the battle against climate change. In fact, the public and private sectors are beginning to embrace voluntary efforts to mitigate GHG emissions and to promote emissions trading as the best policy instrument to achieve these reductions at least cost to society.

There's a history of legislative efforts to promote CO_2 emission reductions in the United States and it continues. During the 106th Congress (1999–2000), more than 20 bills were introduced related to climate change. The sponsors and cosponsors were Republicans and Democrats, representing a substantial bipartisan effort. These bills can be classified as

- proposals to provide credit for "early" reductions of GHG emissions;
- proposals to establish quantified limits on CO_2 emissions, generally from electric power plants as part of a multiple pollutant strategy covering CO_2, SO_2, NOx, and mercury, coupled with emissions trading;
- bills that would provide funding or incentives for activities that measure or sequester carbon in biomass or soils, both at home and abroad; and
- funding for research and development, or subsidies, for renewable energy, energy efficiency, or other low-carbon sources of energy supply.

Most of these proposals did not get out of committee hearings but, taken as a whole, they are significant because they indicate a growing awareness and concern regarding climate change and the policy options to address it. The proposals deemed most important, in terms of establishing the infrastructure or promoting a market for emissions trading, are summarized below and in the table. Also presented are legislative efforts that have been introduced, or are expected to be introduced, during the 107th Congress (2001–2002).

Early Reduction Credits

The Chafee–Lieberman Bill in the Senate (S 547) and the Lazio–Dooley Bill in the House (HR 2520) attempted to provide

Summary of current legislation in the US Congress

Credit for early action:
To provide incentives for companies to make reductions in GHG emissions
through credits that would be recognised in future regulatory regimes in the US.
1999–2000
  Credit for Voluntary Reduction Act (S 547) (Sen. Chafee-Lieberman)
  HR 2520 (Reps. Lazio-Dooley)

4-Pollutant (CO_2, NOx, SO_2 and Mercury):
To establish a cap on CO_2 emissions from the electric power sector in the US
and establish or allow emissions trading.
1999–2000
  HR 2900 *Clean Smokestacks Act of 1999* (Reps. Waxman and Boehlert)
  HR 2980 *Clean Power Plant Act of 1999* (Rep. Allen)
  HR 4861 *Clean Power Act* (Reps. Lazio and Boehlert)
  HR 2569 *Fair Energy Competition Act of 1999* (Rep. Pallone)
  S 1369 *Clean Energy Act of 1999* (Sen. Jeffords)
2000–2001
  The Clean Power Act of 2001 (S 556) (Sen. Jeffords and Lieberman)
  The Clean Smokestacks Act of 2001 (HR 1256) (Reps. Waxman and Boehlert)

Carbon sequestration:
1999–2000
  S 2540 *Domestic Carbon Storage Incentive Act of 2000* (Sen. Brownback)
  S 2982 *International Carbon Sequestration Incentive Act* (Sen. Brownback)
  S 1457 *Forest Resources for the Environment and the Economy Act* (Sen. Wyden,
  Craig and Johnson)
2000–2001
  S 765 *Carbon Sequestration Investment Tax Credit Act* (Sen. Brownback)
  S 769 *International Carbon Conservation Act* (Sen. Brownback)

companies with incentives to make reductions in GHG emissions
through credits that would be recognized in future regulatory
regimes in the United States. Thus, they provide a framework for
future GHG emissions trading. Even if mandatory GHG limits and
trading are imposed on electricity generators through legislation
such as the "four-pollutant" bills, early reduction credit legislation
could provide incentives for industries other than the electric power
industry to take early action.

Tonnage Cap on CO_2

Several bills (e.g., HR 2900, HR 2980, HR 4861, HR 2569, S 1369) were introduced in both the House and Senate to provide a "four-pollutant" or other multi-pollutant approach that includes SO_2, NOx, CO_2, and mercury. All of these would establish a cap on CO_2 emissions from the US electric power sector and establish or allow emissions trading. In mid-March, just days after President Bush's decision to withdraw support for limiting CO_2 emissions from the electric power sector, versions of the four-pollutant bill were reintroduced in both the Senate and House by bipartisan sponsors (S 556 and HR 1256).

Carbon Sequestration

In related legislative initiatives, Senator Sam Brownback (R-KS) introduced the International Carbon Sequestration Incentive Act and The Domestic Carbon Storage Incentive Act. The goals of these Acts are to enhance international conservation, promote carbon sequestration as a means of slowing the build-up of GHGs in the atmosphere, and reward and encourage voluntary environmental efforts that address climate change. Senator Brownback reintroduced both of these bills in late April in the 107th Congress.

In other anticipated developments in the 107th Congress, Senator Smith's (R-NH) Environmental and Public Works Committee appears to be studying ways to develop a multipollutant bill that would include CO_2, perhaps on a voluntary basis, and might receive administration support.

Initiatives have also been undertaken at the state level. Examples include a carbon sequestration bill recently signed in Wyoming and similar efforts in Nebraska, Oklahoma, and South Dakota. Climate change or emissions trading legislation has also been discussed or introduced in Illinois, Michigan, Minnesota, Ohio, and Wisconsin.

In addition to "voluntary" and "emissions trading", the other word that seems to be emerging in Washington, DC is "registry".

It is likely that legislation will emerge from several sources to develop a voluntary registry for GHG reductions — a more rigorous approach to the US Department of Energy's 1605(B) database program that could provide the basis for baseline protection, or early reduction credit, in a later regulatory environment.

This column has previously described a private sector, voluntary initiative for trading GHGs that includes the establishment of a registry — the Chicago Climate Exchange. A report on the Exchange's progress including a few pleasant surprises will be included in this column next month.

Chapter 19

Corporate Giants to Aid Design of US Carbon Market

June 2001

As the United States enters a major debate on energy use and endeavors to develop a policy to reduce carbon dioxide (CO_2) emissions, a project taking shape in the upper Midwest is poised to test market-based solutions to global warming.

The size, diversity, and volume of emissions (1.375 billion tons of CO_2 per year) from this region — Illinois, Indiana, Iowa, Michigan, Minnesota, Ohio, and Wisconsin — make it well suited as a starting point for a robust and representative greenhouse gas (GHG) emissions trading market expandable to include all of North America. The region's economic output of $2 trillion is equal to that of the United Kingdom and the Netherlands combined. A diverse group of major firms has indicated their intent to participate in the design phase of a voluntary pilot trading market for the region, the Chicago Climate Exchange (CCX — see Table 1).

A study of such a market suggests a goal of reducing participants' GHG emissions by 5% below 1999 levels over 5 years. The feasibility study for the CCX was funded by the Chicago-based Joyce Foundation through a special Millennium Initiative grant to the Kellogg Graduate School of Management at Northwestern University. According to Joyce Foundation president Paula DiPerna,

75

1. Companies participating in the design phase of the CCX	
Agriliance	National Council of
Alliant Energy	Farmer Cooperatives
Calpine	NiSource
Carr Futures/Crédit	ORMAT
Agricole Indosuez	Pinnacle West Capital
Cinergy	PG&E National
DuPont	Energy Group
Ford Motor Company	STMicroelectronics
GROWMARK	Suncor Energy
IGF Insurance	Swiss Re
International Paper	Temple-Inland
Iowa Farm Bureau	The Nature
Federation	Conservancy
IT Group	Wisconsin Energy
Midwest Generation	ZAPCO

"the CCX would represent a major step forward while an appropriate regulatory framework for greenhouse gases evolves. A regional success on a global challenge like climate change could be transformational. Because of its variety of economic activities, including its strong agricultural sector, the Midwest is the perfect place to begin demonstrating the regional-global interface".

Trading will help reduce GHG emissions cost-effectively and offer new opportunities for environment-based income for farmers, foresters, and renewable energy firms.

A high-level advisory board consisting of academic, business, environmental, and public sector leaders has been formed with the objective of gathering strategic input (see Table 2).

The notion of trading carbon emissions has long been debated, but the proposed CCX offers the first test of the concept on a scale that has global potential.

As proposed, the exchange could:

- demonstrate that GHG emissions trading can achieve real reductions in emissions across multiple business sectors;
- help discover the price of reducing GHG emissions; and
- develop the frameworks, for monitoring emissions, determining offsets, and conducting trades, needed for a successful market.

2. Advisory board members

David Boren	President of The University of Oklahoma; former US Senator and Governor of Oklahoma
Ernst Brugger	Founding Partner and Chairman of Brugger Hanser & Partners
Jeffrey E Garten	Dean of Yale School of Management
Lucien Y Bronicki	Chairman of ORMAT International
Donald P Jacobs	Dean, Kellogg Graduate School of Management, Northwestern University
Dennis Jennings	Global Risk Management Solutions Leader, PricewaterhouseCoopers
Jonathan Lash	President, World Resources Institute
Joseph P Kennedy II	Chairman and President of Boston-based Citizens Energy Group; former US Congressman
Israel Klabin	President of the Brazilian Foundation for Sustainable Development
Bill Kurtis	National broadcaster, host of Arts & Entertainment cable TV show
Thomas E Lovejoy	Chief Biodiversity Advisor to the President of the World Bank
David Moran	President of Dow Jones Indexes
Les Rosenthal	Former Chairman, Chicago Board of Trade; principal, Rosenthal Collins
Maurice Strong	Chairman of the Earth Council, former UN Under-Secretary General
James R Thompson	Former four-term Gov. of Illinois
Brian Williamson	Chairman, London International Financial Futures and Options Exchange (LIFFE)

The study proposes starting the market in the seven Midwest states, including emission offset projects in Brazil, and expanding over time to include all of the United States, Canada, and Mexico. Participating companies would be issued tradable emission allowances. Emitting firms would commit to a phased schedule for reducing their emissions by 5% by 2005. They could then either cut their emissions directly, buy allowances from companies that have achieved surplus reductions, or buy credits from agricultural or other offset projects. Potential offset projects would include renewable energy systems and the capture and use of agricultural and landfill methane. Offsets could also be generated by carbon sequestration projects such as forest expansion and conservation

3. Proposed market architecture for the Chicago Climate Exchange

Geographic coverage	2002: emission sources and projects in seven Midwest states; 2003–05: emission sources and projects in US, Canada and Mexico; Offsets also accepted from projects in Brazil for both periods.
Greenhouse gases covered	Carbon dioxide, methane and all other targeted GHGs
Emission reduction targets	2002: 2% below 1999 levels, falling 1% per year through 2005
Industries and firms targeted	Primarily 'downstream' participants: power plants, refineries, factories, forestry, vehicle fleets; 40 firms initially targeted. Individual entities or co-operating groups of entities must have emissions exceeding 250,000 tons CO_2e in 1999 to become a participating emission source.
Tradable instruments	Fully interchangeable emission allowances (original issue) and offsets produced by targeted mitigation projects
Eligible offset projects	A. Carbon sequestration in forests and domestic soils; B. Renewable energy systems; C. Methane destruction in agriculture, landfills and coalbeds Offsets must be aggregated into pools of 100,000 tons CO_2e per year; Projects placed into service after 1 January 1999 can qualify.
Emissions/project monitoring	Direct measurement (eg CEMs); fuel flows/emission factors; carbon sequestration: standard tables, case-specific estimates, direct measurement.
Provisions for new facilities	Allowance allocations reflect best technology emission rates
Annual public auctions	2% of issued allowances withheld and auctioned in "spot" and "forward" auctions, proceeds returned pro rata
Central registry	Central database to record and transfer allowances and offsets; interfaces with emissions database and trading platform
Trading mechanisms	Standardised CCX Electronic Market, private contracting
Trade documentation	Uniform documentation provided to facilitate trade
Accounting and tax issues	Accounting guidance suggested by generally accepted accounting principles; precedent exists for US tax treatment
Market governance	Self-governing structure to oversee rules, monitoring and trade

soil management, which remove CO_2 from the atmosphere (see Table 3).

The commitment from the advisory committee and the participating companies is to be commended. Their input in the design phase will help formulate the final rules and procedures for the CCX and determine if this regional program can shape the beginning of a global solution to climate change.

I would like to thank Dr. Michael Walsh, Alice LeBlanc, Rafael Marques, and Scott Baron for their invaluable support and intellectual contributions to this feasibility study.

With special thanks to the Joyce Foundation and Paula DiPerna, Margaret O'Dell, Mary O'Connell, and James Seidita for making all this possible.

Chapter 20

And the Beat Goes on

July–August 2001

It seems to be happening again. The shape of voluntary international emissions trading took one more small step toward clarity in June. Nuon, a Dutch utility company and GSF Energy, an affiliate of the US company DQE Inc., concluded a path-breaking transaction involving Nuon's purchase of greenhouse gas (GHG) emission reduction credits equivalent to 301,252 tons of carbon dioxide (CO_2).

Headquartered in Amsterdam, Nuon is one of the largest multi-utility companies in the Netherlands, providing services such as electricity, gas, water, and heat to 2.5 million residential and commercial customers. GSF Energy, a landfill gas (LFG) recovery firm, currently owns facilities across the United States and provides turnkey design, financing, construction, and operation of LFG recovery systems.

The emission reduction credits are attributable to GSF's methane capture program at a sanitary landfill located in Monmouth County, New Jersey, during 2000, and the destruction of the captured methane to generate 54,113,598 kWh of electricity. GPU Energy, the New Jersey electric utility that sold and distributed the electricity to end users, facilitated the transaction by providing documentation to confirm GSF's unencumbered ownership of the GHG emission reduction credits.

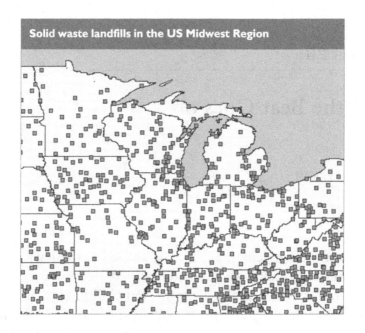

Without installation of the LFG collection systems, the methane would have otherwise been vented into the atmosphere, thereby contributing to global warming. The capture and use of the land-fill methane converts a highly potent GHG to a renewable energy resource.

The purchase by a European company of GHG offsets from an American renewable energy company makes the transaction a landmark trade. Chicago-based Environmental Financial Products arranged the transaction.

It is important to put this trade in a macro context. Emissions from landfills in the United States represent the largest source of methane from human activities. In 1999, emissions were equivalent to 188 million tons of CO_2. This represents a significant decrease from the 1990 level of 236 million tons[1] which is attributable to the large increase in projects associated with capturing methane from landfills.

---

[1]Voluntary Reporting of Greenhouse Gases 1999, US Energy Information Administration.

In 1990, there were only 89 landfill gas-to-energy (LFGTE) projects in operation. This grew to 299 in 2000.[2] Furthermore, significant gains are still possible. There are 6000 landfills scattered across the United States with only 325 LFGTE systems currently operating. The Environmental Protection Agency estimates that there may be up to 700 new landfills with the ability to convert methane to electricity. These LFGTE projects are capable of producing electricity for approximately 3 million houses across the United States. This would be equivalent to offsetting the emissions of close to 24 million cars. These estimates may appreciably underestimate the potential. It is self-evident that the monetization of environmental services through GHG trading will increase the return on projects. This means currently marginal investments could become profitable. Opportunities like this exist elsewhere around the world.

For example, opportunities to generate LFG GHG reductions in Canada have been demonstrated by the successful processing of over half a dozen LFG projects through Ontario's Pilot Emission Reduction Trading project (PERT), which has now been reformed as Clean Air Canada Inc. The World Bank's Prototype Carbon Fund included among its first projects a LFG-energy project in Latvia. And tremendous potential to generate GHG reductions exists in places like Brazil, where a large LFG energy resource is virtually untapped.

In the past, we have promised to transmit in this column information on GHG markets in general, and the Chicago Climate Exchange (CCX) in particular. The illustration shows the potential for landfill methane reduction in the Midwest. The 121 landfills in the seven states targeted for the initial market could generate 5 million tons of CO_2-equivalent reductions per year.

We are pleased to report that a second company with LFG projects — Waste Management — is joining Zahren Alternative Power Corporation in the CCX design phase. Waste Management is

---

[2] 2000 Update of US Landfill Gas-To-Energy Projects, Landfill Methane Outreach Program, US Environmental Protection Agency.

a leading provider of comprehensive waste management services and operates 73 LFG-to-energy facilities. Finally, since our last report, energy giant BP, forest products firm Mead and flooring products company Interface have also agreed to participate in the design of the CCX.

Chapter 21

The Case for Plurilateral Environmental Markets

September 2001

> "Economic history is the story of the gradual extension of the economic community beyond its original limits of the single household to embrace the nation and then the world"
>
> Ludwig Von Mises, *The Theory of Money and Credit*

Diplomats return to the negotiating table this fall in Marrakech to work out further details of the Kyoto Protocol amid a flurry of activity surrounding emissions trading. Individual trades continue to be closed since the last meetings in Bonn. At the same time, individual governments are beginning to take action.

Seeking to become the world leader in emissions trading, the United Kingdom announced that it will launch the first comprehensive market in April 2002. The announcement is significant for several reasons: it represents the first governmental push since the historic agreement in Bonn; it illustrates one particular sovereign approach to domestic goals; and it provides insights into how an international market may evolve.

The motivation was unambiguous. Michael Meacher, the UK Minister of the Environment, indicated that the government's purpose was to give British business a lead in this area — a laudable goal. The United Kingdom had previously announced its goal of reducing

83

greenhouse gas (GHG) emissions by 23% below their 1990 level by 2010.

Several important points should be noted by students of environmental markets. The program was developed by the government and a consortium of businesses known as the Emissions Trading Group. It is a voluntary program. Participating companies agree to take on an emissions cap in exchange for government-funded incentives and their right to sell surplus credits. A government budget of $215 million ($310 million) has been established by the public sector to provide incentives for companies to join. Implementation will begin with a competitive bidding process in the first quarter of 2002 that will establish both the targets and incentives.

Separately, the British government has indicated that it will attempt to merge this domestic scheme into the pilot European Union program scheduled to begin in 2005 with as little friction as possible. The EU program will ultimately be part of the worldwide scheme envisioned in the Kyoto Protocol.

Other individual sovereign efforts are also under way. In the Netherlands, the government plans to set up a CO_2 trading system by 2004–2005. In Japan, a working group comprising members of both the public and private sectors has been meeting for the past few months to discuss setting up an emissions trading market. Denmark launched the first domestic market but it was limited solely to the power sector. The Danish program includes only eight companies and no trades were recorded by the Danish Energy Agency (DEA) in 2000. Several participants in the Danish scheme have expressed an interest in setting up an exchange, according to the DEA.

In the United States, legislation aimed at addressing climate change through the use of market mechanisms continues to appear both at the federal and state levels. Recently, Senators McCain (R — Arizona) and Lieberman (D — Connecticut) have publicly endorsed the establishment of a domestic cap-and-trade program for the United States, later to be expanded to the rest of North America. In the US private sector, the Chicago Climate Exchange (CCX) has just started its design phase, and now includes a total of

35 entities that will help design a market to be expanded to the rest of the North American Free Trade Agreement (NAFTA). All these efforts will start to be harmonized in the next few years. They are summarized in the table below.

Recent sovereign and private initiatives

Country/region	Initiative
UK	Domestic market to be launched in spring of 2002
Denmark	Cap-and-trade system for power sector; some companies plan to set up an exchange
Netherlands	Cap-and-trade system by 2004–05
European Union	EU-wide emissions trading system by 2005
United States	Chicago Climate Exchange; federal and state level legislative initiatives
Japan	Private-public sector working group on emissions trading

We have long both advocated and forecast that the development of an international GHG market would emerge from a "bottom up" and voluntary approach. This mirrors the history of other internationally traded markets. Furthermore, the evolutionary process of market development is also consistent with the history of international political cooperation. International agreements tend to grow from small beginnings — the European Coal and Steel Community has evolved into the Common Market and, now, the European Monetary Union.

In the case of carbon trading, the United Kingdom has taken the first comprehensive step and we believe that a group of countries will coalesce into what we have called a "plurilateral"[1] trading regime. This will require mature individual markets as well as harmonization among them. It is very important to emphasize that the historical record indicates that integration of markets can succeed even

---

[1] A "plurilateral" regime refers to the development of a framework for GHG emissions trading involving a medium-sized set of countries (e.g., 5–20). The concept of a plurilateral regime was first introduced by Environmental Financial Products at the first UNCTAD GHG Emissions Trading Policy Forum in Chicago in June 1997 and at the second Policy Forum in Toronto in November 1997. I would like to thank James Perkaus for first introducing this concept into the discussions while acting as a consultant to Environmental Financial Products in 1997.

if the individual markets exhibit fundamentally different character-istics. The development of efficient markets will probably occupy market participants for the next 5–10 years. Sometime during this first decade of the 21st century we hope to see a truly international GHG market that is as efficient as those of other internationally traded commodities.

Finally, as promised, an update on the CCX. The Joyce Founda-tion in August awarded funding for the design phase of the CCX. Both the foundation and the Kellogg Graduate School of Manage-ment at Northwestern University remain committed to the idea. Westcoast Energy, a Canadian energy group, and Michigan-based CMS Generation have joined the design phase and three more individuals have agreed to join the CCX advisory board. They are Mary Schapiro, head of the regulatory arm of NASDAQ; Elizabeth Dowdeswell, a former executive director of the United Nations Environment Programme; and Dr R K Pachauri, the head of Delhi-based Tata Energy Research Institute (TERI). We extend to them our warmest welcome.

Chapter 22

DJSI World: Two Years on

October 2001

In the inaugural issue of this magazine, and in its first anniversary issue, this column described the impact of sustainability on asset management. We focused on the Dow Jones Sustainability World Index (DJSI World) as the industry leader in sustainable investing. As promised, this is our annual update.

In September 2001, Dow Jones Indexes and the SAM Group announced the results of their annual review. The DJSI World, as of 5 October 2001, will include 311 companies representing 62 industries in 26 countries. They have a market capitalization of approximately €6 trillion ($5.5 trillion). This compares with last year's index of 236 companies and a market capitalization of around €4 trillion. The full list of constituents can be seen on the following web page: http://www.sustainabilityindex.com/djsi_world/components.html.

This year's annual review was marked by greater corporate interest in the indexes. An additional 500 companies were added to last year's universe of 2,000 screened companies. Thousand companies were rated and 500 questionnaires were completed and returned. Companies could also make use of an interactive web-based questionnaire.

Table 1. Leading companies by score and sector

Company (country)	Market sector
Volkswagen (Ger)	Auto
UBS Group (Switz)	Bank
Dofasco (Can)	Basic resources
Dow Chemical Co (US)	Chemical
Skanska (Swe)	Construction
Sony Corp (Jap)	Cyclical goods/services
Royal Dutch Petroleum/ Shell Transport & Trading (Neth)	Energy
ING Groep (Neth)	Financial Services
Unilever (Neth)	Food & beverage makers
Bristol-Myers Squibb (US)	Healthcare
Minnesota Mining & Manufacturing (US)	Industrial goods/services
Swiss Re (Switz)	Insurance
Granada Media (UK)	Media
Procter & Gamble (US)	Non-cyclical goods/ services
Ito-Yokado Co (Jap)	Retail
Intel Corp (US)	Technology
British Telecommunications (UK)	Telecommunications
Severn Trent (UK)	Utilities

The focus on independent verification and transparency was heightened. For the first time, a list of the leading companies in the DJSI World by corporate sustainability score and market sector was published (see Table 1).

Market acceptance of DJSI World continues. The number of licensees has almost doubled in the last year and it includes some of the premier financial institutions in the world (see Table 2). Products range from mutual funds and segregated accounts to equity baskets. Assets managed in these portfolios now amount to more than €2.2 billion.

The reason for this growth appears to be one single factor: performance. The recent bear market suggests that this index is still quite robust during difficult economic times.

Expanding on the success of the DJSI World, Dow Jones Indexes, STOXX Ltd, and SAM Group recently announced the

Table 2. Current licensees

Institution (country)	Product offered
Westpac IM (Australia)	Index fund
Kepler Fonds KAG (Austria)	Fund
Cordius Asset Management (Bel)	Fund
Rothschild & Cie Gestion (Fr)	Fund
HypoVereinsbank (Ger)	Warrant
DWS (Ger)	Fund
Fürst Fugger Privatbank (Ger)	Fund
Gerling Investment KAG (Ger)	Fund
GZ Bank (Ger)	Equity linked note
Invesco (Ger)	Fund
Oppenheim KAG (Ger)	Fund
State Street Global Advisors (Ger)	Fund
Union Investment (Ger)	Fund
BNL Gestioni (Italy)	Fund
Nikko Asset Management (Jap)	Fund
Banque Générale de Luxembourg	Fund
Deutsche Postbank (Lux)	Fund
Aegon (Neth)	Fund
ING Fund Management (Neth)	Fund
Rabobank (Neth)	Certificate
Robeco Groep (Neth)	Fund
Folksam Sak (Swe)	Fund
Skandinaviska Enskilda Bank (Swe)	Fund
SPP (Swe)	Fund
Baloise Insurance (Switz)	Fund
Credit Suisse Asset Man (Switz)	Fund
Sustainable Asset Man (Switz)	Fund
Sustainable Perf Group (Switz)	Investment co
Synchrony Asset Man (Switz)	Certificate

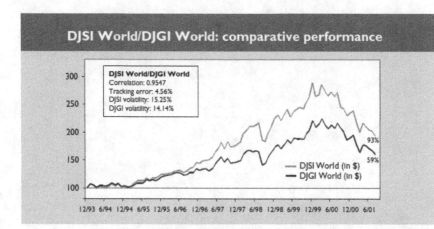

DJSI World/DJGI World: comparative performance

DJSI World/DJGI World
Correlation: 0.9547
Tracking error: 4.56%
DJSI volatility: 15.25%
DJGI volatility: 14.14%

93%
59%

DJSI World (in $)
DJGI World (in $)

12/93 6/94 12/94 6/95 12/95 6/96 12/96 6/97 12/97 6/98 12/98 6/99 12/99 6/00 12/00 6/01

launch of a new set of sustainability indexes for European port-folios, containing only European companies. There will be more on this in a future column.

I would like to thank Alex Barkawi, managing director of SAM Indexes GmbH, for his assistance in the preparation of this article.

IN MEMORIAM

Carlton Bartels (1958–2001)

A dear friend and colleague, Carlton's vision and work on emissions trading will stay with us. Our feelings are perhaps best expressed by John Donne's poem:

> *"No man is an island, entire of itself;*
> *every man is a piece of the continent,*
> *a part of the main.*
> *If a clod be washed away by the sea,*
> *Europe is the less, as well as if a*
> *promontory were,*
> *as well as if a manor of thy friend's or*
> *of thine own were:*
> *any man's death diminishes me,*
> *because I am involved in mankind,*
> *and therefore never send to know for*
> *whom the bells tolls;*
> *it tolls for thee."*
>
> **John Donne** (1624)

Chapter 23

The Convergence of Environmental and Capital Markets: Another Step

November 2001

After a decade of debate within the environmental movement on markets versus command and control there is some good news for the private sector. The European Commission has embraced capitalism as a climate protection policy tool.

On 23 October, the Commission released draft rules for a European Union carbon dioxide (CO_2) emissions trading system. According to Environment Commissioner Margot Wallström, "the emissions trading system will be an important cornerstone in our strategy to reduce emissions in the most cost-effective way". She accurately emphasized that "the proposal on emissions trading represents a major innovation in environmental policy in Europe".

This is a bold and intelligent proposal that resonates with clarity. It recognizes the need to start with a limited pilot program and expand coverage over time. Wallström explicitly acknowledged the guiding principle of any demonstration project, "...as a first step we must establish confidence in a system that is shown to work, with adequate controls".

The salient features of the proposal for the initial period are presented in Table 1. It can generally be described as a greenhouse gas (GHG) emissions trading system. The first phase will begin in 2005 and conclude at the end of 2007.

Table I. Salient features of the initial phase of the European Union GHG emissions trading proposal

GHGs covered	Carbon dioxide only, expressed in tonnes of CO_2 equivalent
Trading period	Beginning of 2005 to end of 2007
Standards	Individual facilities will be granted permits that require the unit to surrender annually allowances that are equal to its emissions and to monitor, verify and report its emissions. Banking of allowances will be allowed during the three-year period. Allowances will have a lifetime not extending beyond the first phase and will be granted free of charge. Each member state may allocate its allowances based on objective and transparent criteria
Targeted activities	Power and heat generation for units of more than 20MW (with the exception of hazardous or municipal waste installations), coke ovens, mineral oil refineries, production and processing of ferrous metals, mineral industry, and industrial plants for the production of pulp from timber and paper and board with a production capacity exceeding 20 tonnes/day
Registry	Member states will establish national registries
Verification protocols	Performed either by "competent authorities" or an "independent verifier" at the discretion of the member state
Non-compliance penalties	Per-tonne penalties for excess emissions will be the higher of €50 or twice the average market price of allowances during a predetermined period
Programme review	By 31 December 2004, the Commission may make a proposal for the inclusion of other activities and gases. Another review may also be carried by 30 June 2006

It will include only CO_2 emissions from limited industrial sectors in an allowance-based program. Individual facilities will be granted permits that require each industrial unit to surrender allowances annually that are equal to its verified emissions and to monitor, verify, and report its emissions. Permits are nontransferable, but each facility will be allocated transferable allowances, or the right to emit a designated quantity of metric tons of CO_2.

Banking of allowances will be allowed during the initial 3-year period. The traded instruments will have a lifetime not extending beyond the 3-year period. Initial penalties for noncompliance will be set at lower levels than those imposed in the subsequent budget period (2008–2012). The penalty for each excess ton emitted in the first phase will be the higher of €50 ($45) or twice the average market price of allowances during a predetermined period. Initially, there will be no legally binding targets limiting emissions by each of the member states. The proposal indicates that facilities will be granted allowances free of charge during the initial period. This is meant to minimize the competitive impacts of different allocation mechanisms among the member states.

Member states will establish national registries. Allowance tracking will be modeled after the allowance tracking system in the US Sulfur dioxide (SO_2) program. Verification will be either by "competent authorities" or an "independent verifier" at the discretion of the member state. The bearer of verification costs will also be determined by the member state. The allowances to cover a prior year's emissions must be surrendered by 31 March the following year.

Member states will periodically be required to report on the progress of the pilot. Issues to be addressed include activities such as allocation experience, monitoring, and verification.

At the outset, the sectors to be covered range from power generation to manufacturing. Specifically excluded are direct emissions from the chemical industry (except from power and heat generation facilities of greater than 20MW) and waste management. The rationale for the former is that emissions in that sector are small and the large number of installations would add to the "administrative burden" of the program. The rationale for the latter is the inability to measure the carbon content of incinerated matter accurately.

The proposal is purposely silent on market organization. It correctly supposes that the structures will arise as the program is delineated. Furthermore, it relies on the private sector to drive solutions in this area.

There are other exclusions that are worth mentioning. The initial proposal specifically excludes credit for project-based mitigation efforts. The proposal is silent on crediting of sequestration in soils and forests as well as credits from renewable energy generated from the use of landfill methane. The commission feels that the enormity of the challenge requires that initially it will exclude project-based credits. However, project-based activities, especially those associated with joint implementation (JI) and the clean development mechanism (CDM), are specifically mentioned as being desirable to include in the future.

The decision of the Commission has been widely praised by those who believe in market-based solutions to environmental constraints. But, whether this program will provide an accurate indication of the cost of reducing GHGs is a far more tricky and complicated question. Its self-imposed limit to initially achieve reductions in GHGs through changes in industrial activity alone and the exclusion of five GHGs may send very inappropriate price signals. Furthermore, while the Commission's motivations are very rational about the exclusion of JI and the CDM at this stage, this sends a less than desirable message to developing countries and economies in transition. There is still hope. The Commission has explicitly indicated that by 31 December 2004 it might make a proposal to include other activities and other gases.

This chapter is dedicated to the memory of Steve Goldstein. He will be sorely missed by friends and family. I would like to thank Michael Walsh, Alice LeBlanc, and Rafael Marques for their assistance in the preparation of this chapter.

Chapter 24

The DJSI — A Story of Financial Innovation

December 2001–January 2002

> **Richard Sandor** and his guest co-author **Alois Flatz** reflect on the birth and development of stock market indexes to aid the growth of sustainable investments

At the beginning of the 1990s, two apparently unrelated financial developments occurred. The first was the launching of the International Chamber of Commerce (ICC) Sustainable Development Charter in 1990. It marked the first time that a group of industry CEOs recognized the importance of positive social and environmental behavior in creating shareholder value. Financial innovation followed, thereby facilitating the flow of billions of dollars into socially responsible investing (SRI) and sustainable investments (SI).

The other was the passage of the US Clean Air Act Amendments of 1990, which provided the legal infrastructure for the successful implementation of the sulfur dioxide (SO_2) "cap-and-trade" program. This scheme's financial and environmental success subsequently led to an understanding that these markets would provide profit-making opportunities for companies, thereby increasing shareholder value.

Both of these developments offer valuable insights into financial innovation. This column provides some personal insights into the inventive process associated with sustainable investing.

The eminent economist Josef Schumpeter divided technological change into three phases: invention, innovation, and imitation or diffusion. The conception of a new product or process is termed invention. Innovation is the commercialization stage, and diffusion is when its use becomes prevalent. It may be useful to trace the development of SI in this context.

Meyer Feldberg, the dean of the Graduate School of Business at Columbia University, took a bold step in the early 1990s and introduced the first course on Environmental Finance taught at a Graduate School of Business, which Richard had the privilege to teach. The students prepared a study in 1992 entitled *Green Investment: Profit or Pain*, which reported that the risk-adjusted performance of SRI funds relative to the S&P 500 index was historically less than stellar. But, in spite of this, they remained optimistic about the future of SRI. They concluded that environmental screening criteria and indexes would become better developed and more widely used and accepted.

Their forecasts proved to be accurate. By 1995, there were 55 socially screened mutual funds in the US with assets totaling $12 billion. Furthermore, 38% of these SRI funds were being screened on environmental performance. This was a change in attitude reflecting a new generation and was not restricted to the United States. That same year, 4000 miles away in Zurich, Switzerland, Reto Ringger, a young Swiss entrepreneur, became the founder and CEO of Sustainable Asset Management (SAM). He persuaded two German entrepreneurs, one of them the influential industrialist Alfred Ritter, to provide seed capital of SFr1.5 million ($900,000) to launch SAM.

Just a year later, Reto invited several academics and businessmen to become founding board members of the Sustainable Performance Group (SPG) (see Table 1). It was to be the world's first sustainable investment company. He hoped to commercialize SI and, being convinced that negative screens would not attract significant capital, he traveled tirelessly to persuade others that a new era was being born.

Table 1: Founding directors of Sustainable Performance Group

Dr Ernst Brugger, Chairman of the Board
Dr Christian Lutz
Dr Richard Sandor
Dr Klaus Woltron
Dr Alexander Zehnder

Ernst Brugger, a personal friend and a leading Swiss academic and practitioner in the environmental field, led a very successful capital-raising campaign that enabled SPG to initially raise SFr79 million. Lead investments came from Swiss Re and the Volkart Group with Andi Reinhart, chairman of Volkart, subsequently becoming chairman of SAM. The fund was officially launched on 8 August 1997.

It was an inauspicious time to launch an innovative financial product. The asset managers were soon faced with a major financial crisis in Russia that affected the worldwide capital markets. But despite this poor timing, the SPG started to outperform its benchmark, the MSCI World Index. At the first board meeting of the SPG, Richard suggested the development of a sustainability index as a tool for demonstrating that the performance of the SPG was not only superior to the MSCI, but to other competitors that might enter the SI field. As time passed, it became clear that the superior performance of the SPG needed to be explained in terms of SI if clarity was to be achieved in the minds of its investors. The board discussed the idea and concluded that it would be a very valuable tool. Its involvement stopped at that time. SAM would not officially inform the SPG board of the status of its research until a suitable partner had been found.

One year after the launch of the SPG, Alois Flatz from SAM began exploring the possibility of developing an international sustainability index. SAMs management and the research staff started to develop a detailed concept of the index. They sought the assistance of a handful of outside experts, including John Elkington, the founder of UK consultancy Sustainability.

The concept was simple but convincing. The sustainability index would track the financial performance of the top sustainability companies. The selected companies would be leaders in their industries, reflecting the "best of class" approach. They would be chosen from a ranking of the world's biggest companies based on a relatively simple corporate sustainability assessment system. Initially, it was anticipated that a five-page questionnaire would be sufficient for assessing these companies.

It was also decided that the index could be developed internally but calculated and branded by a third party. SAM's management therefore contacted the major index companies but all rejected the concept. However, a combination of skill, determination, and luck resulted in a partner being found.

The Swiss stock exchange provided the impetus to finding the partner. It was interested in branding the index but the global nature of the index didn't fit the exchange's strategy. It then introduced SAM management to STOXX, a joint venture of the Swiss, French, and German stock exchanges and the Dow Jones Index Co. A newly hired managing director, Michael Schanz, introduced the SAM team to the Dow Jones management.

The critical decision-maker in these first meetings was the chief editor of Dow Jones Indexes, John Prestbo. John was both a distinguished writer as well as a seasoned veteran of Wall Street. If he were intellectually convinced about the validity of SI, then SAM would have its most credible advocate at Dow Jones. John was initially skeptical, but later became convinced that a sustainability index could be differentiated from SRI and would be consistent with the mission of Dow Jones Indexes.

During this time, Andi Reinhart became a significant investor in SAM and chairman of the board. The original investors had supported the development of the index since 1997. Andi also strongly believed that a strategic relationship with Dow Jones would be helpful in legitimizing the concept of sustainability and raising the visibility of SAM. Fortuitously, Richard had worked with David Moran, president of Dow Jones Indexes, in the licensing of the Dow Jones Industrial Average to the Chicago Board of Trade, where he served as its vice-chairman for strategy. David, with the advice of his colleagues, would ultimately make the final decisions about the new venture. His vision and leadership would ultimately determine the viability and success of any partnership.

Final negotiations took place in New York in October 1998. David and John were joined by Mike Petronella, a very promising and bright member of the Dow Jones team. It was at that lengthy meeting that all of the issues were discussed. The green light was finally given.

But it was only the start. As Goethe said: "The genius is in the detail". Through scenario planning and the assessment of trends and driving forces, various criteria were applied to all 64 industries. From those general and industry-specific criteria, questions were devised. The sustainability questionnaire amounted to 14 pages, compared to the initial estimate of five. Armed with a questionnaire and a defined corporate sustainability methodology, SAM invited the largest 2000 companies in the Dow Jones Global Index — drawn from 64 industry groups and 36 countries — to participate in the first annual assessment.

Companies' reactions varied greatly. Some welcomed the index and provided SAM with completed questionnaires accompanied by boxes of supporting documentation. Others refused to even return the questionnaire because of their skepticism about sustainability. The questionnaires prompted self-assessments among corporates and concomitantly provided an educational tool for sustainability efforts. Companies that did not respond to the questionnaire were ranked using publicly available information.

Over a period of 6 months, SAM management and a team of 15 analysts completed the assessment of 600 companies. To facilitate the analysis, SAM developed an extensive database. It has been upgraded over the past three years and has become the world's first and largest database tracking global corporate sustainability.

By the spring of 1999, the stage was set for the final determination of the index. Reto and Richard met with the Dow Jones' team. For the better part of a day the final details of the index were completed. There was significant debate about the weapons industry. European investors wanted negative screening to exclude this. However, sustainability measures required the inclusion of companies that produced military equipment if it was only a part of their sales. The solution to the dilemma was to reduce the weight of these companies by the percentage of weapons related turnover. The salient features of the index were fully debated and only finalized when there was unanimity. It was a familiar scene that occurs in investment banks, stock and futures exchanges on a regular basis. The inventive process in the capital markets is collaborative. This was the process at its finest.

Next came the acid test — the historical performance of the index was determined by backcasting.

There was great uncertainty about how it would perform. After hours of calculation the results were unambiguous. The sustainability index outperformed the general Dow Jones Group Index overall, in all three regions, and in eight out of the nine sectors. The calculations were run through the night to double-check the results. Nothing changed. In the Schumpeterian sense the inventive process was completed.

Next came innovation — the commercialization of this new financial product. The index was launched on 8 September 1999. At the outset, there were five licensees for the index but that number has now grown to 31 with more than €2.2 billion ($2 billion) under management. We are not only in the midst of a Schumpeterian innovation with diffusion, but have also witnessed imitators. That is the final stage of the inventive process.

There has been a dramatic increase in SRI. Figure 1 shows the growth in assets under management from 1995 through 2001 for three categories of SRI: investments selected through screening

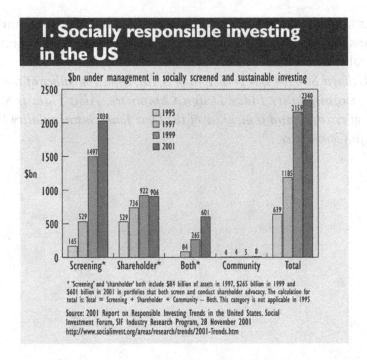

1. Socially responsible investing in the US

$bn under management in socially screened and sustainable investing

Source: 2001 Report on Responsible Investing Trends in the United States. Social Investment Forum, SIF Industry Research Program, 28 November 2001 http://www.socialinvest.org/areas/research/trends/2001-Trends.htm

* 'Screening' and 'shareholder' both include $84 billion of assets in 1997, $265 billion in 1999 and $601 billion in 2001 in portfolios that both screen and conduct shareholder advocacy. The calculation for total is: Total = Screening + Shareholder + Community – Both. This category is not applicable in 1995

criteria; shareholder advocacy investing; and investing to support local community development by entities such as credit unions.

Although SRI and SI differ greatly in methodology, approach, and investors, they have been driven by similar trends. In both cases, the driving forces behind their growth fall into three categories:

• the need to manage environmental and social risk exposure;
• shareholder pressure; and
• sustainability and maximization of shareholder value.

Nothing illustrates the last point more clearly than the fact that the DJSI significantly outperforms all other indexes with virtually no increase in risk.

We began with the premise that financial innovation could be viewed as a Schumpeterian process. The development of the DJSI in this context seems to follow this pattern. The mixture of entrepreneurship by capital providers and management helped this process. Inventive activity is ultimately a response to latent or overt demand. The reasons for growth in sustainable investing, and the success of this index, are simple: higher risk-adjusted rates of return. Capital markets have eyes.

Richard Sandor is a principal of SAM, and a member of the Dow Jones Sustainability Index Design Committee. Alois Flatz is SAM's head of research and a member of the Dow Jones Sustainability Index Design Committee.

Chapter 25

Chicago Climate Exchange Progress Report

February 2002

The Chicago Climate Exchange (CCX), an 18-month-old project with the goal of designing and implementing a voluntary "cap-and-trade" market for greenhouse gases (GHGs), began its first industry meetings last month.

These meetings, coming after 15 months of research that included site visits to virtually all of the participants, signify the beginning of a new stage of the research that will continue to build consensus among the members and finalize the design of the exchange.

This project was initially funded by the Chicago-based Joyce Foundation through a special Millennium Initiative grant to the Kellogg Graduate School of Management at Northwestern University. New funding was granted 6 months ago when the success of the exchange was deemed to be likely. As promised, this is our semi-annual update on CCX's progress.

Since our last progress report (see "Corporate giants to aid design of US carbon market", June 2001, Chapter 19), 23 new entities have agreed to participate in the design process. Table 1 contains the current full list of participants.

The new additions are of interest for three reasons: CCX's increased penetration of existing sectors in both the United States and Canada as well as European Union (EU)-based companies with

1. Current list of CCX participants

Energy	Industry	Ormat
Alliant Energy	Cemex	*Pronatura de Mexico*
American Electric Power	DuPont	The Nature Conservancy
BP	Ford Motor Company	
Calpine	*Grupo IMSA de Mexico*	**Service providers**
Cinergy	*Interface*	American Agrisurance
CMS Generation	ST Microelectronics	IT Group
DTE	*Waste Management Inc*	Swiss Re
Exelon		Carr Futures/Crédit Agricole
FirstEnergy	**Offset providers**	
Manitoba Hydro	Agriliance	**Forest products companies**
Midwest Generation	*Cataguazes-Leopoldina*	International Paper
NiSource	*Ducks Unlimited*	Temple-Inland
Ontario Power Generation	Growmark	*Mead Corp*
PG&E National Energy Group	Iowa Farm Bureau Federation	*Stora Enso*
Pinnacle West Corporation (APS)	National Council of Farmer	
Suncor Energy	Cooperatives	**Municipalities**
TXU Energy Trading	*Navitas Energy*	*City of Chicago*
Wisconsin Energy	*Nuon*	*Mexico City*

Names in italics denote additions since June 2001

North American operations; new participants in Mexico and Brazil; and the addition of a totally new sector — municipalities.

Six new companies have joined from the power sector including three of the top 10 US utilities. The participants from this sector now account for 180,000 MW of capacity representing 20% of US generation. This is equivalent to the entire generating capacity of France. In Canada, we have expanded to include OPG and Manitoba Hydro from the power sector. In the EU, the inclusion of Nuon adds to our design capabilities. Furthermore, Finland-based Stora Enso (the second largest forest products company in the world) is an important addition to the CCX forest products sector which already includes International Paper, Temple Inland, and Mead.

We now also have the first Brazilian company, Cataguazes-Leopoldina, a leading generator of electricity based in the state of Minas Gerais, joining the CCX. Cemex, the largest Mexican cement company and the second largest cement company in the United States, and Grupo IMSA de Mexico, a leading diversified steel and manufacturing group, have recently agreed to participate. Pronatura de Mexico, a major national conservation group, is joining us as well.

One of the most exciting new developments has been the addition of two major cities in North America — Chicago and Mexico City. The commitment of these two municipalities provides us with the expertise to deal with GHG emissions from transportation systems as well as city-operated energy and power production. Cities also manage landfills, offering opportunities for the capture and destruction of methane, a major GHG.

The advisory group of the CCX also continues to expand. Table 2 provides a complete list of current members.

The addition of Mary Schapiro, President of NASD Regulation, and Robert Wilmouth, President of the National Futures Association, provide us with the acknowledged leaders among US-based self-regulatory organizations (SROs). The CCX is devoted to market architecture that will unambiguously emphasize transparency and oversight. Finally, the Honorable Richard M. Daley, mayor of the City of Chicago, has agreed to become the honorary chairman of CCX. His energy plan, released last November, emphasized the role of financial institutions in facilitating the city's goal of becoming the "greenest city" in the United States.

Look for some important new additions in all of these areas in the next few months.

On 10 January 2002, the electricity generation and gas transmission/distribution sectors committee of the CCX held its first meeting. The next day the landfill gas (LFG) sector committee also met. Both agendas were driven by broad issues of baselines, the facilities covered, monitoring, reporting, and verification.

Why were these the first groups chosen? The answer is simple. CCX will be an allowance-based system but will also include offsets. The electricity sector is a major participant in the emission allowance segment of the market, and the LFG sector can be a significant source of offsets generated from the destruction of methane, which is 21 times more potent than carbon dioxide as a GHG. Furthermore, they are related because the destruction of methane is a principal source of renewable energy, and some members of the electricity generation sector are also in the LFG business.

2. Current advisory board members

Honorary chairman
The Honourable Richard M Daley, Mayor, City of Chicago

David Boren	President of University of Oklahoma; former US Senator and Governor of Oklahoma
Ernst Brugger	Founding Partner and Chairman of Brugger Hanser & Partners
Elizabeth Dowdeswell	*Former Executive Director of UNEP*
Jeffrey E Garten	Dean of Yale School of Management
Lucien Y Bronicki	Chairman of ORMAT International
Donald P Jacobs	Dean, Kellogg School of Management, Northwestern University
Dennis Jennings	Global Risk Management Solutions Leader, PricewaterhouseCoopers
Jonathan Lash	President, World Resources Institute
Joseph P Kennedy II	Chairman and President of Boston-based Citizens Energy Group; former US Congressman
Israel Klabin	President, Brazilian Foundation for Sustainable Development
Bill Kurtis	National broadcaster, host of Arts & Entertainment cable TV show
Thomas E Lovejoy	Chief Biodiversity Advisor to the President of the World Bank
David Moran	President of Dow Jones Indexes
R K Pachauri	*Director-General of the Tata Energy Research Institute*
Les Rosenthal	Former Chairman, Chicago Board of Trade; principal, Rosenthal Collins
Mary L Schapiro	*President of NASD Regulation Inc*
Maurice Strong	Chairman of the Earth Council, former UN Under-Secretary General
James R Thompson	Former four-term Gov. of Illinois
Sir Brian Williamson	Chairman, LIFFE
Robert Wilmouth	*President and CEO of the National Futures Association (NFA)*

Names in italics denote additions since June 2001

Members of both groups recognized that this was only the beginning of what would be a long series of meetings. Nevertheless, there was a great sense of optimism. However, this was the time for questions rather than answers. We'll report on some of those questions and answers in this column in the future.

I would like to thank Michael Walsh, Alice LeBlanc, and Rafael Marques for their assistance in the preparation of this chapter.

Chapter 26

Observations on Enron

March 2002

It didn't make the headlines when Enron collapsed. It didn't have the human interest stories of financial ruin associated with the loss of jobs and pensions. It lacked political drama and there was no need to debate legislative and regulatory action because it wasn't associated with investor protection, fraudulent accounting, or inadequate corporate governance. It was only a story about market architecture that ended the same way others ended. However, its effect on risk management and the efficiency of energy markets may prove to be profound.

Two totally different market architectures were competing for the order flow in the energy and power sectors when Enron met its demise.

In one of them, purportedly invented in modern times, there is a dominant principal (buyer or seller) for a wide variety of energy and power products and their derivatives. That dominant economic actor provides liquidity in hundreds of products to thousands of participants. In the case of Enron, the principal appeared to have a virtually endless capacity to extend credit in all of these markets and to all of the participants. It appeared to be infinitely scalable in new products because the dominant player's corporate culture fostered innovation.

In the alternative market architecture, which has emerged over many centuries, there is either a significant number of bilateral trades in an over-the-counter (OTC) market or a centralized multilateral market. Principals, or their agents (brokers), consummate transactions relying on the creditworthiness of their counterparties. The creation of an independent clearing service occurred when the supply of credit could not satisfy the demand for credit. Increases in the capacity for credit were limited by the totality of capital of the individual participants and/or their clearing corporations.

The scalability of new products in the bilateral market depends on the creativity of the individual buyer or seller. In the multilateral market, new products' scalability depends on the innovative capacity of all buyers or sellers exercising their creative skills through trade associations or exchanges.

EnronOnline embodied the first type of market architecture. It was a dominant principal in the energy and power markets and their derivatives. It was commonly accepted by a significant part of the investment community that the company could dominate several existing and new markets. Enron came from relative obscurity to be the seventh largest corporation in the US in terms of sales. Its model seemed to be infinitely scalable with no credit constraints and a boundless ability to innovate. The proof lay in its market power in markets as diverse as natural gas, weather derivatives, and bandwidth. The company's ability also seemed boundless because of the emergence of the Internet — a key facilitating technology of the 1990s.

Enron's sudden demise was a surprise to all of us except for a few very wise short sellers. In retrospect, a simple study of a few commodity and capital markets would have revealed that this type of market architecture generally has a short life. Variants of this story occurred in both the grain markets and the bond markets during the 20th century.

While the halcyon days of Enron captured huge amounts of attention, the second type of market architecture quietly proceeded to grow, transform and mature into a deep market that is effectively filling the gap left by Enron's collapse.

Both the New York Mercantile Exchange and the International Petroleum Exchange (IPE) — traditional examples of the multilateral, voice-brokered format — experienced substantial volume growth during the 1990s. The OTC markets continue to thrive and are being transformed by the introduction of new approaches to trading. In the latter part of the decade, the industry experienced a move toward electronic marketplaces. The Atlanta-based Intercontinental Exchange (ICE) and TradeSpark are two examples of this new trend. At ICE, the number of participating firms and users soared by more than 400% last year, while the number of trades it executed grew 15-fold. With the acquisition of the IPE, ICE added a broad range of exchange traded energy-based futures and options markets to its extensive roster of energy and metals-based OTC derivatives markets. Last year, ICE also signed an agreement to offer optional clearing services through the London Clearing House. These recent events indicate a move towards a "fusion" of these two types of OTC/multilateral markets.

Though some may have feared that the collapse of a dominant player like Enron would have caused massive disruption to the market(s), this was not the case. After the firm's demise its business was seamlessly transferred to other markets, as evidenced by the huge increase in deal flow at the ICE. Despite the fact that Enron's collapse could have caused major disruption to the energy markets, this smooth transition during the busy winter trading season was barely noticed by the media. With the exception of a 15 February article in *The Economist*, it was not a headline story.

What lessons can we learn from a brief look at history when the dominant actor no longer exists? First, the collapse of the dominant player can cause financial ruin for its counterparties (in addition to its creditors, employees, and community) and may introduce systemic problems that cause economy wide damage. However, it is also a time when its market shares are divided among other participants. To the extent that trading migrates to public exchanges, market participants will benefit from more transparent prices and the steady flow of data on volume and open positions. The self-regulating markets may again enjoy expanded benefits from the market confidence provided by their systems of rules, checks and balances, and exposure to external inspection. The results are greater profitability for the survivors and more efficient markets. This ultimately leads to lower transactions costs. Improved efficiency in these markets will help ensure economically rational allocation of energy resources.

I would like to thank Michael Walsh, Rafael Marques, and Julie Sandor for their assistance in the preparation of this chapter. Special thanks to Les Rosenthal for providing the inspiration.

Chapter 27

A Decade of SO₂ Allowance Auctions

April 2002

It hardly seems newsworthy. The Environmental Protection Agency's (EPA) 10th annual auction of sulfur dioxide (SO_2) allowances conducted by the Chicago Board of Trade (CBOT) on 25 March provided no surprises. But, we think it is newsworthy precisely because of its routine results. It also provides us with an opportunity to describe the anatomy of an auction.

A decade is not a sufficient period to reach final judgement on a tool of public, social, or environmental policy. However, during that time the price discovery and related information that is published by the CBOT has significantly altered the nature of the debate and possibly the future of emissions trading.

The last issue of this magazine indicated that, following an increase in prices associated with the current administration's Clear Skies initiative, "prices levelled off around $170.00 for the rest of the month on low volume as the market prepares for the EPA's auction of 2002 and 2009 vintage allowances on 25 March". Data provided by the CBOT provides us with both price discovery and a different kind of insight into the recent quiescent market (see Tables 1 and 2).

The clearing price in the spot auction was $160.50, whereas the weighted average of winning bids was $167.74. This was consistent

111

1. Allowances available for auction

Origin	Spot auction (first usable 2002)	7-year advance auction (first usable 2009)
EPA	125,000	125,000
Privately offered	2,388	2,388
Total	127,388	127,388

Source: CBOT and EPA

2. Spot auction results

Allowances	Number of bids	Number of bidders	Bid price
Bid for: 302,285	Successful: 46	Successful: 21	Highest: $215
Sold: 127,388	Unsuccessful: 7	Unsuccessful: 6	Clearing: $160.50 (the clearing price is the lowest price at which a successful bid was made)
Total	53	27	Lowest: $150
			Average: $167.74 (weighted by the number of allowances in each bid)

Source: CBOT and EPA

3. Seven-year advance auction results

Allowances	Number of bids	Number of bidders	Bid price
Bid for: 273,388	Successful: 13	Successful: 5	Highest: $120
Sold: 127,388	Unsuccessful: 3	Unsuccessful: 3	Clearing: $68 (the clearing price is the lowest price at which a successful bid was made)
Total	16	8	Lowest: $60
			Average: $81.87 (weighted by the number of allowances in each bid)

Source: CBOT and EPA

with recent pricing in the over-the-counter (OTC) market. Furthermore, the difference between the highest and lowest bid was $65.00, which compares with $120.00 last year. The results confirm the reduction in OTC volatility that has occurred in recent months. The number of successful bidders was 21, whereas six were unsuccessful. This also reflected a more uniform set of expectations by market participants. By comparison, last year's auction had 14 successful and 71 unsuccessful bids.

The clearing price in the 7-year advance auction was $68.00, whereas the weighted average of winning bids was $81.87 (see Table 3).

Despite the proliferation of market intermediaries, the forward OTC market still appears to be inefficient and price discovery is insufficient, making price information from the CBOT forward auction even more important. The profile of price ranges and the relationship of successful to unsuccessful bids followed the same patterns as the spot auction. There was a greater range in bids than in the spot market but a narrower range than last year. In contrast to last year, there was also a similar ratio of successful to unsuccessful bids, as in the spot market. Furthermore, there was a higher number of successful bidders than last year.

In a pattern that has continued for the last few years, the difference between spot and forward prices remained much higher than it was during the 1990s. Some market participants attribute this specifically to regulatory uncertainty. Others say it is due to general market uncertainty.

What can we infer from this particular auction and the 10-year history?

This year's results specifically suggest that the SO_2 market is functioning very effectively. Prices continue to be well below levels that were forecast in 1992. In that year, the median forecast was $600 with a low of $309 and a high of $981. During the past 10 years, spot prices have averaged $135.8 and forward prices $106.1 (see Table 4). This is well below what experts had predicted. Furthermore, sulfur emissions have fallen faster than required. Recent analysis by the EPA and others suggests that the total cost of the program ranges from $750 to $2 billion. Benefits range from $25 to $40 billion. It is hard to imagine many policies and tools that could match this level of success.

If imitation is the highest form of flattery, then the most recent SO_2 "cap-and-trade" development flatters the concept and illustrates how far the environmental movement has come in embracing market-based solutions to pollution. This year, Slovakia witnessed the first trade of SO_2 allowances in its own domestic programme. This is quite remarkable to any student of politics and economics. When the US program was being designed in the latter part of

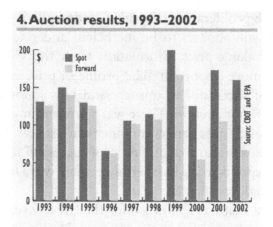

4. Auction results, 1993–2002

the 1980s, Slovakia was a region of another country in the Soviet bloc. At the time of the CBOT's first auction, it became a sovereign nation. And now, nearly a decade later, it has launched what appears to be a successful trading programme of its own.

What a shining example to us all of how any country can successfully build institutions and implement market-based solutions to environmental problems. In this light, solutions to global warming are much less daunting than is often proclaimed. Despite widespread predictions that SO_2 trading would fail in the US, annual turnover in the cash and derivative markets is now equal to the value of the US wheat crop. Successful uptake of the concept in a former Soviet satellite reminds us that the naysayers have often made the mistake of selling short the potential for innovative environmental markets to succeed.

I would like to thank Michael Walsh, Alice LeBlanc, and Rafael Marques for their assistance in the preparation of this chapter.

Chapter 28

The Road to Price Discovery

May 2002

There are at least two different market-based approaches now being undertaken to address the problem of climate change: multi-sector and voluntary versus single-sector and mandatory. Over time both should provide valuable insights into the cost of mitigating the problem. Little attention has been given to the process of developing these approaches as opposed to the specifics of each. It is our objective to look at the different approaches in this light.

As multi-sector voluntary programs go, the United Kingdom's Emissions Trading Scheme (ETS) is complex and therefore, a bit difficult to analyze. This does not detract from its value. It simply requires students of markets to carefully analyze its multiple objectives and measure its progress against these objectives. Too much of the early discussion has focused on the inadequacies of the architecture and the nature of price discovery to date. Not enough dialogue has been devoted to the process of building institutions. Our purpose here is to highlight the success of the process as opposed to the details of the ETS (see Chapter 27 "A decade of SO_2 Allowance Auctions", April 2002, for a more detailed discussion of the scheme).

The initial objective of the United Kingdom was to develop a voluntary "cap-and-trade" scheme. The UK Emissions Trading Group was established to achieve a consensus on the mechanics of the program and to build institutions which would facilitate the achievement of the objectives. Some of these objectives have already been unambiguously accomplished. The British government, private sector, and nongovernmental organizations (NGOs) together developed a three-part participation framework: absolute reductions from a predetermined baseline; the meeting of efficiency targets to reduce the impact of the Climate Change Levy; and participation for domestic project-based reductions of greenhouse gases (GHGs). A gateway mechanism was also developed to manage trading between the absolute and efficiency-based sectors. This was done to ensure that total GHG emissions would be reduced. We are only at the beginning of the process of determining whether all or parts of the participation framework will ultimately be successful.

Consensus was also built regarding a specific financial incentive of £215 million ($312 million) for participating companies as well as a mechanism for allocating this sum. As an aside, practitioners and institutional economists would benefit greatly from a fuller description of this process.

We can infer from the results released in mid-March that the incentive auction has been highly successful. The multiple-round Dutch auction attracted 34 successful participants. Some expectations were that only six or seven companies would take part. The incentive auction began at a price of £90 and after nine rounds a

---

Example: UK ETS auction incentive payments

● An 'annual target' of 100,000 tonnes means the target falls by 100,000 tonnes a year
● An 'overall target' means the reduction in the fifth year relative to the baseline, ie, an 'overall target' of 500,000 tonnes means the year 5 emissions target is 500,000 tonnes below the baseline

Hypothetical example of 100,000-tonne 'annual target'

Baseline	1,000,000 tonnes	Cut relative to baseline
2002 target	900,000 tonnes	100,000
2003 target	800,000 tonnes	200,000
2004 target	700,000 tonnes	300,000
2005 target	600,000 tonnes	400,000
2006 target	500,000 tonnes	500,000
Total tonnes cut (relative to baseline)		1,500,000

Per-tonne incentive payment at £53.37 clearing 'price'	£5,337,000 × 5 = £26,685,000
Total cuts:	1,500,000 tonnes
Incentive payment per tonne (pre-tax)	£17.79

clearing 'price' of £ 53.37 was achieved. The true per-tonne auction incentive level is in fact one-third of this value, or £ 17.79 (see box).

But, it is important to emphasize that this is not the "price" of allowances. It is simply a point on the road to price discovery. This was an incentive payment to induce participants to commit to specific emission reduction targets. There has been considerable misunderstanding of this number. The purpose of the incentive money was to insure that the volunteers did not put themselves in an uncompetitive position within their industry relative to the nonvolunteers. Market participants and economists can debate whether the incentive was too high, but the price of allowances will ultimately be determined only when the participation framework is fully actualized.

Another significant by-product of the process was the emergence of a consensus on the need for a centralized registry system. The successful building and operation of this institution is very significant.

The other market approach — single-sector and mandatory — already exists in Denmark. That process required political consensus which enabled legislation to be passed. Its restriction to the power sector and the relatively small size of this industry (eight participants) provided for a quicker launch. The market cap has already been achieved, so the process was successful in relation to this objective. On the other hand, there has been no need to trade. The Danish system has initialized a process that can eventually provide another point on the road to price discovery. As announced by the Danish Energy Agency, several participants have expressed a desire to form an exchange. It too has created a registry. It is noteworthy that the United Kingdom's multi-sector voluntary program does not directly address emissions from power production, while the simpler Danish program addresses only power sector emissions.

Variations on both of these approaches are already in progress in the United States. The Chicago Climate Exchange (CCX) is a voluntary and comprehensive program, while the states of Massachusetts and New Hampshire are pursuing the mandatory single-sector approach. Both should provide us with insights into how flexible mechanisms can be used to mitigate GHG emissions. We believe in the wisdom of Eugene O'Neill — "All God's chillun got wings".

- Finally, as promised, here is an update from the CCX. Its newest members include Baxter International, representing the pharmaceutical sector, while The Carbon Fund and Conservacion Mexico have recently joined as offset providers. New members Det Norske Veritas, SCS Engineers and Edelman Worldwide will help provide market infrastructure. We are also glad to announce that Gerard Pannekoek has joined Environmental Financial Products as a senior vice president and chief operating officer.

I would like to thank Robert Routliffe of DuPont Canada for his assistance in the preparation of this chapter.

Chapter 29

Here Come the States

June 2002

> "You shall not press down upon the brow of labor this crown of thorns, you shall not crucify mankind upon a cross of gold".
>
> — William Jennings Bryan, 19th century American orator and politician in a speech to the Democratic National Convention of 1896

Following 5 years of talk in the US Congress — but no legislation — the American debate over cutting greenhouse gas (GHG) emissions has moved to the state level. As another example of the "bottom-up" approach previously discussed in this column, two states have passed laws to establish GHG "cap-and-trade" systems. Several others have passed, or are debating, laws establishing the infrastructure to facilitate trading. However, one particular state is considering legislation that has the potential to create a highly fractured US approach to climate change.

It all began with Oregon. This was the first state to initiate a public policy aimed at mitigating GHG emissions. In 1997, legislation required new power plants to avoid, sequester, or displace a portion of their previously unregulated carbon dioxide (CO_2) emissions. As a result, the Climate Trust, a nongovernmental organization whose main purpose is to implement CO_2 offset projects, was established. The program provided flexibility to power suppliers. A company could offset its CO_2 emissions by making a contribution to the Climate Trust, in lieu of establishing its own offset program.

Massachusetts was the first state to legislate a cap on CO_2 emissions. Under this law, existing electricity generating facilities are subject to two types of cap — historic and output based. After 1 October 2004, a power plant's CO_2 emissions cannot exceed its 3-year average emissions over 1997–1999. After 1 October 2006, its CO_2 emissions rate cannot exceed 1800 Clean Power Act (HB 284) pounds/MWh. Both historic and output-based limits can be met through off-site CO_2 reductions. In addition, any new facility of more than 100 MW capacity must offset 1% of its emissions per year for the next 20 years.

New Hampshire, a neighbor of Massachusetts, has also passed legislation providing for a cap-and-trade system (see Chapter 28 "The road price to discovery", May 2002). The law provides for a statewide cap of 5.4 million tons of CO_2. Emissions must be reduced by 7% below 1990 levels beginning in 2006 (see Table 1). Coverage applies to the state's three fossil-fuel plants, which are owned by Public Service of New Hampshire, a division of Northeast Utilities. The utility can reduce its emissions or buy credits from other approved programs or sources.

It is interesting to note that legislation in both Massachusetts and New Hampshire was preceded by significant interaction between the government and a variety of stakeholders. However, it is not clear that those affected by these laws put forth the argument that the multiple GHG limits and flexibility provisions should be coordinated.

Table I. Salient features of Massachusetts and New Hampshire trading programmes

Massachusetts	New Hampshire: Clean Power Act (HB 284)
● Signed by Governor 23 April 2001	● Signed by Governor 9 May 2002
● Capped at historic CO_2 emissions (3-year average of 1997–99)	● Applies to three power plants in the state
● Facilities will also have an output-based limit of 1,800 lb/MWh	● Reduce CO_2 to 1990 levels by 2006
● Both historic limit and output-based limit can be met through off-site CO_2 reductions	● Caps are annual, output-based, with trading for CO_2
● Must meet historic cap by 1 October 2004; output rate-based cap by 1 October 2006	

Climate change initiatives/ proposed legislation	Registries	Multi-state initiatives
Massachusetts	California	New England governors
New Hampshire	New Hampshire	Eastern Canadian provinces
Oregon	New Jersey	
New York	Wisconsin	
Pennsylvania	Massachusetts	
Illinois		
Michigan		
Minnesota		
Ohio		
California		

Table 2. Selected states with recent GHG activity

Although Massachusetts and New Hampshire have similar types of programs, another state is following a different course (see Table 2). The great-granddaughter of William Jennings Bryan — who was staunchly opposed to the "command-and-control" gold standard in his Democratic convention speech quote — has introduced legislation in California that would require the reduction of tailpipe emissions of GHGs.

The proposed legislation would require the State Air Resources Board to develop regulations that would achieve the maximum feasible reductions of GHG's by vehicles used for personal transportation. The regulations could take effect as early as 2006, but the application of the law would be limited to vehicles that are made in the model year 2009 and later. In response to a specific question, a staff member of the California State Assembly informed us that no trading is foreseen.

A law of this type carries with it the danger of reverting to a command-and-control system, as opposed to a more flexible and cost-effective cap-and-trade system. It is ironic that California's "cross of gold" may turn out to be inflexible command-and-control legislation with a potential long-term deleterious impact on its economy. A significant coalition has mobilized against the passage of the bill. This may in fact be round one in the GHG mitigation battle of command-and-control versus markets.

I would like to thank Michael Walsh, Alice LeBlanc, and Rafael Marques for their assistance in the preparation of this article.

Chapter 30

Lies, Damned Lies, and Statistics

July–August 2002

> "I don't get it"
> — Tom Hanks in the film *Big*

Recent reports on greenhouse gas (GHG) emissions in the United States can be summarized in two words: confusing and paradoxical. The situation reminds us of the importance of caution when interpreting environmental data. But, a close examination of recent US data reveals some modest cause for optimism as we begin the multi-decade efforts needed to manage the risks of climate change.

A headline from the 14 June issue of the *Wall Street Journal* (*WSJ*) reads: "Power-Plant Emissions Exceed Worst-Case Forecasts of 1996". The article states: "Emissions of carbon dioxide jumped 20% to 2611 tons in 2000 from 2175 in 1995, or double the increase forecast by the Federal Energy Regulatory Commission in 1996, according to the report by the Commission for Environmental Cooperation of North America (CEC)". However, it should be noted that the full *WSJ* article includes a graph of US emissions by year from 1995 to 2000. This indicates that emissions from the electricity sector were flat from 1999 to 2000.

Two weeks later, a 1 July Reuters news item stated: "US energy-related emissions down first time in decade". It goes on to say: "US carbon dioxide emissions totaled the equivalent of 1,540 million metric tons carbon equivalent in 2001, down from

1,558 million metric tons...the year before, according to preliminary estimates from the Energy Information Administration". It goes on: "...industrial emissions were down 9.1% and transportation and residential sector emissions decreased by 0.6% and 1.8%, respectively".

Both articles are from impeccable sources. They are well written and accurate. However, the first article deals with the power sector only and ends with calendar year 2000, while the second deals with total GHG emissions in 2000 and 2001. The latter cites changes in the industrial, transportation, and housing sectors with no reference to electricity. They initially both confuse us and present a paradox. Ultimately, they challenge us to examine the data.

These articles prompt this student of climate change to ask two questions: What is the overall trend in GHG emissions in the United States and how has it been affected by recessions? And what is the trend of emissions in the electricity sector and how has it been affected by recessions? The data yield some surprising conclusions.

There is an unmistakable upward trend in GHG emissions in the United States since 1990 as shown in Table 1. The average yearly increase in carbon dioxide (CO_2) emissions was 1.2%. In the 1990–1991 recession both emissions and gross domestic product (GDP) declined. During the downturn of 2001, GDP increased,

Table 1. US CO_2 emissions vs GDP

Year	US CO_2 emissions (m tonnes)	US GDP real $ ($bn)	Emissions/ GDP
1990	4,956.68	6,707.90	738.93
1991	4,889.11	6,676.40	732.30
1992	4,982.35	6,880.00	724.18
1993	5,078.06	7,062.60	719.01
1994	5,166.07	7,347.70	703.09
1995	5,211.91	7,543.80	690.89
1996	5,397.46	7,813.20	690.81
1997	5,475.93	8,159.50	671.11
1998	5,482.90	8,508.90	644.37
1999	5,563.21	8,856.50	628.15
2000	5,713.19	9,224.00	619.38
2001	5,647.18	9,333.80	605.02

Source: US DOE – Energy Information Administration, US Bureau of Economic Analysis

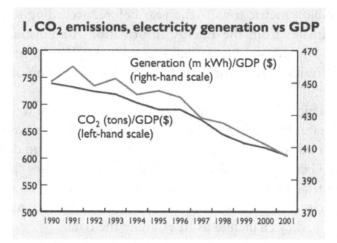

but emissions declined. This, at the very least, is curious. It suggests further research into the composition of GDP may be fruitful for forecasting future trends.

The other peculiarity is that emissions per unit of GDP show an uninterrupted decline (see Figure 1). Recessions seem to have no impact on this trend. As suggested in this column previously (see article "The US and EU — Closer than you think", September 2000, page 36) this may be a result of the growing share of the technology and service sectors in the US economy. We continue to witness a "dematerialization" of the US economy.

Table 2 shows that emissions from US electricity generation were also on the rise during the 1990s. The average yearly increase in emissions from power generation was 1.8%.

The average yearly increase in electricity generation was 2%. In the economic downturn of 1990–1991, however, power generation actually increased while GDP decreased, while in 2001 the opposite happened. This sounds as confusing as the two articles. We have to be cautious about inferences from these data because of the importance of weather as a determinant of electricity production. Figure 1 also shows the same unambiguous declining trend regarding electricity generation per unit of GDP. Perhaps, this is just another view of "dematerialization".

Table 2. Emissions from electricity generation

Year	Total US electricity generation (m kWh)	US GDP real $ ($bn)	Electricity generation/ GDP	Emissions from electricity generation (m tonnes CO₂)
1990	3,024,766	6,707.90	450.93	1,859.17
1991	3,071,201	6,676.40	460.01	1,855.50
1992	3,083,367	6,880.00	448.16	1,877.50
1993	3,196,924	7,062.60	452.66	1,952.31
1994	3,253,799	7,347.70	442.83	1,982.75
1995	3,357,837	7,543.80	445.11	1,989.35
1996	3,446,994	7,813.20	441.18	2,061.22
1997	3,494,222	8,159.50	428.24	2,138.23
1998	3,617,873	8,508.90	425.19	2,226.60
1999	3,704,545	8,856.50	418.29	2,246.40
2000	3,799,944	9,224.00	411.96	2,352.75
2001	3,776,986	9,333.80	404.66	2,258.87

Source: US DOE – Energy Information Agency, US Bureau of Economic Analysis

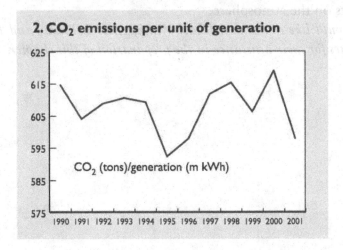

2. CO₂ emissions per unit of generation

CO₂ (tons)/generation (m kWh)

At the same time, Figure 2 shows that CO_2 emissions per unit of generation have fluctuated over the decade, with no clear trend. The apparent disparity between the two articles cited earlier does not exist. If the CEC report had included 2001, the two news items would have reached the same conclusion. In addition, the data seem to support the concept of "dematerialization" of the US economy. We can draw two major conclusions:

- Environmental data must always be interpreted cautiously, and doing so often reveals consistency among apparently conflicting reports; and

- Continuing reductions in US GHG emissions intensity provide cause for optimism that emissions can be restrained in the face of economic growth, but the challenge now is to begin restraining absolute emissions.

As a final caveat, it is clear that existing data have some important gaps. Full emissions accounting would routinely include offsets such as sinks, as well as non-CO_2 gases. Markets create demand for data, and these demands will help improve the clarity of the data. The emergence of GHG trading programs will be an important step in moving towards data and management systems that reflect overall impacts on the atmosphere.

I would like to thank Michael Walsh, Alice LeBlanc, and Rafael Marques for their assistance in the preparation of this chapter.

Chapter 31

DJSI World Index — Three Years on

September 2002

In the inaugural issue of this magazine and its two subsequent anniversary issues, this column described the impact of sustainability on asset management. We focused on the Dow Jones Sustainability World Index (DJSI World) as the industry leader in sustainable investing. As promised, this is our annual update.

This month, Dow Jones Indexes, STOXX Ltd., and SAM Group announce the results of their annual review of the DJSI family. The new composition of the DJSI World will again include over 300 companies representing the world's sustainability leaders across all industries. They have a market capitalization of close to €5 trillion ($4.9 trillion). The full list can be seen on www.sustainability-indexes.com.

This year's review was marked by continued strong interest in DJSI membership and significant improvements in terms of corporate sustainability performance. The integration of economic, environmental, and social criteria is moving up the management agenda in all industries and has reached a high degree of sophistication in some sectors. A growing number of companies are publishing sustainability reports to inform their stakeholders on their achievements and targets in this field.

At the same time, market acceptance of the DJSI family continues. The list of DJSI licensees has seen the addition of nine new

Table 1. Current DJSI licensees

Institution (country)	Product
Sagitta Wealth Management (Austral)	Fund
Kepler Fonds KAG (Austria)	Fund
Dexia Asset Management (Belgium)	Fund
Credit Union Central of Ontario (Canada)	Certificate
Danske Invest (Denmark)	Fund
Sparinvest (Denmark)	Fund
DWS (Finland)	Fund
CIC Asset Management (France)	Certificate
Rothschild & Cie Gestion (France)	Fund
HypoVereinsbank (Germany)	Warrant
Gerling Investment KAG (Germany)	Fund
DZ Bank (Germany)	Certificate
Invesco (Germany)	Fund
Oppenheim KAG (Germany)	Fund
State Street Global Advisors (Germany)	Fund
Union Investment (Germany)	Fund
WestLB (Germany)	Certificate
BNL Gestioni (Italy)	Fund
Banca Advantage (Italy)	Fund
Zenit (Italy)	Fund
Nikko Asset Management (Japan)	Fund
Banque Générale de Luxembourg	Fund
Deutsche Postbank (Luxembourg)	Fund
Aegon (Netherlands)	Fund
Rabobank (Netherlands)	Certificate
Robeco Groep (Netherlands)	Fund
Folksam Sak (Sweden)	Fund
Skandinaviska Enskilda Bank (Sweden)	Fund
SPP (Sweden)	Fund
Baloise Insurance (Switzerland)	Fund
Credit Suisse Asset Management (Switz)	Fund
Sustainable Asset Management (Switz)	Fund
Sustainable Performance Group (Switz)	Invest Co
Swiss Life Asset Management (Switz)	Fund
Synchrony Asset Management (Switz)	Certificate
VZ VermögensZentrum (Switzerland)	Fund
Merrill Lynch International (UK)	Certificate

members over the past 12 months and it includes some of the premier financial institutions in the world (see Table 1). Products range from mutual funds and segregated accounts to equity baskets. Assets managed in these portfolios now amount to almost €2 billion.

These licensees cater to the demands of a rapidly growing number of investors that seek to include sustainability criteria in their asset allocation. Recent corporate governance scandals have reemphasized the need to look beyond annual reports and financial statements when analyzing companies. Moreover, the floods, which continental Europe experienced in August, were a frightening example of current environmental developments and the effects they have on companies. Investors are increasingly taking these and other sustainability trends into account to assess their impact on the long-term performance of investments.

In that context, the performance of the DJSI World over the past 12 months shows encouraging results. We should note that although the index has underperformed the DJGI during the past year, it has outperformed the MSCI.

Separately, a 9 August article in the *Wall Street Journal* reported recent data from Lipper and Morningstar that suggest that socially responsible funds have also produced better returns than the average domestic fund during the one-year period ending 31 July (see the figure).

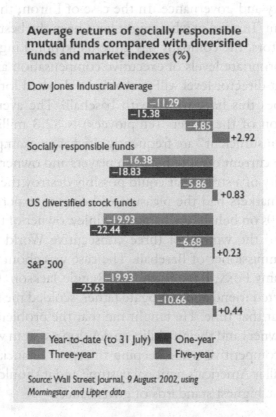

Average returns of socially responsible mutual funds compared with diversified funds and market indexes (%)

Dow Jones Industrial Average
−11.29
−15.38
−4.85
+2.92

Socially responsible funds
−16.38
−18.83
−5.86
+0.83

US diversified stock funds
−19.93
−22.44
−6.68
+0.23

S&P 500
−19.93
−25.63
−10.66
+0.44

■ Year-to-date (to 31 July) ■ One-year
■ Three-year ■ Five-year

Source: Wall Street Journal, 9 August 2002, using Morningstar and Lipper data

In late July, the Social Investment Forum indicated that 72% of the funds it tracks achieved the highest rankings for performance from both Morningstar and Lipper for the one and/ or 3-year periods ending 30 June 2002. Furthermore, the Forum's most recent study shows that socially and environmentally responsible investing in the US grew 8% from $2.16 trillion in 1999 to $2.34 trillion in 2001.

Finally, recent events in the US corporate world and the above average performance of sustainable and socially screened funds seem to strengthen the linkage between good corporate governance and stock performance. Three recent, and seemingly unrelated, stories in the US media might be illustrative. They concern Enron, Major League Baseball, and United Airlines. This observer would argue that they are all part of a three-legged stool called shareholder responsibility and governance. In the case of Enron, the argument is self-evident. In spite of what might have been the best judgement of the directors, the company has gone bankrupt. Lingering questions of appropriate levels of executive compensation and conflicts of interest at director level will probably be debated for years.

What does this have to do with baseball? The average annual compensation of the players (employees) is $2.3 million. Claims that this is "insufficient" are frequently cited as an example of player avarice. The current dispute between players and owners is creating the possibility of a strike that could possibly destroy the sport. This student of markets had the pleasure of being an expert witness in the late 1970s on behalf of Charles O. Finley, owner of the Oakland Athletics and the winner of three consecutive World Series, versus the Commissioner of Baseball. The case was about the relative value of Jimmy Foxx, Babe Ruth, and Reggie Jackson. Charlie, my dearly departed friend and surrogate father, scolded me for blaming the players at that time. He taught me that the problem was really about the owners and their inability to develop a system where teams could stay competitive while keeping the sport financially sustainable. Baseball is America's national pastime and it should be capable of setting the highest standards of governance.

The same story applies to United Airlines. The perception is that the pilots and machinists are on the verge of driving the company into bankruptcy. The press is quick to point out that the former can earn as much as $300,000 for 12 hours of work a week. It certainly appears that, unlike baseball players, there is a more than ample supply of good pilots. However, the representatives of these groups are also owners and directors of this company. Isn't it ultimately the responsibility of the representatives of the shareholders to insist that management develop a business model that is sustainable? This is a great company that should be doing better.

Enron, Major League Baseball, and United Airlines are the three different faces of the same problem: lack of good corporate governance and shareholder responsibility.

I would like to thank Alex Barkawi, managing director of SAM Indexes, and Rafael Marques for their assistance with this chapter.

Chapter 32

NASD Agreement Boosts Chicago Climate Exchange

October 2002

In September 2001, global warming was pushed off the US national agenda and left for dead. It had fallen victim to terrorism, a falling stock market and the first recession in nearly a decade.

However, in September 2002, in spite of these same conditions, the creation of a market for reducing and trading greenhouse gas (GHG) emissions moved one significant step closer to reality. The Chicago Climate Exchange (CCX) selected the National Association of Securities Dealers (NASD) as the provider of regulatory services for the exchange.

The CCX is a self-regulatory organization that will administer a voluntary pilot GHG emission reduction and trading programme for emission sources, carbon sinks, offset projects, and liquidity providers in the US starting in the first quarter of 2003. Offset providers in Brazil will be part of the programme and Canada and Mexico will also be integrated into the market next year, thereby creating a North American GHG market.

The development of the CCX resulted from feasibility and design studies that were funded by grants from the Chicago-based Joyce Foundation and administered by Northwestern University's Kellogg Graduate School of Management. Environmental Financial Products conducted the research.

The market architecture reflects an agreement that emerged from the efforts of 30 emitting companies in the power generation, forest products, manufacturing, oil and gas, and agricultural industries. It incorporates input from technical experts representing 18 design phase participants in the engineering, forestry, agricultural, academic, NGO, and public sectors. In addition, it reflects expertise drawn from domestic and international capital, commodity, and environmental markets. In total, more than 50 entities and hundreds of experts have contributed to the design phase.

The goals of the exchange are to

- Demonstrate unambiguously that a cross section of US industry can reach agreement on a voluntary commitment to reduce GHGs and implement a market-based emission reduction programme.
- Establish proof of concept by demonstrating the viability of a multi-sector GHG emissions "cap-and-trade" program supplemented by project-based offsets.
- Establish a mechanism for achieving price discovery as well as developing and disseminating market information.
- Allow flexibility in the methods, location, and timing of emission reductions so that GHG emissions can be reduced cost effectively.
- Facilitate trading with low transaction costs.
- Build market institutions and infrastructure and develop human capital in GHG emissions trading.
- Encourage improved emissions management.
- Harmonize and integrate with other international or sovereign trading regimes.
- Develop a market architecture that rewards innovative technology and management and encourages sustainable farming and forestry practices.

It is appropriate to ask three important questions at this point: What is the NASD? What will it do? And how will this agreement with the NASD help the CCX achieve its goals?

The NASD is the leading private-sector provider of financial regulatory services in the United States. Following the stock market crash of 1929 and the subsequent depression, Congress passed the Securities Exchange Act of 1934 to promote efficiency in equities markets and prevent abusive practices. In what appeared to be an afterthought, the Maloney Act amendments were passed. These created the NASD which is now responsible for regulating the securities industry and the NASDAQ stock market.

NASD also regulates the International Securities Exchange and the NASDAQ Liffe Markets (NQLX). The latter is a joint venture with the London International Financial Futures and Options Exchange. The NQLX is creating a market for single stock futures, which will be launched shortly.

Also of note is NASD's recent work following the Enron debacle. The NASD reach is extensive and its responsibilities include "registering and educating all industry participants . . . examining securities firms, enforcing both NASD rules and federal securities laws, and administering the largest dispute resolution forum for investors and member firms". Its staff numbers over 2000 with a geographical presence in more than 23 cities, including Chicago.

According to the terms of the historic agreement announced last month, NASD will assist in the development of registration, market oversight, and compliance procedures for members of the CCX. It will audit emissions baselines, the annual "true-up", and offset verification and certification procedures. NASD will assist in translating the recent agreement on the architecture of the CCX — a document named The Chicago Accord — into the exchange's rulebook.

In addition, NASD will use its state-of-the-art market surveillance technologies to monitor CCX trading activity for fraud and manipulation.

Although no regulatory framework is needed for the operation of the CCX, the decision was made to seek the services of NASD as an independent regulator in the belief that it will further the goals of the exchange by providing transparency, liquidity, and the highest degree of market integrity for this pilot programme. This should also facilitate the harmonization of the CCX with other international markets.

We believe that the importance of NASD's role in furthering the goals of the CCX is self-evident. It is encapsulated in the words of its top management. Mary Schapiro, NASD's president of regulatory policy and oversight, said: "The CCX is a market with a commendable purpose, and its investors will be best served by a well-regulated, transparent market". NASD's chairman and CEO, Robert Glauber, said: "The relationship with CCX promotes NASD's goal of becoming the regulatory services provider of choice to financial markets, exchanges, and regulators". We agree.

This historic agreement and the enthusiasm of NASD management and staff have significantly increased the momentum for the CCX. It is a milestone in the effort to bring market-based solutions to global warming.

I would like to give special thanks to Mary Schapiro, Joe Glauber, and the staff of NASD for their support of the CCX. Also thanks to Gerard Pannekoek, Michael Walsh, Alice LeBlanc, and Rafael Marques for their assistance in the preparation of this chapter.

Chapter 33

How Emissions Can Make Wind Power Pay

November 2002

We've come a long way since Don Quixote tilted at windmills. Wind is an important form of sustainable energy in some countries and has significant growth potential in the largest energy market in the world.

Energy from wind now provides approximately 4% of the power generated in Germany and 15% in Denmark. Even in the US where wind provides only 0.5% of the power, a dramatic increase is taking place. Since 2000, wind power capacity in the US has increased by almost 2,000 megawatts (MW) to 4,261 MW in 2001. Although Texas and California dominate US capacity, wind farms exist in approximately 30 states (see map).

Furthermore, the growth appears to be exponential. Florida Power and Light recently announced the addition of 350 MW in California and New Mexico. This project alone would boost US capacity by 8%. Projects in Washington and Oregon will increase capacity by an additional 830 MW in 2003. The Rolling Thunder wind farm in South Dakota, which will come on line in 2006 with 3,000 MW of capacity, will be the largest project in the country. The nation's first proposed offshore project off New England may add another 420 MW.

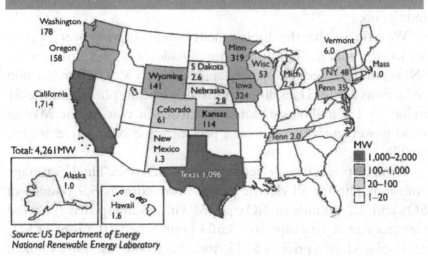

US wind power capacity (MW, end-2001)

Washington 178
Oregon 158
California 1,714
Total: 4,261 MW
Alaska 1.0
Hawaii 1.6
Wyoming 141
Colorado 61
New Mexico 1.3
Minn 319
S Dakota 2.6
Nebraska 2.8
Kansas 114
Texas 1,096
Wisc 53
Iowa 324
Mich 2.4
Tenn 2.0
Vermont 6.0
NY 48
Penn 35
Mass 1.0

MW
1,000–2,000
100–1,000
20–100
1–20

Source: US Department of Energy
National Renewable Energy Laboratory

There are three principal drivers in the growth of wind power. Technological gains have driven the cost of wind production down more than 80% in the last decade. More than a dozen states now have laws requiring that between 3% and 8% of their power comes from renewables. Finally, the wind energy Production Tax Credit of 1.5 cents per kilowatt hour is part of the national energy policy. In addition, current and potential gains associated with emissions trading are also contributing to this growth of wind power.

Wind has an inherent weakness. It is intermittent. As a result, transmission lines may go unused more than 60% of the time, imposing higher costs. Furthermore, this uncertainty requires that buyers have alternative sources of power. But, even after factoring in the latter difficulties, growth continues. Here's why. A single MW of capacity requires an investment of approximately $1.2 million. Operating at 40% capacity, with a prevailing price of $39 per MWh, and a debt/equity ratio of 70/30, wind development can provide a competitive rate of return on capital.

We typically spare our readers the tedious arithmetic of emissions values and their relationship to investment. However, in this case it really provides some interesting insights into the trends toward the monetization of environmental gains and we therefore ask for your indulgence.

We estimate that the displacement benefits of wind over 20 years are worth about $220,000. Sulphur dioxide (SO_2) and nitrous oxide (NOx) emission reductions total approximately $95,000 and carbon reductions about $125,000. This is a significant portion of the $1 million – 1.2 million estimated construction cost of one MW of wind power capacity, even on a present value basis. Here are the details.

Wind displaces other electric power generation. The US average emissions rate for all electric power production is 5.9 pounds of SO_2 and 2.7 pounds of NOx per MWh. Assuming that the wind turbines run at 40% capacity (3,504 hours) then 10.3 tons of SO_2 are displaced. At a price of $125/ton, this would result in a value of avoided emissions of $1,287 per year or $25,740 for a 20-year life. Similar reasoning yields $70,950 for NOx emissions. The combined emissions displacement value is therefore approximately $96,690 over the 20 years. Even using present values this represents a meaningful number relative to the investment.

Furthermore, the case becomes even more dramatic if we include carbon. The average emissions rate for all power generation in the US is 0.61 tons of carbon per MWh. Using similar reasoning, a price of $3.00 per ton of carbon dioxide creates a displacement value of $128,246. The emerging restrictions on mercury emissions from the electric power sector will add another point of value to this zero emission power source.

There are, however, some clouds on the horizon. Environmentalists in the tiny Cape Cod area are trying to block the development of the first US offshore wind farms. Their position is that 40-storey turbines, distributed along just less that 30 miles of coastline, will both destroy their views and endanger sea birds and animals. They claim that this would result in significant damage to tourism. As this is a critical part of the economies of Cape Cod and nearby Nantucket and Martha's Vineyard, the battle is raging in the US courts.

It is also a battle that is being fought in less opulent communities. Residents of Cherry Valley, in New York state, are also opposing the development of wind farms in their area.

While the siting of wind farms in certain areas may generate controversy and possibly be constrained on a rational basis, the trend seems inexorable. The middle of the US and its coastal areas offer a large potential for renewable energy. It's our view that these resources will ultimately be developed for both the private and public good.

• Also, as promised, here is another update on the Chicago Climate Exchange (CCX). The exchange has retained Rothschild as its investment banker, marking another milestone in its development.

I would like the thank Michael Polsky, CEO of Invenergy, which specializes in wind energy development, for his valuable input. I would also like to thank Michael Walsh and Nathan Clark for their assistance in the preparation of this article.

Chapter 34

Markets Everywhere

December 2002–January 2003

> "Economic history is the story of the gradual extension of the economic community beyond its original limits of the single household to embrace the nation and then the world"
>
> Ludwig Von Mises, *The Theory of Money and Credit*

One year ago, this column discussed the plurilateral evolutionary path of international environmental markets. That column opened with the above quote from the great neoclassical Austrian economist. He continues to be correct.

In yet another sign of the trend toward plurilateral[1] environmental markets, in December, European Union (EU) environment ministers agreed to establish a greenhouse gas (GHG) emissions market for the years from 2005 to 2007. This "cap-and-trade" system still must be approved by the European Parliament. However, that appears to be a formality.

The cap-and-trade system is the critical component of the EU's plan to meet its Kyoto Protocol target of cutting GHG emissions to 8% below 1990 levels by 2012.

---

[1] A 'plurilateral' regime refers to the development of a framework for GHG emission trading involving a medium-sized set of countries (e.g., five to 20). The concept of a plurilateral regime was first introduced by Environmental Financial Products at the first UNCTAD GHG Emissions Trading Policy Forum in Chicago in June 1997 and at the second Policy Forum in Toronto in November 1997.

We have long postulated that environmental markets would emerge in different regions and would ultimately be integrated through a common set of rules or arbitrage.

The establishment of the European market continues the trend established by the emergence of distinct GHG markets in Denmark and the United Kingdom. There has already been a trade between entities in these two sovereign nations. The EU market extends the multi-sector approach initiated in the UK programme. Sectors initially covered include energy, production and processing of ferrous metals, the mineral industry, and pulp and paper production. Initially, the scheme only covers carbon dioxide (CO_2) emissions.

December also witnessed further evidence of the extension of the plurilateral market concept. The government of Slovakia sold Kyoto allowances equivalent to 200,000 tons of CO_2 to a private sector firm in Japan.

A casual reading of the popular press suggests that the actions of the EU will create a single GHG market. An exposition of the text of the political agreement reveals a somewhat different inference. Each country will establish its own reduction targets and schedules in the initial period. Furthermore, there will be different registries for each nation. A proviso states that there will be a general registry for the EU. Transfer of allowances among member states is provided for in the agreement.

Member states will separately establish monitoring and verification procedures in accordance with an overall set of guidelines. The noncompliance fines will be €40 ($40) per excess ton from 2005 to 2007, rising to €100 from the start of the Kyoto Protocol in 2008. Ultimately, agreements should be reached with other industrialized countries participating in the Kyoto Protocol to provide mutual recognition of allowances.

This agreement is the beginning of the movement from a plurilateral to a multilateral environmental market.

The establishment of an EU-wide GHG market is an important step in the development of an international trading regime. It is easy to criticize the specifics of any new market and we should refrain from this. Markets must initially be limited. They will not be comprehensive at the outset. Efforts to be comprehensive can prevent progress in building the essential foundation.

Financial innovation often begins with a limited model, which is then refined. In this spirit, it is important to note that the EU scheme starts as an allowance-only market. Although it does not initially provide for project-based offsets, it allows for their eventual inclusion from both domestic and international projects.

The targets that the EU and the member states must achieve represent a significant challenge. Inclusion of offsets will provide the opportunity to reach these objectives in a least-cost manner. Projects in the agriculture, forestry, and landfill gas sectors are just some of the low-cost mitigation opportunities presented via projects. Agricultural subsidies have been a significant source of dissension within the Union and worldwide. There appears to be an enormous opportunity to enhance net farm income by rewarding the provision of environmental services such as soil carbon sequestration. This may provide a better way to allocate resources within the agricultural sector than the current system (while also enhancing farm productivity and water quality).

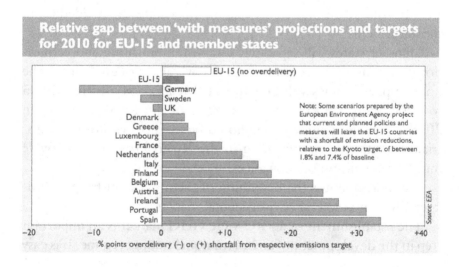

Relative gap between 'with measures' projections and targets for 2010 for EU-15 and member states

Note: Some scenarios prepared by the European Environment Agency project that current and planned policies and measures will leave the EU-15 countries with a shortfall of emission reductions, relative to the Kyoto target, of between 1.8% and 7.4% of baseline

% points overdelivery (−) or (+) shortfall from respective emissions target

Source: EEA

The 1990 baseline for the 15 members of the EU is approximately 3.6 billion tons of CO_2. The addition of 10 EU candidate countries would also expand the emissions market. Independent forecasters predict the value of the EU market could reach €8 billion by 2007. If, and only if, the market architecture is designed appropriately (allowances, offsets, clearing and settlements, liquidity provisions, etc.) we believe that this could prove to be a conservative estimate.

The EU's use of established terminology (e.g., "allowances") and proven procedures (e.g., primarily free allocation and provisions for public participation) are simple, but important elements that bode well for market success and eventual linkage with other trading blocs.

The recent ratification of the Kyoto Protocol by New Zealand, imminent ratification by Canada, and earlier ratification by Japan, provides the EU with emissions trading partners with whom successful commercial relations already exist. Those countries would be well advised to closely examine the EU directive as it provides a good starting point for the formation of a global carbon market.

I would like to thank James Perkaus for first introducing this concept into the discussions while acting as a consultant to Environmental Financial Products in 1997.

Chapter 35

Chicago Shows the Way

February 2003

> "Nothing is as powerful as an idea whose time has come"
> — Victor Hugo

It floats out there in popular culture as "America's heartland"; home to a vast amount of soybean and corn production; a dreary and cold continental climate; its great fame achieved from gangsters such as Al Capone and John Dillinger; and the region is far from the east and west coasts that link the United States with Europe and Asia. Yet, Chicago could become the proving ground for the concept of market-based solutions to environmental and social issues.

Efforts to develop market-based solutions to global warming reached a milestone on 16 January when, at a press conference hosted by the City of Chicago in City Hall, leading United States and international companies and the City of Chicago announced they will be the founding members of Chicago Climate Exchange (CCX), a voluntary "cap-and-trade" program for reducing and trading greenhouse gas emissions. In an unprecedented voluntary action, these entities have made a legally binding commitment to reduce their emissions of greenhouse gases by 4% below the average of their 1998–2001 baselines by 2006, the last year of the pilot program.

The announcement marks the first time major companies in multiple industries have made a voluntary binding commitment to use a

Table 1. Founding members of CCX
Automotive
Ford Motor Company
Chemicals
DuPont
Commercial real estate
Equity Office Properties Trust
Environmental services
Waste Management
Electric power generation
American Electric Power
Manitoba Hydro
Electronics
Motorola
Forest products companies
International Paper
MeadWestvaco Corp
Stora Enso North America
Temple-Inland
Municipalities
City of Chicago
Semiconductors
STMicroelectronics
Pharmaceuticals
Baxter International

rules-based market for reducing their greenhouse gas emissions (see Table 1). CCX will enable them to receive credit for such reductions and to buy and sell credits in order to find the most cost-effective way of achieving reductions. Trading is targeted to begin in the spring of this year. The private sector's response to the initiative has been incredible. These companies have demonstrated tremendous leadership. They really believe that a proactive approach to climate change advances everyone's long-term interests.

CCX will administer this pilot programme for emission sources, farm and forest carbon sinks, offset projects, and liquidity providers in North America. To foster international emissions trading, offset providers in Brazil can also participate. The development of CCX resulted from feasibility and design studies that were funded by grants from the Chicago-based Joyce Foundation and administered by Northwestern University's Kellogg Graduate School of Management. Environmental Financial Products conducted the research and development effort.

CCX market architecture incorporates input from a wide range of economic sectors as well as technical experts in the engineering, forestry, agricultural, academic, nongovernmental organization, and public sectors (see Table 2). In total, more than 50 corporate entities and hundreds of experts have contributed to the design phase.

CCX selected NASD to provide regulatory services and Rothschild Inc., an affiliate of the London-based bank NM Rothschild & Sons, to provide investment banking services. Detailed discussions are under way with more than 80 additional corporations who are interested in becoming members of CCX. More news about the trading platform as well as clearing and settlement will appear in this column in the coming months. A second group of members is expected to be announced in the next 90 days.

There have been years of discussion about the potential for trading carbon emissions, but the CCX will offer the first test of the

Table 2. CCX key features

Geographic coverage	US emission sources and offset projects in the US and Brazil. Sources and projects in Canada and Mexico to be added during 2003
Emission targets and timetable	Emission reduction commitments for 2003–06. Emission targets are 1% below baseline during 2003, 2% below baseline during 2004, 3% below baseline during 2005, 4% below baseline during 2006
Emission baseline	Average of annual emissions during 1998–2001
Gases included	CO_2, CH_4, N_2O, PFCs, HFCs, SF_6
Emission offsets	Landfill and agricultural methane, sequestration in soils and forest biomass. Other project types accepted from Brazil
Early action credits	Credits from specified early projects to be included starting in 2004
Registry, electronic trading platform	Registry will serve as official holder and transfer mechanism, and is linked with the electronic trading platform on which all trades occur
Exchange governance	Self-regulatory organisation overseen by committees comprising exchange members, directors and staff

concept on a scale with global potential. A representative carbon trading market can yield lessons that may be relevant for economies worldwide for years to come.

On a sentimental note, I want to personally thank the founding members of Chicago Climate Exchange and my colleagues at Environmental Financial Products. They were all the true heroes.

Chapter 36

Institutional Innovation (Part I)

March 2003

A flimsy transparency introducing the title of the talk was placed on an old-fashioned overhead projector in Gleacher Hall at the University of Chicago. The organizers of the conference had purposefully chosen a low-tech teaching tool. Institutional innovation is itself a very disruptive idea: a compelling story best told without Power-Point. I was to address guests of the Ronald Coase Institute. We discussed the evolution of institutional innovation and how these innovations have helped to form the intellectual basis for environmental markets and the Chicago Climate Exchange. The institute and its members provided a most fitting audience, as its principles and the ideas of one of the greatest thinkers of the 20th century — Nobel prize–winning economist Sir Ronald Coase — on the significance of transaction costs and property rights provide the intellectual basis for environmental markets. This column shares some points of that discussion and provides three examples of such institutional innovations leading up to the current market for carbon dioxide (CO_2).

Numerous elements are necessary when establishing financial institutions: academic involvement, nongovernmental organization (NGO) or funding entity participation, trade associations, advisory groups, banking, clearing, legal, exchange organization (electronic or open outcry), speeches and lectures, and media awareness and education (see the table). This chapter focuses on three of the elements:

- NGOs or industry and trade groups promoting the concept and becoming funding entities;
- media coverage of the innovation to provide public education and awareness; and
- introducing the innovation into the academic curriculum.

Building innovative markets

	Pacific Commodity Exchange	Financial Futures (GNMA, T-Bonds)	SO_2	CO_2
Academic	Univ. of California, Berkeley (1971)	Northwestern (1977)	Berkeley (1971)	Columbia (1992) Northwestern (2003)
NGO/funding entity	Commodity Club of San Francisco (1969)	Center for Real Estate and Urban Economics	Coalition for Acid Rain Equity	Joyce Foundation, WRI
Trade associations	Commodity Club of San Francisco	IAFE	EMA	IETA
Advisory groups	Pacific Vegetable Oil; RJ Reynolds; Bank of America; Merrill Lynch	GNMA Committee and Bond Committee (Preston Martin, Eli Broad, ARAC Tony Frank)	Clean Air Committee, CBOT, ARAC	CCX Advisory Committee
Banking	Bank of America	Settlement Bank: GNMA CDR; T-bonds: existing repo market	Self-evident property right (CCAA)	Settlement bank
Clearing	Pacific Commodity Exchange	Extension of agricultural clearing	Existing law, banking systems: ATS, EPA	Clearing corp: allowances and offset registry
Legal	Commodity Exchange Authority	CFTC Act (1975)	CAAA (1990)	Exchange and NASD
Exchange organisation	Corporations with professional chairmen and management	Mutually-owned	CBOT auctions, OTC market	Corporations with professional chairmen and management
Electronic/open outcry	Electronic	Open outcry	Electronic	Electronic
Speeches and lectures	Coffee, Sugar and Cocoa Exchange; Int'l commodities conference	Public Securities Association; Mortgage Bankers Association	Utility Conferences	Environmental Finance, Utility conferences
Media awareness and education	FT, Journal of Commerce, San Francisco Examiner	WSJ, Business Week, FT	NY Times, WSJ, FT	Environmental Finance, FT, WSJ

Academic institutions and NGOs have been the workhorses of new and innovative markets. The intellectual basis of the Chicago Climate Exchange can be traced back to a grant given by the Commodity Club of San Francisco.

This grant financed a study of the feasibility of a new exchange in San Francisco called the Pacific Commodity Exchange. Since the organizers of the exchange had chosen coconut oil as the first commodity, the task was straightforward. There were two components to the feasibility study: design an institution that minimized the general cost of price discovery and develop a system that minimized the specific cost of negotiating and consummating each transaction on the exchange.

Although the recommendations of the study were radical departures from the business model of the time, they are the current practice of many of the most successful exchanges of today. Exchanges have evolved from mutual organizations with multiple parties and open outcry auctions to for-profit organizations with electronic trading.

The prospect of the novel idea of a fully automated trading system caught the eye of the *Financial Times, The Journal of Commerce,* and several other publications. This helped advance the second element.

The third element was addressed in 1971, a time when futures markets were taught only in departments of agricultural economics. The School of Business Administration of the University of California boldly allowed a course on futures markets to be introduced into its curriculum. The trade group promotions and media coverage built short-term education for market participants, while uptake in the academic sector would theoretically provide long-term human capital for the innovation through the education of future business leaders.

Further evidence of the role of academic institutions and NGOs in institutional innovation emerges from a study of the origins of financial futures in general and interest rate derivatives specifically. Shortly after the research on the Pacific Commodities Exchange had been concluded, the Center for Real Estate and Urban Economics at the University of California provided a grant to study the feasibility of developing a futures market for mortgage interest rates. This research ultimately led to the development of interest rate derivatives. They were introduced at the Chicago Board of Trade on 20 October 1975.

The same challenges were present in this innovation and the same approach was used. Hundreds of speeches to industry and trade groups, vast media coverage and a course at Northwestern University helped successfully propel interest rate futures to a daily trading volume of trillions of dollars spread over five continents.

Academic institutions and NGOs continued their role of workhorses in the development of the US sulfur dioxide (SO_2) allowance market. In this instance, an Ohio public interest organization called the Coalition for Acid Rain Equity funded a study that ultimately helped convince lawmakers to include emissions trading in the Clean Air Act of 1990. This Act created the property right that is the basis of a multi-billion-dollar US market.

The same methods were used to educate practitioners and develop human capital. A fledgling over-the-counter (OTC) market in the early 1990s was complemented by the first annual SO_2 allowance auction conducted jointly by the US Environmental Protection Agency and the Chicago Board of Trade. This was the first organized spot and forward market. The SO_2 environmental market is now providing us with insights into the development of a CO_2 market in the US and internationally.

Academic institutions and NGOs have also been, and will continue to be, driving forces in the new market for CO_2. Hundreds of conferences are being held worldwide. The media continues to play a vital role in public awareness and education. Lectures are being held at major universities. And the curriculum of universities is being changed to reflect this institutional innovation.

All practitioners in the emerging CO_2 emissions markets should remain confident in their objectives. The institutions they are building are based on the thoughts of one of the greatest economists of the 20th century and are supported by many of the leading economic and environmental minds around the globe.

I would like to dedicate this column to my wife, Ellen, my children, and grandchildren. They have been my biggest supporters throughout this great adventure.

Chapter 37

The Power of an Idea

April 2003

Stories about the demise of sulfur dioxide (SO_2) emissions trading appear routinely every year. This year was different — there seemed to be more of them. Some implicated the program in local mortality rates; others predicted the complete failure of the program while erroneously linking it to unsuccessful lawsuits that would have brought older plants under new regulation. Forward prices were going to collapse and the entire SO_2 allowance market with it. However, it now appears that the death of "cap and trade" systems are tomorrow's story and, parenthetically, promise to always be so.

This year's 11th annual Environmental Protection Agency (EPA) auction, conducted by the Chicago Board of Trade (CBOT), once again proved newsworthy because of its routine nature. This observer found the fact that three elementary schools were winning bidders to be about the most entertaining event of the day.

Nevertheless, there were some interesting developments. The spot auction clearing price of $171.80 was far above the preauction spot market of $158.00 for 5000-ton trades. This divergence suggests that liquidity in the over-the-counter (OTC) market for high-volume trades is still suffering from the exit of market markers. Tables 1–3 summarize this year's auctions.

The clearing price in the spot auction was $171.80 while the weighted average of winning bids was $171.81. The number of successful bidders was 20 while the unsuccessful totaled 18.

1. Allowances available for auction

Origin	Spot auction (first usable 2003)	7-year advance auction (first usable 2010)
EPA	125,000	125,000
Privately offered	10	–
Total	125,010	125,000

Source: Chicago Board of Trade and EPA

2. Spot auction results

Allowances	Number of bids	Number of bidders	Bid price
Bid for: 618,565	Successful: 20	Successful: 20	Highest: $250
Sold: 125,000	Unsuccessful: 62	Unsuccessful: 18	Clearing: $171.80 (the clearing price is the lowest price at which a successful bid was made)
Total	82	38	Lowest: $2.06
			Average: $171.81 (weighted by the number of allowances in each bid)

Source: Chicago Board of Trade and EPA

3. Seven-year advance auction results

Allowances	Number of bids	Number of bidders	Bid price
Bid for: 438,500	Successful: 6	Successful: 2	Highest: $92
Sold: 125,000	Unsuccessful: 34	Unsuccessful: 5	Clearing: $80 (the clearing price is the lowest price at which a successful bid was made)
Total	40	7	Lowest: $10
			Average: $86.40 (weighted by the number of allowances in each bid)

Source: Chicago Board of Trade and EPA

By comparison, last year's auction had 21 successful and six unsuccessful bids. The clearing price in the 7-year advance auction was $80.00 while the weighted average of winning bids was $86.40.

Despite the proliferation of market intermediaries, the forward OTC market still appears to be inefficient. Price discovery in the OTC market is inefficient, making price information from the CBOT forward auction even more valuable to the market. The profile of forward price ranges and the relationship of successful to unsuccessful bids followed the same patterns as the spot auctions. This is consistent with last year's forward auction.

In a pattern that has continued for the last few years, the difference between spot and forward prices remained much greater than it had been during the 1990s. Some market participants attribute this difference to regulatory uncertainty; others to general uncertainty. The interest rate implied by the difference between spot and forward prices is 10.9%. This far exceeds the rates on 10-year medium quality corporate debt (6.5%) and is roughly equal to the current rate on high-yield bonds. The high cost of capital now faced by the financially distressed elements of the electric power sector may be influencing the forward pricing curve in the allowance markets.

The 2003 auction results suggest that the SO_2 market continues to function very effectively. Prices continue to be well below levels that were forecast in 1992. In that year, the median forecast was $600 with a low of $309 and a high of $981. Over the 11-year history, the spot prices now average $139.08 and forward prices $103.72. Most importantly, sulfur emissions have fallen faster than required, while the health and social benefits have been impressive. The latest EPA environmental assessment of the Acid Rain Program was released in November 2002. It amplifies the earlier findings of tremendous environmental improvement since the launch of the program (see www.epa.gov/airmarkets/cmprpt/arp01/index.html).

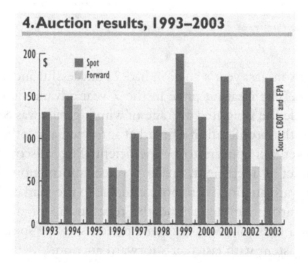

4. Auction results, 1993–2003

In last year's article, we highlighted Slovakia's experience with the development of an SO_2 "cap-and-trade" program. This was an example of the spread of the emissions trading model to other countries. Now, we witness market-based solutions to environmental problems being embraced in a demonstration program in Tayuan, the capital of Shanxi province in China.

This program was designed with the help of a team of experts from Resources for the Future (RFF). In a city once considered by the World Bank to be one of the most polluted in the world, it is heartening to see such an important policy experiment. Recently, we had the privilege of witnessing Asia's enthusiasm first hand at a conference in Hong Kong sponsored by the Association for Sustainable and Responsible Investment in Asia. Here, local entrepreneurs and officials expressed a strong interest in learning more about, and becoming further involved in, trading programs.

The SO_2 auctions at the CBOT remain a testimony to the power of an idea. This breakthrough program has helped build institutions and implement a successful market-based solution to a major environmental problem. Now the model and its lessons are being taken up by other initiatives around the world. China's experience with an SO_2 program, the European Union's plans to implement a CO_2 emissions trading program by 2005, and the upcoming launch of the Chicago Climate Exchange, prove that ongoing trading initiatives are continuing to drive much of the environmental policy debate. Environmental markets are here to stay.

I would like to thank Michael Walsh, Rafael Marques, and Nathan Clark for their assistance in the preparation of this article. Richard Sandor is chairman and chief executive of Environmental Financial Products.

Chapter 38

Institutional Innovation (Part II)

May 2003

> "This was an important ... historic meeting. It has brought together officials, negotiators and private sector participants actively involved in the market who are creating the potential for this kind of trading to take place in practice".
>
> — Nobel Laureate Ronald Coase, Chicago, June 1997

Ronald Coase wondered out loud why this organizer of the event had asked him to deliver the opening remarks as he lacked any specific knowledge of greenhouse gas (GHG) emissions trading. However, in the next 30 minutes he would put the purpose of our 2-day seminar and subsequent work into a context that we all understood.

It was also inspirational. He reminded us about how he had been publicly derided for decades when he thought, as a matter of public policy, that broadcast spectrums should be auctioned to the private sector. The practice has now been widely accepted. Theoretically sound mechanisms using markets would ultimately prevail. They simply required the building of institutions that minimize transaction costs. Those opening remarks by Ronald Coase at the June 1997 Policy Forum sponsored by the Earth Council and United Nations Conference on Trade and Development (UNCTAD) and hosted by Centre Financial Products, the forerunner of the Chicago Climate Exchange (CCX), marked the beginning of the process of building the first professional association devoted to international emissions trading.

In the March 2003 article, we promised to discuss specific components of the institution-building matrix. For this article, we would like to focus on the role played by professional trade associations in the development of human capital. This development is critical to the success of any new market. We should not assume that human capital suddenly appears. Institutions which educate professionals and promote a greater understanding of the markets themselves have to be built from scratch.

A description of three different professional associations provides some insight into the scope and purposes of these institutions.

In the field of financial futures, the International Association of Financial Engineers (IAFE), founded in 1992 by Robert Schwartz and Jack Marshall, congregates financial professionals dedicated to fostering the practice and advancement of quantitative finance. The IAFE brings together academics and practitioners from a wide-variety of institutions across the globe and is active in the organization of conferences, seminars, and publications that support its mission.

Environmental markets have benefited from the leadership of two organizations that continue to provide support and education to the trading concept in both the United States and abroad.

The Emissions Marketing Association (EMA) was founded in January 1997. Dan Chartier (Wisconsin Electric), Andy Ertel (Natsource), and Linda Clemmons (Enron) were instrumental in the groundwork necessary to create this organization. In May of that year, the EMA held its first meeting in New Orleans. At that time, membership stood at 30 companies. Today, the EMA boasts some 300 members from nearly 200 companies worldwide. Initially created to serve firms involved in the sulfur dioxide market, the EMA's focus has evolved to encompass other emerging markets such as nitrogen oxides, renewable energy credits and GHGs. The association promotes market-based initiatives by supporting the advancement of policy and regulation related to environmental markets and by an extensive educational and outreach campaign to its members and the general public.

The International Emissions Trading Association (IETA) is a nonprofit organization created in June 1999 to establish a functional international framework for trading GHG emission reductions. Its membership includes some of the leading international companies involved in carbon trading. IETA members seek to develop an international emissions trading regime, and work in informing members of the public and private sectors in seminars and conferences around the world. Our friends Paulo Protasio and Andrei Marcu have devoted countless hours to build and strengthen IETA's role in the emissions trading market. Frank Joshua, then at UNCTAD, was also very active in the formative years of the organization.

IETA was the first professional association devoted to international emissions trading. The seeds for the formation of IETA were planted a few years earlier, in a fortunate conjunction of initiatives then taking shape at the policy and business levels worldwide. By 1996 individuals from The Earth Council, UNCTAD, and CFP had a long history of promoting a market-based solution to climate change. During one of our conversations, Maurice Strong and I agreed that we had to formalize the dialogue on emissions trading that had been taking place in disparate settings by developing a policy forum. The forum would be sponsored by the Earth Council and UNCTAD and organized and hosted by CFP (see box).

The attendees would go on to play critical roles in the emerging carbon market, ranging from the negotiations in Kyoto to the development of the voluntary GHG market in the United Kingdom and the first private sector market in the United States. In addition to Professor Coase, the then US Secretary of Commerce, the Hon. William Daley, also provided a keynote luncheon address. Other senior officials present at the event included Michael Zammit-Cutajar, the head of the United Nations Framework Convention on Climate Change (UNFCCC) who presided over the Kyoto negotiations; Dr. R. K. Pachauri, the future director of the Intergovernmental Panel on Climate Change (IPCC), and Luiz Gylvan Meira

POLICY FORUM ON GREENHOUSE GAS EMISSIONS TRADING

Critical Issues and Practical Steps for Implementation

Organised by UNCTAD and the Earth Council
and hosted by Centre Financial Products
Inaugural Session 19–20 June 1997
Venue: Union League Club, Chicago, US

Opening Session
Chairmen: Maurice Strong and Richard Sandor
Addresses by:
Maurice Strong, Chairman, Earth Council
Michael Zammit-Cutajar, Executive Secretary,
  UNFCCC Secretariat

Keynote Address
By Professor Ronald Coase, Nobel Laureate,
  Economics, 1991

**International GHG Emissions Trading: Benefits
of an Initial-Phase Cap & Trade Market**
Richard Sandor, Centre Financial Products
Panel
Dirk Forrister, Chairman, White House Climate
  Change Task Force, US
Ambassador Ole Kristian Holthe, Royal Ministry of
  Foreign Affairs, Norway
Ambassador John Fraser, Ambassador for the
  Environment, Canada

**The US SO₂ Allowance Trading Programme:
Are There Lessons for GHG Trading?**
Brian McLean, Director, Acid Rain Division, USEPA
Panel
Michael Shields, Detroit Edison, US
Grzegorz Peszka, Advisor, Ministry of Environment,
  Poland
Stuart Calman, Ministry for the Environment, New
  Zealand

Round-Table Discussion
Perspectives on an Initial-Phase Cap & Trade
  International GHG Emissions Trading Programme

Summing up: by Maurice Strong

Filho, the president of the Brazilian Space Agency. It is interesting to note that 6 months before the Kyoto meeting, Zammit-Cutajar offered encouragement to the Chicago gathering but warned that there was significant opposition to including trading in the Kyoto Protocol.

The second and third forums were held in Toronto and London in the next two years. The programs continued with the format and sponsors of that first event. It had become clear after the London event that these forums should be morphed into a professional trade association. This was formalized over a dinner at Conference of the Parties (COP 4) in Buenos Aires. IETA was officially incorporated in 1999.

The formation of the other trade associations have similar rich histories. The vision of the founders and the amount of work required to launch them were prodigious. Their subsequent activities play an ongoing role in ensuring that markets function efficiently. The CCX is proud to be a member of all three organizations.

Special thanks to Tanya Beder of the IAFE, Dan Chartier of the EMA, and Andrei Marcu of IETA.

Chapter 39

Flexibility is the Key

June 2003

Two distinct, yet closely related, stories made headlines in the early part of May. In one, the UK government announced the results of the first year of its voluntary emissions trading program. Meanwhile, a report from the European Environment Agency (EEA) revealed that emissions of greenhouse gases (GHGs) in the European Union (EU) are on the rise for the second consecutive year. The underlying message of these two, apparently, distinct stories can shed some light on the importance of encouraging flexibility in the design of emissions trading programs.

According to UK government figures released on 12 May, the first year of the program has seen allowances equivalent to 7 million tons of carbon dioxide (CO_2) traded in about 2000 transfers. More than 800 companies participated in trading. The government also reported that 5,000 firms had reduced their GHG emissions by an equivalent of 13.5 million tons of CO_2 in 2002, three times greater than the original reduction target of 3.5 million tons. The United Nations has said that Britain is well positioned to meet its GHG emission goal under the Kyoto Protocol of an average 12.5% reduction from 1990 levels over 2008–2012.

Meanwhile, the EEA reports that GHG emissions from the EU are on the rise for the second year in a row. This indicates that the EU is moving further away from meeting its commitment to reduce GHG emissions by an average of 8% below 1990 levels over the same period. Ten of the 15 EU members will have difficulties meeting their targets, with Ireland, Spain, and Portugal being the farthest away from their goals. In the case of Ireland, a recent news item indicated that the Irish Business and Employers Confederation clearly recognizes the benefits of Kyoto's flexible mechanisms as a way to achieve low-cost emission reductions that could be realized outside Ireland.

Why are these recent news items relevant to the debate on the design of emissions trading pilot programs? An article we wrote in this magazine in September 2000 discussed the trends that the United States and Europe were facing in terms of "decoupling" of emissions and economic growth. We thought it would be helpful to update this information.

Economic growth in the United States has become largely decoupled from increases in GHG emissions. The rapid growth in the US economy during the 1990s has not been matched by an equivalent growth in GHG emissions. From 1990 to

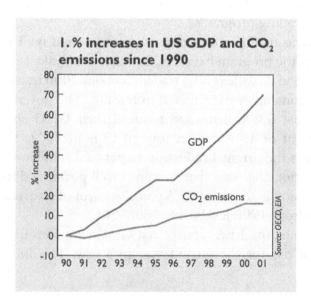

1. % increases in US GDP and CO_2 emissions since 1990

the end of 2001, gross domestic product (GDP) rose by 74% (in current dollars) whereas GHG emissions grew by only 16% (see Fig. 1).

Absolute GHG emissions in the EU declined during the early 1990s, but are now experiencing an upswing blamed on weather conditions and an increase in road transportation. The belief that public policies are a main driver in bringing the EU closer to its goal of an 8% reduction from 1990 levels is not accurate. Similar to the US experience, these gains are largely (but not exclusively) the by-product of other developments (e.g., weather, fuel switching at UK power stations, and the economic decline and retooling of the former East Germany). Although economic fluctuations in the EU have been less dramatic than in the United States, there has been an even more pronounced decoupling of economic growth and GHG emissions. Figure 2 illustrates the percentage increases in GDP and CO_2 emissions in the EU during the 1990s.

It is interesting to examine the emissions per unit of GDP in the United States and the EU. Figure 3 shows a long-term declining trend among these major economies.

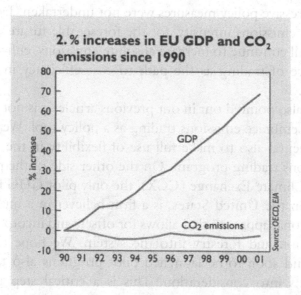

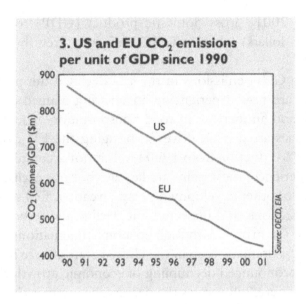

3. US and EU CO_2 emissions per unit of GDP since 1990

The economies of both the United States and Europe are becoming less carbon intensive. In 2000, we warned that since this "decoupling" is not yet fully realized, it would probably be difficult to keep emissions below 1990 levels in the next few years if more aggressive policy measures were not undertaken. Despite the decline in emissions intensity, for the foreseeable future economic growth will continue to increase absolute emissions, enhancing the importance of trading as the path to cost efficiency in reducing emissions.

As we also pointed out in our previous article, it is not sufficient merely to embrace emissions trading as a policy tool. We believe it is fundamental also to make full use of flexibility in the design of an emissions trading program. On the other side of the pond, the Chicago Climate Exchange (CCX), the only pilot GHG reduction program in the United States, is a firm believer in a multi-sector, multi-national approach that allows for offsets and incorporates soil sequestration and forestry into the system. We hope that other existing and soon-to-be launched pilot programs also take these suggestions into consideration. This is a critical step to ensure that countries will have the opportunity to make the best use of this important policy mechanism to achieve their environmental goals.

I would like to thank Michael Walsh, Rafael Marques, and Nathan Clark for their assistance in the preparation of this article.

Chapter 40

Water Rights and Wrongs

July–August 2003

Water markets are on the move. New ones are emerging and those that already exist are being modified. Energy and emissions brokers are entering the market and this once arcane business continues to attract a widespread following. The reasons are obvious. Water is scarce and becoming more so. Command and control has had little success in achieving the best possible use of this commodity.

There are two key issues to consider — the quantity of water available and its quality. It seems reasonable to start by focusing on issues of quantity. We will deal with quality in a subsequent column.

A few facts help in understanding why water rights will continue to see significant demand and why there is a role for transparent markets in these rights. According to the UN Environment Program (UNEP), 2.5% of the world's water is freshwater but the vast majority of it is locked in the polar regions and glaciers. Approximately 0.01% of the water on earth is freshwater that can be readily used for human consumption. This small and fixed supply must be used to satisfy an ever-growing demand. Officials at the Third World Water Forum held in Kyoto in March this year reported that water demand is growing approximately three times as fast as the current rate of population growth.

This supply-demand imbalance is one of many factors causing desertification. According to the UN Convention to Combat

Desertification (UNCCD), an area of 4 billion hectares, roughly equal to a third of the planet's land surface, is affected by desertification. The United Nations estimates that this figure is increasing by some 5.25 million hectares each year.

But, the problems go far beyond desertification. According to officials at the WaterForum, nearly 1.2 billion people lack a safe water supply and virtually all regions of the planet face water problems. It is expected that many of the conflicts in the 21st century will involve disputes over water rights. One example is the current battle between the United States and Mexico over water from the Rio Grande.

Such disputes are not only international in nature, but are also taking place at the state level. Water rights have always been a hugely contentious issue among the western US states that draw from the Colorado River. As scarcity increases, water markets are expected to becoming more prevalent and sophisticated.

Water rights are expressed in terms of acre-feet, a volume of water equal to one acre, one foot deep (equivalent to 326,000 gallons). Rights to acre-feet of water can be bought outright or leased temporarily. Trades almost always go through a third party. In the course of our research for this article, it became clear that the market is fragmented and lacks price transparency.

Two states provide relevant examples of the status of water rights trading. In California, industrial and residential users compete with agriculture for ever scarcer water resources. According to the Pacific Research Institute, agriculture uses almost 80% of the state's water resources, whereas urban areas consume 20%. The state has experimented with water markets and informal local transactions led to the creation of WaterLink, an electronic trading platform on which buyers and sellers can post bids and offers. In response to these initiatives and other enabling legislation introduced by the government, brokers and other market participants are entering this nascent market.

New Mexico is another state that has experimented with informal water markets. A system based on private or municipal ownership of irrigation ditches called acequias was brought to the region by Spanish settlers in the 1500s. Users of water from another person's acequia had to compensate the owner. This remains the model for water allocation in the state. Today, all the water rights associated with private lands have been assigned. Farmers, manufacturers, power producers, or any other type of private landowner in need of water must buy rights from a municipality or private entity. The figure shows the breakdown of water consumption in the state of New Mexico by sector. Similar to the situation in California, tension exists between agricultural water users and industrial and residential users.

Problems of water scarcity further complicate an interstate dispute between New Mexico and Texas. New Mexico has to maintain a specified flow rate in the Pecos River to fulfill the Texas–New Mexico Pecos River Compact. In 2003, New Mexico expects it will have to send 17,000 acre-feet over the State line. In 2002, the State Legislature appropriated $70 million in public funds to finance purchases to meet this obligation. In order to deliver, New Mexico has to buy at least 12,000 acres worth of land and water rights from landowners. One is led to believe that more informed and cost-effective public decisions could be made if better price information was available.

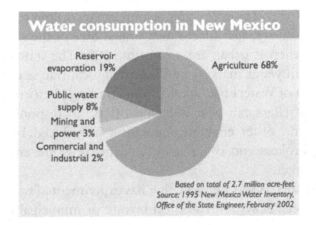

Based on total of 2.7 million acre-feet
Source: 1995 New Mexico Water Inventory,
Office of the State Engineer, February 2002

New Mexico has a major opportunity to become a leader in the emerging water markets due to the commitment of Governor, Bill Richardson and John D'Antonio, New Mexico's Secretary of the Interstate Stream Commission.

For students of markets, it appears that, similar to the current state of the carbon market, the buying and selling of water rights is fragmented and suffers from high transaction costs. This lack of price transparency complicates policy and business decisions. The status of water rights in the Western United States exemplifies the need for organized markets that can help inform the debate on this issue by creating agreed standards and practices. Current efforts by private, public, and academic participants can help form the necessary institutions that will pave the way for an organized exchange model.

I would like to thank Jeff Sterba, CEO of Public Service Company of New Mexico, for facilitating a meeting with key leaders in New Mexico.

Thanks also to Claire Jahns, Nathan Clark, Rafael Marques, and Michael Walsh for their assistance in the preparation of this article.

CCX update: we are pleased to announce two new members representing important new sectors for the exchange. Bayer Corporation is the first North American entity owned by a German company to join and Tufts University is CCX's first US private university member.

Chapter 41

The CCX Auction: 20 Questions

September 2003

The Chicago Climate Exchange (CCX) has reached several milestones in the past few months, fulfilling its first objective of proving that a cross-section of private and public entities in North America (including 17 companies, one university and the City of Chicago) could reach agreement on a voluntary commitment to reduce greenhouse gas (GHG) emissions.

In addition, the recently completed CCX rulebook will serve as the set of procedures and guidelines for the operation of the exchange. This document marks the first articulation of the structure and governance of a multisector and multinational GHG trading program, including modalities of emission quantification, monitoring, verification, offset definitions, and trading.

In an effort to achieve its goals of establishing a mechanism for achieving price discovery and disseminating market information, an auction of CCX allowances will be held on 29 September. This month's column will answer frequently asked questions about the auction.

1. *Why hold an auction?* Auctions play a significant role in the US financial and environmental markets. They provide both a distribution and price discovery function. Their prevalence in the huge market for US Treasury securities indicates their importance. In the sulfur dioxide (SO_2) market, the annual auction

helped generate price and volume information for this market in its early stages, and still serves as an indicator of market trends. Periodic auctions also help focus attention on market conditions and may foster additional trading and market liquidity.

2. *Why hold an auction before the market opens?* An auction will provide price and volume information needed by CCX members and other exchange participants. This data will be one of many indicators that they can use to develop least-cost strategies for complying with their CCX emission reduction commitments or for their trading strategies.

3. *What is the CCX auction?* It is an organized and periodic sale of CCX allowances using a sealed-bid process. Allowances represent 100 tons of carbon dioxide equivalent (CO_2e) emissions. A schedule of future auctions is forthcoming.

4. *Will the results be transparent?* One of CCX's main goals is to foster market transparency by providing widespread dissemination of price and volume information. CCX will make public all successful bid prices, the associated quantities and the identity of the successful bidders.

5. *What unit of measurement will be used?* CCX chose to use tons of CO_2e emissions as this conforms to the most widely used international unit of measurement. It provides standardization in a system that also involves Canada, Mexico, and Brazil, thus helping foster international trade links.

6. *What is available for auction?* The allowances being auctioned by CCX are withheld from the allowance allocation distributed to each CCX member. This first auction makes available 100,000 tons worth of allowances having a 2003 vintage (i.e., 1000 allowances) and 250 allowances of the 2005 vintage.

7. *What if demand is greater than the available supply of allowances?* If demand at the auction is greater than the initial available supply, CCX will have a mechanism for increasing the size of the auction.

8. *What is the auction style?* CCX will employ a discriminating price auction style. Starting with the highest bidder, continuing with

the next highest, and so on, until the quantity of allowances available for auction is exhausted, each successful bidder will pay the price it bids for the quantity it requests.

9. *Is there a minimum or maximum bid or purchase quantity?* The minimum that can be bid for and purchased is one CCX allowance, which represents 100 tons of CO_2e. The maximum will be announced no later than 15 September. If a bidder succeeds in buying the maximum quantity, any further bids from that bidder will be canceled.

10. *Is there a maximum or minimum price?* There is no maximum or minimum bid price and no limit on the highest or lowest successful bid price.

11. *What are the price increments?* All CCX trades are priced in increments of 1 cent ($0.01) per ton of CO_2, which translates to an increment of $1 per CCX allowance.

12. *Who can bid in the CCX auction?* CCX members (entities that emit GHGs and have committed to the CCX reduction schedule); participant members (liquidity providers, such as market-makers and brokers), and associate members (electricity consumers that have committed to the CCX reduction schedule to achieve or maintain carbon neutrality).

13. *Can exchange participants and non-CCX members bid in the CCX auction?* Further clarification regarding the participation of exchange participants and CCX nonmembers will be made available before the auction.

14. *Can bidders submit multiple bids?* Yes. Bidders may submit as many bids as they wish.

15. *Will auction participants be able to buy allowances at the average price?* Yes. CCX will accept average-price bids. This is an agreement to buy at the weighted average price of successful bids.

16. *What if multiple tied bids are submitted at the clearing price?* If there are multiple bids at the price that clears the market (i.e., the combined bid quantities at the clearing price exceeds the total quantity of CCX allowances remaining), then the quantity

of allowances remaining after filling the next highest bid would be divided among the tied bids in proportion to the quantity that each bid represents relative to the total quantity of tied bids.

17. *Can CCX member or others offer allowances or exchange offsets for sale in the auction?* For the first CCX auction no additional sale offers will be accepted. CCX may allow additional offers to be included in future auctions.

18. *How are bids submitted and payments handled?* For the first auction, bids are submitted on forms provided by CCX. The auction forms will be sent in both hard copy and electronic formats. Monies associated with the bids must be placed in an escrow account held by CCX.

19. *When is the deadline for submitting bids?* 12 p.m. CDT on 29 September.

20. *When will the results be announced?* 9 a.m. CDT on 30 September.

Example of the auction process

If 100 CCX allowances were offered for sale in the auction and the four highest bids were:
- Member 1 bids for 30 allowances at a price of $X.90/tonne;
- Member 2 bids for 40 allowances at $X.75/tonne;
- Member 3 bids for 40 allowances at $X.65/tonne, and
- Member 4 bids for 10 allowances at $X.60/tonne.

then the auction clearing price would be $X.65/tonne. Members 1 and 2 would be successful in acquiring the allowances they bid for and each would pay the price they bid. Member 3 would succeed in acquiring 30 allowances (not 40) as the total bids by members 1 and 2 leave only 30 allowances for sale to the next highest bidders. Member 4's bid is below the clearing price, making its bid unsuccessful. In this scenario member 1 is required to pay an amount equal to 30 x 100 x $X.90 for its successful bid, as each allowance represents 100 tonnes of CO_2. Each CCX member would then receive $X.65 for each tonne of allowances that were withheld and placed in the auction pool.

Chapter 42

The Benefits of Corporate Sustainability and Responsibility

October 2003

The trend is unmistakable. From ethical investing to socially responsible investing and now sustainability. Each year, we update readers on the status of the Dow Jones Sustainability World Index (DJSI World), the industry leader in this field. This year we will do the same, and also comment on the increasingly prevalent role that environmental considerations play in the day-to-day decisions of firms that use corporate sustainability as their guide.

The DJSI World comprises more than 300 companies in 22 countries that are sustainability leaders in their respective industries. These companies represent the top 10% of the leading sustainability companies in 59 industry groups, and have a market capitalization of more than $5 trillion.

There are new DJSI-based products in Austria, Denmark, Finland, France, Italy, the Netherlands, and Canada, giving investors a broader range of certified sustainable investment opportunities than ever before. Since the DJSI was launched in 1999, 45 licenses have been issued in 14 countries. Current license holders are shown in Table 1.

The assets managed in DJSI-based portfolios are up €2 million ($2.2 million) since this time last year, bringing the new total to €2.2 billion. This growth occurred in spite of some of the most

Table I. Current DJSI licensees

As of 31 August 2003

Institution (country)	Product
Sagitta Wealth Management (Australia)	Fund
Kepler Fonds KAG (Austria)	Fund
Raiffeisen (Austria)	Fund
Dexia Asset Management (Belgium)	Fund
Credit Union Central of Ontario (Canada)	Certificate
Danske Invest/BG Invest (Denmark)	Fund
Sparinvest (Denmark)	Fund
Mandatum Asset Management (Finland)	Fund
OP Fund Management Company (Finland)	Fund
CIC Asset Management (France)	Certificate
Rothschild & Cie Gestion (France)	Fund
DWS (Germany)	Fund
DZ Bank (Germany)	Certificate
Gerling Investment KAG (Germany)	Fund
HypoVereinsbank (Germany)	Warrant
Invesco (Germany)	Fund
Oppenheim KAG (Germany)	Fund
State Street Global Advisors (Germany)	Fund
Union Investment (Germany)	Fund
WestLB (Germany)	Certificate
BNL Gestioni (Italy)	Fund
Gestnord (Italy)	Fund
Zenit (Italy)	Fund
Nikko Asset Management (Japan)	Fund
Deutsche Postbank (Luxembourg)	Fund
Aegon (Netherlands)	Fund
Rabobank (Netherlands)	Certificate
Theodor Gilissen Bankiers (Netherlands)	Fund
Folksam Sak (Sweden)	Fund
SPP (Sweden)	Fund
Baloise Insurance (Switzerland)	Fund
Credit Suisse Asset Management (Switz)	Fund
Sustainable Asset Management (Switz)	Fund
Sustainable Performance Group (Switz)	Invest Co
Swiss Life Asset Management (Switz)	Fund
Synchrony Asset Management (Switz)	Certificate
VZ VermögensZentrum (Switzerland)	Fund
Merrill Lynch International (UK)	Certificate

difficult and volatile equity markets in decades. The DJI, STOXX, and the SAM Group publish an annual review of the DJSI family every September, and this year's review shows that companies and funds that pass through the DJSI filter for corporate sustainability consistently outperform their competitors.

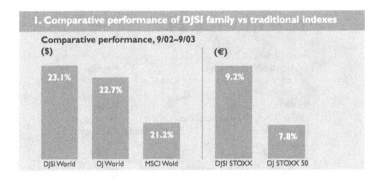

Over the 12 months to September 2003, the Dow Jones World Index increased (in dollar terms) by 22.7%, while the DJSI World rose by 23.1%. Over the same period, the DJSI World index grew almost two percentage points more than the MSCI World (again, in dollar terms), which was up 21.2% on the previous year. The DJSI STOXX (calculated in euros) grew 9.2% over that period, versus 7.8% for the DJ STOXX 50 (also in euros). Figure 1 shows that investments that go through the DJSI corporate sustainability filter have a higher performance than traditional investments.

The 2003 DJSI World review shows not only higher-than-average market returns for sustainability, but also those issues of economic, social, and environmental sustainability are becoming increasingly important within the corporate framework. These two findings go hand-in-hand. It is becoming clear that corporate sustainability has moved beyond "green-washing" and is truly getting down to business.

This year's review found that environmental and social standards are being articulated at every level of operation from the executive office to the factory floor, and that companies are undertaking the necessary measures to quantify previously ignored metrics, such as the greenhouse gas emissions that contribute to global climate change.

The analysts also found competition for DJSI World sustainability certification to be at an all-time high. The increasingly competitive quest for certification seems to be driving more and more companies to internalize what had previously been disregarded as external costs, such as air and water pollution, and other negative community impacts of company operations.

Company executives are seeing their sustainability initiatives translate into higher shareholder value and more robust long-term economic health for their companies. More executives are beginning to understand that setting an environmental sustainability goal, such as reducing greenhouse gas emissions, for example, is actually a business discipline. With such a goal in place, managers are given the incentive to find wasted energy and save it, thus reducing emissions and moving toward environmental sustainability — while saving on energy costs in the process. Visionary executives and creative, hard-working staff members are finding that environmentalism and profits can go hand-in-hand.

New incentives to engage in environmentally sustainable actions have prompted industrious companies to further explore the opportunities. Emissions trading systems like the Chicago Climate Exchange (CCX) provide companies with the incentive to reduce greenhouse gas emissions above and beyond the level demanded for compliance with CCX rules. A company that sells CCX allowances benefits directly from its sustainable action: first by generating the allowances by reducing fuel use and/or energy purchases and, second, by selling excess reductions on the exchange.

As this year's review of the DJSI World indicates, companies that engage in environmentally sustainable activities can also see their stock prices rise relative to their competitors. If a company leader chooses to take the reins and factor into his or her decision increases in shareholder value, savings from previously undiscovered inefficiencies, and risk reduction from hedging against the unpredictable nature of global and local politics, the choice becomes obvious: sustainability pays. And, as more and more companies engage in sustainable behavior, the bar — and the benefits — will only rise.

I would like to thank Claire Jahns, Michael Walsh, and Alex Barkawi for their assistance in the preparation of this chapter.

Chapter 43

Water — New Horizons for Markets

November 2003

> "Whiskey is for drinking and water is for fighting"
> — Mark Twain

Almost 12 years ago, in 1992, countries involved in an international water conference held in Dublin issued a statement that "Water has an economic value and should be recognised as an economic good". The other "Dublin Principles" recognized the finite nature of fresh-water and called for a participatory approach to water development and management.

We're still waiting for the ultimate tools to implement those principles, but progress has begun. A recent accord finally addressed the allocation of water from the Colorado River. It took almost 10 years to arrange approximately 30 separate agreements. In simplistic terms, farmers will have to sell water and the city of San Diego will have to pay for it. This is perhaps the beginning of an evolution toward water markets.

The same battle is raging in the south-eastern United States. Prospects for a quick resolution seem remote. Georgia, Alabama, and Florida are waging war over the allocation of water from the Apalachicola–Chattahoochee–Flint river basin.

The efficient allocation of water is a question of both quantity and quality. We have some reasons to hope we are making progress in the quality area.

Nutrients, such as nitrogen and phosphorus, are substances that occur naturally in water, soil, and air. Nitrogen and phosphorus in fertilizer aid the growth of agricultural crops, but excessive presence of nutrients in watersheds can have harmful consequences. High concentrations of phosphorus or ammonia in lakes, streams, and reservoirs are often responsible for fish mortality, foul odors and excessive aquatic weed growth. For humans, exposure to excessive levels of nitrate (a form of nitrogen) can reduce oxygen transport in the bloodstream.

Water pollution sources can be divided into two types. Point sources can be attributed to a specific physical location such as nutrient discharges from wastewater treatment plants, industries, or municipalities. Nonpoint sources — the main cause of nutrient pollution — are a diffuse source of pollution that cannot be attributed to a clearly identifiable, specific physical location, or a defined discharge channel. This includes the nutrients that run off the ground from any land use — croplands, lawns, parking lots, streets, forests etc. — and enter waterways. It also includes nutrients that enter through air pollution, through groundwater, or from septic systems.

Climate change mitigation and water quality improvements are also interrelated. Any decreases in nitrogen reaching waterways from agricultural land have implications for emissions of nitrous oxide, a potent greenhouse gas (GHG). For instance, lower nitrogen fertilizer use reduces both the nitrogen that is leaked into waterways and the amount that is released as GHGs. Moreover, agricultural practices and management decisions that slow the rate of nutrient losses to waterways frequently improve carbon sequestration and storage in the soil. Thus, a single environmental strategy has the potential to address multiple environmental problems simultaneously.

Analysis and research undertaken by the World Resources Institute (WRI) shows that the use of market mechanisms like nutrient trading provides not only the greatest overall environmental benefits, but is also the most cost-effective approach.

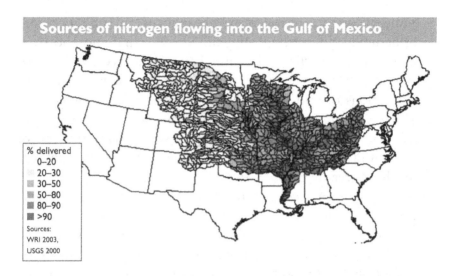

Sources of nitrogen flowing into the Gulf of Mexico

% delivered
0–20
20–30
30–50
50–80
80–90
>90
Sources:
WRI 2003,
USGS 2000

The concept is remarkably simple. Programs can take the form of a mandatory cap on the total quantity of nutrients entering the water, or the goal could also be a percentage reduction pursued through a voluntary, open program. The total amount of allowable pollution is then allocated among the participating sources.

Once pollution allowances are allocated, sources with low-cost pollution reduction options have an incentive to reduce nutrient loadings beyond what is required of them and to sell the excess credits to sources with higher control costs. Through a series of trades, pollution reduction efforts get reallocated to the sources that have the lowest-cost opportunities to reduce pollution. This flexibility greatly reduces the cost of improving water quality, while freeing up resources for other pressing social needs. Water quality trading in the United States is usually considered within the Total Maximum Daily Load (TMDL) process under the Clean Water Act.

The WRI has also taken the trading concept to its ultimate practical outcome — the development of NutrientNet, a web-based marketplace for nutrient reduction and trading. Currently, Nutrient Net is operational for phosphorous in the Kalamazoo Watershed in Michigan and is to be extended to nitrogen trading in the Potomac Watershed of Chesapeake Bay.

Worksheets on the market's website enable interested parties to assess whether or not they should participate in the nutrient reduction market. The worksheets allow a first assessment of the quantity of reductions that might be possible. A market section reviews and posts offers to buy and sell nutrient reductions. The section also provides the trading rules, a standard contract, and a summary of market activity for each watershed.

Market-based initiatives in nutrient trading underscore the importance of three critical points when building markets: transaction costs, transparency, and credibility. Transaction costs can impede trading if they are too high. For credibility to exist in the reduction credits generated by agriculture and other nonpoint sources, standard estimation methods must be used. Essentially, the public and the buyers need to be assured that all credits are estimated in the same way. Lastly, there has to be a relatively simple way to record trades so that policy-makers and the general public are provided with transparent information.

Markets need champions. Institutions like the WRI and individuals like David Batchelor of the Environment Trading Network help advance the cause of building the necessary infrastructure that makes markets, and therefore social and environmental improvement, possible. The possibilities to further expand this market program for nutrient pollution are very exciting. In a future article, we hope to explore how markets can assist in other pressing problems such as over-fishing.

I would like to thank Paul Faeth and his staff at WRI and Claire Jahns for their assistance in the preparation of this chapter. For more information about nutrient trading, please visit http://www.wri.org/ wri/water/nutrient.html and www.nutrientnet.org.

Chapter 44

"The British are Coming!"

February 2004

The United Kingdom's national allocation plan (NAP) should be heard as a wake-up call.

The 19 January release of the first phase of the United Kingdom's draft NAP, slightly less than a year before the European Union's Emissions Trading Scheme (EU ETS) is set to begin, marked the beginning of a new era in climate change policy: implementation. Official release of the Dutch and German draft NAPs is expected to follow close behind (they had not been released as of 28 January). Release of the draft NAPs is important to the success of the EU ETS, because it imposes the sector- and facility-level caps that will facilitate trading in the first-ever mandatory, international emissions reduction, and trading market.

It is not surprising that the United Kingdom was first out of the gate with its NAP release; given that it was the first government to pilot a functional multi-sector ETS, which was launched in 2002. What is notable about the UK draft NAP, however, is that it begins to layout protocols for the combination of an externally (EU and Kyoto Protocol) imposed mandatory cap on emissions with a nationally (United Kingdom) imposed cap on emissions that is voluntary. It sets an abatement target beyond that of the externally imposed cap.

The United Kingdom's strategy for emissions reductions and trading takes into account the EU-mandated commitment to reduce UK emissions by 12.5% below the 1990 baseline level by 2010, but it is really designed to achieve a more enterprising national abatement target of 20% below 1990 levels by 2010–2012. The German NAP, on the other hand, is not expected to prompt reductions below the levels required for Kyoto compliance.

Of the 7.3 million tons (Mt) of carbon dioxide (CO_2), the United Kingdom needs to abate by 2010 for compliance with its nationally imposed target, 1.8 Mt will be achieved within the United Kingdom by the same sources that have been involved in the pilot UK ETS. These reductions are projected to bring the United Kingdom's emissions to 15.3% below 1990 levels, which would surpass the requirements of the Kyoto Protocol. Participation in the EU ETS is projected to reduce the United Kingdom's greenhouse gas (GHG) emissions by an additional 5.5 Mt of CO_2. This would bring projected 2010 emissions down to a level 16.3% lower than in 1990. The United Kingdom's participation in the EU ETS will add functionality to the United Kingdom's own ETS and enhance the country's ability to achieve its 20% reduction target.

The United Kingdom's draft NAP places an emphasis on flexibility and cost effectiveness in achieving reduction targets. It leaves emissions trading as an option open to all UK companies, not just those in the power sector. The UK government has written the guidelines for a compliance program that authorities believe will achieve, at a minimum, Kyoto compliance at the lowest possible cost to its citizens.

The UK power sector has been cited as the area with the biggest potential for low-cost reductions, and the NAP; therefore, adjusts power plants' allowance allocations downward every year. It reflects their potential to achieve reductions at marginal costs lower than those of facilities in other sectors of the economy.

Carbon-intensive industries outside the generating and refining sectors have options as to how they will comply with UK carbon laws. Those rules will not be fully formulated until the final UK

NAP is submitted to the European Commission by 31 March 2004. These other polluting facilities have the choice of enrolling their direct emissions in the first phase of the EU ETS and paying a carbon/energy tax on indirect emissions as part of their climate change agreements (CCAs), or opting out of the EU ETS altogether and paying the tax on both direct and indirect emissions. The option allows individual manufacturers in the cement, glass, chemicals, pulp and paper, and other energy-intensive industries to choose their own least-cost method of compliance.

The United Kingdom is using emissions trading for exactly what it was intended to do: provide flexibility in achieving significant cuts in emissions of GHGs. The UK authorities have allocated emission allowances with a focus on steering abatement to the sectors and individual facilities that will face the lowest marginal costs of compliance. This strategy may very well lead to a compliance period that has the smallest possible burden on the economy as a whole. Moreover, the United Kingdom's participation in the EU ETS leaves open the possibility that UK companies might actually make money out of the Kyoto Protocol, by selling excess allowances to companies within those EU member states that fall short of their own abatement targets.

Of course, the United Kingdom's draft NAP is not without its problems and it should by no means be viewed as the final cut. Sections dealing with monitoring mechanisms, the potential for discrimination between companies or sectors, competition from non-EU states, implementation of the allowance auction, and the impact of certain national legislative acts on emissions have not been fully articulated. These issues must be publicly debated and resolved before the 31 March deadline. In particular, the United Kingdom has decided to reserve a portion of the annual allocation that is to be held back for new entrants for the exclusive use of combined heat-and-power (CHP) facilities. International scrutiny has suggested that this reserve might be viewed as "state aid" toward CHP facilities, which is frowned upon by the European Commission.

Despite these problems, the United Kingdom's draft NAP represents an important step in the right direction, for the successful implementation of the EU ETS as well as for cap-and-trade systems in general. It shows that voluntary emissions mitigation commitments can easily be integrated into existing mandatory legislation. This fact has significant positive implications not only for the United Kingdom, but also for those companies, organizations and government entities, or municipalities that wish to voluntarily reduce their negative climatic impacts in the absence of mandatory regulation. The United Kingdom has gotten over the hurdle that voluntary environmental commitments cannot exist within mandatory legislative frameworks. I think this will put the United Kingdom in good stead for the second phase of the EU ETS and beyond.

Chapter 45

Industrial Policy Skews EU Allocation Plans

March 2004

In country after country of the European Union, serious debates are taking place as member states have to finish their national allocation plans (NAPs) for carbon dioxide emission allowances by 31 March. As this column is being written, only a few countries have produced drafts. The rest of the participating nations are working out major technical and political issues surrounding allowance allocation. EU NAPs are emerging as a combination of industrial policy and emissions trading.

If the NAPs were allocating allowances for a straightforward "cap-and-trade" system, then the process would not be complicated. Cap-and-trade emissions trading, as a policy tool, is designed to achieve a given quantity of emission reductions at the lowest possible per-unit and total cost.

Programs like the US Environmental Protection Agency's Acid Rain Program and the Kyoto Protocol are based on the premise that this tool can achieve significant emission reductions at a cost far below what it would have been under a command-and-control policy. The success of the Acid Rain Program to date has proven the practical outcome of this theory.

The general rules of the Acid Rain Program are relatively simple: set a program-wide abatement target and let the facilities within the program divide up the abatement responsibilities based on their own individual cost curves and the price of allowances. This is the same principle that was used for allocating countries' abatement targets under the Kyoto Protocol. Both the Kyoto Protocol and the Acid Rain Program use simple, straightforward methods of allocation. The EU NAPs are not that simple.

Given the target set by the EU Emissions Trading Scheme (ETS), each carbon dioxide-emitting electric power generating facility, manufacturing plant, and so on, should be given a quantity of allowances equal to its baseline (1990) emissions, minus the abatement target set for that country by the ETS. For example, in Germany, every facility would have to have on-paper emissions of 21% below their 1990 baseline levels by the compliance period, 2008–2012. The abatement burden would be shared equally across sectors, and those facilities that had already taken measures to reduce their emissions between 1990 and the compliance period would be rewarded by the ability to sell excess allowances.

The EU Emissions Trading Scheme

From January next year, more than 15,000 industrial installations across the European Union will face caps on their emissions of carbon dioxide (CO_2). The Emissions Trading Scheme, designed to help the EU meet its targets under the Kyoto Protocol, explicitly covers facilities in five sectors: electricity production; ferrous metals; pulp and paper; building materials and oil refineries. Combustion plants with a thermal input of more than 20MW in other sectors are also included. All told, these account for around 46% of EU CO_2 emissions.

Member state governments are responsible for setting targets and allocating allowances to industry – these national allocation plans must be submitted to the European Commission for approval by the end of the month for the 15 existing members, and by the end of April for the 10 Accession Countries.

The Commission will assess these plans against 11 criteria, ensuring that they meet the environmental objectives of the scheme, and EU rules on state aid and competition. The final allocations to industry will be announced by October.

If every emitting facility in a country faces the same below-baseline percentage abatement target, then each facility will end up paying (or receiving) the average, aggregate marginal cost of abatement. This economy-wide, average marginal cost of abatement, which would also equal the average cost of allowances, would reflect the true social cost of reducing greenhouse gas emissions. Students of markets will note that the current allocations being debated in Germany and other EU member states will most likely result in higher allowance prices.

The reports surrounding the preliminary proposal for the German draft NAP, which was produced by the German Ministry of Environment and is being coauthored with the German Ministry of Economy, suggests that trade and other lobbying groups will end up editing the German draft NAP to further the domestic industrial agenda.

The proposed NAP calls for an average 7.5% reduction in carbon dioxide emissions below baseline levels by 2007 (the German base years are set in the early 2000s). According to reports of the proposal, it distributes the abatement responsibilities relatively equally among facilities in the energy and industrial sectors, with some small adjustments made for process emissions from noncombustion, chemical processes. Producers of steel and aluminum are not faced with abatement targets, but will have to buy allowances if their emissions increase in the future.

Both German ministries are facing conflicting pressures from the energy and industrial sectors to rewrite the draft NAP. According to some reports, coal industry unions, cement, chemical and steel manufacturers, and environmental groups are all weighing heavily in the debate. The coal interests, recognizing that coal will become more expensive to burn if the associated emissions are factored into the fuel's price tag, argue that the NAP will cost union jobs. Manufacturing industries are worried that breaks for the energy sector will end up costing them. These lobbying groups have gone so far as to boycott NAP negotiations, and they will almost certainly end up skewing the allowance allocation.

Economists will note that a politically skewed allocation will most likely cause an upward trend in allowance prices and may impact the technological choices of industry. There is almost no doubt that the final German draft NAP will take into account the concerns of other interest groups. Indeed, this will probably be the case with all the EUNAPs. In the final analysis, we believe policymakers will choose an intelligent balance between industrial policy and market efficiency.

Chapter 46

SO$_2$ Auctions — An Even Dozen

April 2004

For the past 11 years, it has been one of the most highly reported events in emissions markets. In the early days, nay-sayers and protesters were rife. This writer had the privilege of being actively involved in the first sulfur dioxide (SO$_2$) auction in his role as chairman of the clean air committee at the Chicago Board of Trade (CBOT) and witnessed numerous headlines referring to "smut traders" and picketers outside the CBOT building with banners that read "trading pollution is not the solution".

It was ironic that, five years later, the same picketers and their organizations endorsed the Kyoto Protocol and its emissions trading mechanisms. In spite of early market inefficiencies, as measured by the bid-ask spreads, the 1993 auction still provided the first price discovery for this bold new market. SO$_2$ emissions trading had arrived with great fanfare and the results were presented to a packed press room.

For the next 11 years, the press conferences were attended by leading members of industry and the academic world. At the 1995 auction, a sixth-grade class from Glens Falls, New York was a winning bidder. As an exercise for a science project the class studied acid rain and considered ways they could participate in solving the problem. They determined that the best way to do this was to buy SO$_2$ emission allowances and retire them through a donation to a charity.

They raised $3,171 and bought 21 allowances. The next year they spent over $20,000 and bought 292 allowances at an all-time low price of $66 per allowance. Their example spawned an outpouring of student involvement, with six other schools participating in 1996.

As the years rolled by the market became more and more efficient. The press conferences and the auction itself have become more and more routine. A final testimony to the maturity of the market came at the last auction when, for the first time, there was no need for a press conference and the auction results were routinely absorbed by the market. The SO_2 market has finally come of age. It has matured and clearly demonstrated that market-based instruments can be employed to solve environmental problems efficiently.

In this year's auction, a total of 125,011 allowances was released for the spot auction. The clearing price of $260 was the highest in the history of the program. However, it was much lower than market expectations, considering that spot allowance prices in the over-the-counter (OTC) market during the week prior to the auction climbed to $273–276. Limited adoption of emissions-reducing equipment, such as scrubbers, and the exhaustion of banked allowances may all lead to upward pressure on prices in the current compliance year.

Bids in the auction ranged from $107 to 300 with an average bid price of around $273. The spot auctions had a total of 25 successful and 39 unsuccessful bids (see table). It appears that, as the market matures, the price of the allowances can now be seen as approaching the marginal abatement cost of SO_2 mitigation.

The seven-year advance auction, for allowances usable from 2011, had 125,000 allowances and a clearing price of $128. The difference between the spot and forward prices was the highest recorded. As has been previously noted, the forward price has been falling in recent years, increasing the spread between the spot and the forward markets. This could imply greater operational and regulatory uncertainty in the energy sector. Another interesting fact is that the interest rate implied by the difference between spot and forward prices is 10.12%. This is in the same range as in the previous

Results of the 2004 Acid Rain allowances auction

	Spot auction (First usable in 2004)	7-year advance auction (First usable in 2011)
Total available	125,011	125,000
Allowances bid for	288,537	275,053
Allowances sold	125,011	125,000
Total bids	64	8
Number of bidders	21	5
Highest bid price ($)	300.00	129.11
Clearing bid price ($)	260.00	128.00
Average winning bid price ($)	272.82	128.00

Source: Chicago Board of Trade and US EPA

auction but much higher than returns from the high-yield corporate bond market.

Looking at the big picture, the SO_2 auction program provides the platform from which future trading programs for environmental derivatives will emerge. It has proved a great success, judged by the criteria of environmental improvement and economic efficiency as well as its demonstration effects and the trading activity it has stimulated. The Environmental Protection Agency (EPA) reports that fewer than 1% of the lakes in the US Midwest are acidic — a direct consequence of the program.

There is no question that emissions trading is going to occupy a predominant position as the optimal policy choice in the future. Several private and public programs emerging around the world have embraced emissions trading as the central feature to achieve their environmental goals. In this context, many operational lessons are to be gained from the acid rain program. It is now well established that any market-based trading system needs to have transparency, credible verification, and standardized protocols for its success.

Another reason for the success of the acid rain program involves the technology to monitor SO_2 emissions from smokestacks continuously. While challenges remain in designing similar systems for

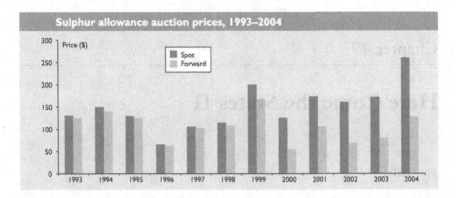

nonpoint source pollutants, growth in verification and monitoring technology will prove invaluable for any future trading mechanism. Once such technologies are developed, there is great potential for providing the right incentives to adopt more environmentally friendly practices. We may not be too far from the day when rice producers in Vietnam could use a trading mechanism to reduce methane emissions from their deep water paddy fields, leading to more sustainable production practices. The opportunities seem endless and the benefits to society tremendous, thanks to the SO_2 trading program. We've come a long away from the days of picketers.

I would like to thank Dr. Murali Kanakasabai, Rafael Marques, and Dr. Michael Walsh for their assistance in preparation of this article.

Chapter 47

Here Come the States II

May 2004

In 1787 and 1788, a series of 85 letters called the Federalist Papers was written by James Madison, Alexander Hamilton, and John Jay. The essays, originally published to encourage New Yorkers to rat- ify the recently drafted US Constitution, are now often cited by those who advocate for states' rights. The United States, a federal republic, continues today to rely on state-level initiatives for national leadership on many fronts, just as it did in the late 1700s.

In June 2002, I wrote an article for this publication discussing state-level initiatives to address climate change in the United States. Two years later the states continue to be very active.

To date, six states have passed legislation setting concrete goals for reducing greenhouse gas (GHG) emissions. Massachusetts was the first state to legislate a cap on carbon dioxide (CO_2) emissions. Its power plants are subject to a two-tier reduction commitment. From October, a power plant's CO_2 emissions cannot exceed its three-year average emissions of 1997–1999. After October 2006, a facility's CO_2 emissions rate cannot exceed 1800 lb/MWh. Both historic and output-based limits can be met through off-site CO_2 reductions. In addition, any new facility with more than 100 MWh of capacity must offset 1% of its emissions each year for the next 20 years.

In 1997, Oregon promulgated legislation mandating the off- setting of roughly 17% of emissions from new power plants.

New Jersey has established the goal of reducing GHG emissions to 3.5% below their 1990 levels by 2005, and plans to be more comprehensive in its scope, including sectors outside of electricity generation. In May 2002, New Hampshire enacted legislation allowing trading with output-based caps that require the state's three major power plants to reduce emissions to 1990 levels by 2006. More recently, on 31 March, Washington state governor Gary Locke signed a regulation into law that requires owners of new power plants to make reductions or buy offsets equal to 20% of their plant's CO_2 emissions.

On the regional level, the New England states and eastern Canadian provinces are promoting a plan to reduce the region's emissions to 1990 levels by 2010 and then to 10% below 1990 levels by 2020. Maine has become the first of the group to pass such a plan into law. New York, New Hampshire, Vermont, Massachusetts, Rhode Island, Connecticut, Delaware, and New Jersey continue to further the plan by preparing the groundwork for a CO_2 cap-and-trade program for electric power plants in their states. Maryland and Pennsylvania have classified their status as "observers" of the group. The group is considering the possibility of trading among its members and is calling for standardized inventories and a regional registry.

GHG inventory and registry initiatives continue to make progress, with at least 11 states establishing mandatory or voluntary registries. Among the most widely recognized are the California Climate Action Registry and the Wisconsin registry.

In Georgia, the Carbon Sequestration Registry Act was recently sent to the governor's desk for approval. Expected to be passed, the Act will provide for an offsets registry for CO_2 mitigation projects related to forestry and agriculture. The voluntary program will provide standardized reporting procedures, including forms and software, as well as third-party verification, to ensure the legitimacy of the offsets. In addition, the state has instituted a conservation tillage assistance program, which leases no-till equipment to participating farmers. To date, the program has sequestered an esti-mated 25,000 tons of CO_2, in addition to reduced fuel usage from no-till farming.

State-sponsored sequestration efforts in Minnesota and New Mexico promote forestation, reforestation, and maintenance and plantation improvement by providing grants to communities, orga-nizations and others for their efforts. The Oregon legislature has created the Oregon Forest Resource Trust, open to landowners owning 10–5000 acres of eligible under-producing forest. The trust pays for 100% of plantation establishment costs in return for the landowner's obligation to share a portion of the harvest revenues with the trust, should the landowner decide to harvest the planta-tion. Ownership of the CO_2 offset credits lies with the trust until the end of the 200-year contract. Additional state-level sequestra-tion initiatives include geologic sequestration efforts taking place in West Virginia, Ohio, and Illinois.

Selected US states with recent climate change activities

Climate change initiatives/ Proposed legislation	Registries	Multi-state initiatives
Massachusetts	California	New England governors/
New Hampshire	New Hampshire	Eastern Canadian provinces
Oregon	New Jersey	**Northeast states, including:**
New York	Wisconsin	Maine
Pennsylvania	Massachusetts	New Hampshire
Illinois	Maine (proposed)	Vermont
Michigan	Northeast states	Massachusetts
Minnesota		Rhode Island
Ohio		Connecticut
California		Delaware
New Jersey		New Jersey
Washington		Maryland (observer)
Maine		Pennsylvania (observer)
Vermont		**Western states governors' initiative,**
Rhode Island		**including:**
Connecticut		California
Delaware		Washington
Maryland		Oregon

Red type indicate initiatives undertaken since 'Here come the states' (Environmental Finance, June 2002)

Just as they have in many areas of public policy in the United States, state-level initiatives on climate change will continue to move forward and inform the public debate at the federal level. The importance of such initiatives should not be underestimated.

Although the state-level efforts are certainly commendable, it must be remembered that efficient markets require coordination, cohesiveness, and standardization. A company taking part in the various state level initiatives will find itself in the unenviable position of having to comply with multiple reduction targets, registry requirements, offset project protocols, trading rules, reporting, monitoring, and verification procedures, along with a variety of other rules and regulations. I am a firm believer that markets are built from the bottom-up. However, this market-building process requires coordination from potential market participants to increase participation and market activity by creating homogenized protocols. It should be an overall goal of the interested parties to strive for such homogenization.

I would like to thank Nathan Clark and Michael Walsh for their assistance in the preparation of this article.

Chapter 48

A Tale of Two Continents

June 2004

> "It was the best of times, it was the worst of times..."
> — Charles Dickens, *A Tale of Two Cities*

It is a tale of two continents. One pilot is mandatory and the other is voluntary but legally binding. While much has been made of the apparent difference between European and US approaches to climate change policy, a closer look indicates that things are not necessarily what they seem.

Over the past few years, Europe has embraced the concept of greenhouse gas (GHG) emissions trading as a policy tool to address climate change cost-effectively. The European Union (EU) emissions trading scheme (ETS) is due to begin next year. And, in the US heartland, the Chicago Climate Exchange (CCX) started continuous electronic trading in December 2003. These separate and seemingly distinct events could be pointing toward a common thread.

In preparation for the launch of the EU ETS, 14 of the 25 member states have submitted their national allocation plans (NAPs) to the European Commission. Slowly but surely, all signs indicate the emergence of a major global market for emissions. While the NAPs and final allocations are yet to be approved by the commission, some interesting thoughts arise on how different societies have responded to address the global challenge of climate change, and how their outcomes compare. In other words, we have seen two parallel developments in the creation of carbon emissions markets.

The EU ETS and the CCX have followed strikingly different paths. The EU framework has largely been a top-down approach, partially driven by private sector input, with an impending mandatory process in 2005. The absence of regulation has rendered the CCX pilot a voluntary and bottom-up, private sector, consensus-driven approach. Could one expect these divergent processes to converge in their ultimate objectives? Do the origins and the paths of the market evolution process really matter? These questions can only be answered when the commission announces its judgments on the NAPs — expected by the end of June — and when the results of the programs are known in a few years.

To put this idea in perspective, consider the background of the two programs. In March 2000, the EU embarked on a policy of using emissions trading to help achieve the overall 8% common GHG reduction target accepted by the EU under the Kyoto Protocol. As part of the program, a pilot phase is expected to operate from 1 January 2005 to December 2007. The European experience has largely been directed by governments in member states in consultation with stakeholders.

Charles Lindbloom, a public policy economist, might consider the European process to be one in which society arrives at optimal outcomes by muddling through various solutions and allocations. The European Commission recently sent letters to at least one member state requesting a tightening of its initial allowance allocation plans. One would expect many more such revisions and consultations before the final allocations emerge. This iterative process will, in some sense, result in an optimal first-round allocation process.

The CCX, on the other hand, is a pilot, voluntary, legally binding effort for GHG emissions trading for emission sources and offset projects in North America and Brazil. It requires participating entities to commit legally to reduce their GHG emissions, or trade, to achieve annual 1% reductions below a 1998–2001 baseline for the pilot period of 2003–2006 (resulting in 2006 emissions 4% below the baseline).

A unique feature of the Chicago experiment is that it has been a consultative and collaborative process with the participating members, which represent a host of stakeholders including private, academic, and nongovernmental agents. The outcome of this process marks the first articulation of the structure and governance of a multisector and multinational GHG trading program, including modalities of emissions quantification, monitoring, verification, offset definitions, and trading.

As discussed below, the expected societal outcomes of both markets are more or less similar. However, there are some differences in the provisions of these markets (see table).

Comparison of the preliminary NAP allocations with the CCX reduction targets gives some credence to the notion that the two markets are converging. While it is still too early to come to a conclusion, market economics suggests such a movement is to be expected, all things remaining equal.

Finland's proposed allocation for the pilot phase represents a cut of 4% below business-as-usual emissions, which suggests little, if any, cut in absolute emissions. While Germany has committed to a 2% cut, Ireland allows a 5% increase relative to the baseline. The United Kingdom has by far the most ambitious reduction goal — 15.2%

Comparison of EU and CCX emissions markets

	EU Pilot Market (2005–07)	Chicago Climate Exchange
Type	Mandatory and regulated	Voluntary, legally binding and regulated
Gases involved	Carbon dioxide only	All greenhouse gases
Compliance regions	25 states of the EU	Volunteer members in North America and Brazil
Membership	Combustion and some industrial processes	Electric power, manufacturing sectors as well as universities, NGOs and office establishments
Emission reductions	Individual country targets vary from −16% to +7%	1% reduction from individual member baselines each year until 2006; −4% at 2006
Baseline period	Country specific: mostly 2001–02	1998–2001
Offsets	No provision for offsets in pilot phase	Provision for limited offsets from methane and sequestration projects
Initial allocation	For pilot phase at least 95% of allowances allocated free	100% of allowances allocated free
Compliance deadline	30 April each year	10 May each year

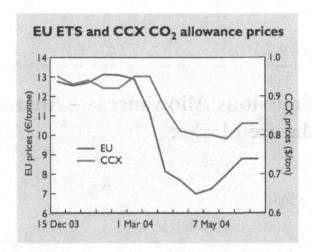

EU ETS and CCX CO_2 allowance prices

below its baseline. Austria proposes to allow a 7% rise in emissions. It remains to be seen what the final allocations will be after the commission's review of the NAPs. A reasonable hypothesis is that the average emissions cap for Phase I of the EU ETS will be fairly similar to the 4% reduction that CCX members commit to.

The generosity of the NAPs has also had an impact on EU carbon prices, which have dropped to around €8/ton ($14.32/ton). Carbon allowance prices in the CCX have been around $0.85 per ton. The figure shows a recent pattern of comovement between prices in the two systems and a narrowing of the price differential. Given that the program designs and regulatory structures are quite different, some level of deviation is to be expected. If the final EU allocations resemble the targets set forth by the participatory process followed by CCX, it should indicate the fascinating process of two markets converging to similar outcomes. Time will tell.

Special thanks to Murali Kanakasabai, Michael Walsh, Claire Jahns, and Rafael Marques for their assistance in the preparation of this article.

Chapter 49

SO$_2$ Emissions Allowances — Anatomy of a Mature Market

July–August 2004

Shortly after the passage of the Clean Air Act of 1990, critics of sulfur dioxide (SO$_2$) emissions trading in the United States were quick to point out the lack of activity in the market. It took almost three years for the first trades to occur. It seemed irrelevant to sceptics that the first compliance period didn't begin until 1995.

Nine years later, the situation has completely changed. For those unfamiliar with the roots of the program, SO$_2$ emission allowance trading was established by Title IV of the 1990 Clean Air Act Amendments, which called for reducing overall SO$_2$ emissions by 50% from 1980 levels, representing a cap of about 8.95 million tons. Phase I of the program started in 1995, and applied to 263 generating units at 110 electric utility plants. Its success led to Phase II, from January 2000, which applied to most fossil fuel-fired electric power plants.

The economic logic is quite simple. By permitting allowance holders to trade, those that can reduce emissions at the lowest cost have an incentive by sell surplus allowances to those that find emission reduction an expensive option. The expected result is that the marginal abatement costs will be equated across sources, thereby achieving the environmental goal at the lowest cost.

The environmental consequences have been tremendous. In 2002, SO$_2$ emissions from power plants were 41% lower than the baseline 1980 emissions. The outcomes have resulted in reduced human risk of premature mortality from exposure to sulphates. In fact, a study by the Federal Office of Management and Budgets indicates that the program accounts for the single largest quantified human health benefits of any federal program in the past decade, of about $70 billion annually.[1] In addition, acid deposition has reduced in lakes and streams in the Northeast.

Many opponents who argued that the program created regional hot spots — where trading created a concentration of polluting sources — have been proved wrong. Studies have found no significant regional trends in the flow of traded allowances. Net interregional trades of allowances constitute only 3% of all used allowances.

Even more remarkable is the cost of achieving the stated environmental goals. The Environmental Protection Agency (EPA) reports the cost of compliance to be just $1 billion to $2 billion a year, just a quarter of original estimates. That reflects an economically efficient program by any standard. Since the start of trading, the SO$_2$ allowance market has seen considerable activity. The volume of trading between economically distinct entities has grown around 40% on an annualized basis over the years, while the average dollar value of transactions has grown 46% over the years (see Fig. 1). Trading activity has been vibrant with half of business days recording 15 or more trades in the past two years (see Fig. 2).

More interesting is the wide range of participants that the program has attracted. The volatile nature of sulfur prices and their lack of correlation with other asset classes have attracted many noncompliance participants such as speculators, hedge funds, brokerages, and investment banks. The top participants in trading for 2003 included leading financial firms such as Morgan Stanley, Cantor

---

[1] See www.epa.gov/airmarkets/capandtrade/ctresults.pdf.

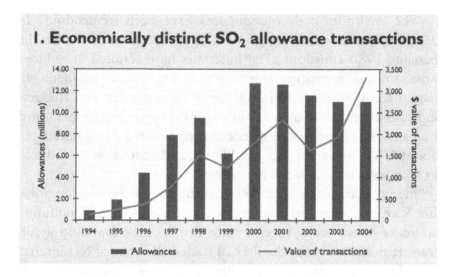

I. Economically distinct SO₂ allowance transactions

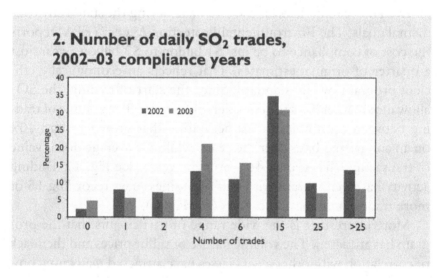

2. Number of daily SO₂ trades, 2002–03 compliance years

Fitzgerald, Millennium Energy, and Barclays Capital. Major compliance participants in 2003 include PPL, PSEG, and APS among others.

What does the future hold for the sulfur program? Recently, allowance prices reached all-time highs of $630/ton, and some analysts expect them to continue to rise. Much of the increase in prices is attributed to anticipate regulatory cuts in future phases of the program, continued depletion of previously banked permits and widespread participation by speculative buyers. Recent trends in allowance auctions indicate a stabilization in the number of allowances auctioned by the EPA each year, and even potential reductions.

Market conditions in the future are likely to be driven more by fundamental physical factors such as weather, cost of inputs, and substitution possibilities. Economics suggests that allowance prices would eventually stabilize at levels of substitute compliance costs, such as the cost of installing pollution controls.

The SO_2 trading program has shown in a remarkably short time that tradable permits and market-based methods can prove to be valuable policy tools to manage environmental pollution. The lessons learnt from the Acid Rain Program come at a particularly important time when developing countries like China and India are grappling with high pollution and when some pessimists question the success of EU's planned greenhouse gas (GHG) emissions reduction program, due to start in January.

The first issue is serious global concern. On 9 July, the *Wall Street Journal* reported that SO_2 emissions in China reached 21.6 million tons. Even more troubling is the large population potentially affected in these regions. The SO_2 allowance trading program provides a valuable framework for regional emissions programs elsewhere in the world. It has proved beyond doubt that a clearly defined structure that allows for flexibility, transparency, and simplicity enables private entrepreneurs to establish a thriving market that achieves stated the environmental goals.

And for those pessimists who question GHG trading programs, the lesson from the SO_2 programme is simple: with patience come great dividends. It took almost three years for the first trade to occur in the Acid Rain Program, and now the same market is worth $4 billion. History has taught us that environmental markets need time to mature and great benefits to society await their arrival. Be patient with the EU Emissions Trading Scheme.

I would like to thank Dr. Murali Kanakasabai for his assistance in the preparation of this article.

Chapter 50

Pricing Crude Oil Price Volatility: Can Markets Help?

September 2004

It's front page news around the globe. Everyone seems to be talking about it but few seem to be analyzing it. Some associate it with both national security and economic growth.

The recent bullish ride taken by world crude prices is breaking records every day. Crude oil futures at the New York Mercantile Exchange (NYMEX) on 22 August settled at $48.70/barrel with the market still showing a strong momentum to break the psychological $50/barrel mark. The high price of crude oil has contributed to higher prices of gasoline, jet fuel, and other crude derivatives, raising fears of its impact on economic growth.

While some analysts rightly attribute the rising price and increased volatility in the crude oil market to the political situation in the Middle East, woes of the Russian oil giant Yukos and the uncertain Venezuelan political situation, one must not forget that this is not an entirely new concern. An examination of crude prices over the past 20 years reveals considerable price volatility as well as a substantial overall price increase.

As we prepare to deal with potentially high oil prices for the foreseeable future, we would like to bring readers' attention to the far more important factor issue of future energy security. This issue is of crucial importance to the United States but is also very relevant to much of Western Europe and developing economies in Asia.

Two crucial economic questions remain unanswered: what is the impact of the cost of crude oil price uncertainty? And what is the cost of supply uncertainty to the economy? We will focus on the first question. It is important for many reasons. First, from a purely academic standpoint, it is important to price the cost of oil price volatility to the tax-payer. Second, as successive governments contemplate resolving the issue of energy security, one needs to know the economic cost of this disruption. The fact that more than half of US crude oil imports comes from politically sensitive regions of the world causes significant friction in the supply-demand balances of this important commodity. To compound this, a recent report from the US Energy Information Agency projects oil imports surging from 54% to 70% of consumption in 2025.

So the problem remains: how to price the cost of crude oil volatility to the economy. One potential approach is to use complex econometric modeling to arrive at estimates. For example, one econometric analysis, using the S&P DRI energy model, estimates crude oil volatility to have reduced average annual gross domestic product (GDP) growth rate by ~0.2 percentage points and to cost the US economy $20 billion/year. However, being a strong believer in the markets and their ability to capture price expectations, we look to them to provide answers. More specifically, the crude oil futures market can provide valuable information to this end.

Over the years, futures markets have served two related purposes. First, they have provided an organized platform for efficient hedging or speculating. Second, the price of futures contracts provides a valuable consensus view on market expectations of future price movements. In fact, the cost of hedging oil price volatility to the US economy can be derived using forward option pricing, as shown by the following exercise.

A five-year forward at-the-money Asian option is constructed for West Texas Intermediate crude (which serves as the US marker crude) using Nymex futures prices. Such an option gives the holder the right to buy (call) or sell (put) at the specified exercise price. An Asian option,[1] also called an average option (as opposed to American[2] and European[3] options), uses expected average prices for the term of the option. Asian options are less expensive because the volatility associated with an average value is less than the value for any single time period. Parameters used to price the option using modified Black–Scholes option calculators, as of 2 June 2004, are presented in footnote 4.[4] Under these conditions, the market value for the five-year Asian call was $3.31/barrel and the Asian put was $0.52/barrel.

The interpretation is that the Asian option call-plus-put prices serve as a market estimated metric to value crude oil volatility. In other words, the holder of the Asian put and call options has paid the sum of these instruments' cost to eliminate price risk and is subjected only to the secular trend. In this snapshot, over the five-year time horizon, the market value of the oil price volatility is ~$3.8/barrel in year 2000 dollars. Extending these numbers to the annual US economy's consumption of crude oil that is subject to price risk — around 4–5 million barrels/day[5] — equates to around $7 billion/year. This is relatively in significant when compared to the US real GDP for first quarter of 2004 ($10,716 billion in 2000 dollars).

The obvious question in the readers' mind is why such hedging avenues are not being employed to manage crude oil volatility in the economy. One answer is that the market cannot stand the hedging of such a large volume. Moreover, there exists no private counterparty large enough or creditworthy enough to cover this kind of hedge. But the more important lesson from this exercise is that markets can

---

[1] An Asian option is an option whose payoff is linked to the average value of the underlier on a specific set of dates during the life of the option.

[2] An American option is one that can be exercised any-time during the life of the option.

[3] A European option is one that can be exercised only at the end of the life of the option.

[4] The parameters used for the options calculation were a five-year forward price volatility of WTI crude of 17% (obtained from personal communication from Lewis Nash, Morgan Stanley), five-year forward price as of 2 June 2004 of $31.80, a spot price of $40, riskless interest rate of 5%.

[5] Personal communication from Lewis Nash, Morgan Stanley.

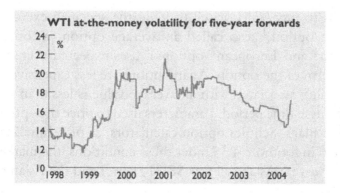

efficiently be used to price risk from crude oil volatility. Risk sharing among market participants can reap major benefits for the economy, both from a development as well as a national security standpoint.

I wish to thank Michael Walsh and Rafael Marques for their assistance in preparation of this article. Special thanks go to Amory Lovins, Rocky Mountain Institute, for his insights and contributions to our analysis of this issue.

Chapter 51

An Economist's Progress

October 2004

Five years? That's nothing. Richard Sandor looks back at a 12-year
odyssey — from the beaches of Rio, to the launch of the world's
first exchange for carbon credits.

Fifteen years ago, climate change was a concern to a limited number of scientists and environmentalists. An even smaller number
of individuals were thinking about a market-based solution to climate change. Today global warming is the subject of international
treaties and sovereign law. It's discussed in the media, journals, and
books. The movie *The Day After Tomorrow* grossed $70 million on
its opening weekend.

Less heralded, but perhaps more significant, was the launch
late last year of the Chicago Climate Exchange (CCX). This
market-based solution to global warming has attracted corporations whose greenhouse gas (GHG) emissions are approximately
equal to those of the companies in the United Kingdom covered
by the European Union (EU) Emissions Trading Scheme, which
commences next year.

Its more than 60 members include such domestic corporations
as Ford, DuPont, IBM, Motorola, International Paper, and the
largest utility in the United States, American Electric Power. International corporations with North American operations, such as
Rolls Royce, Bayer, ST Microelectronics, and Manitoba Hydro,

have also joined. Each emitter has voluntarily taken a legally binding commitment to reduce emissions by 4% from a baseline of
1998–2001. Members also include environmental organizations
such as the World Resources Institute, consulting firms including
Natural Capitalism and Domani, and the law firm Foley & Lardner.
These associate members commit to purchase and retire emission
allowances to fully offset their carbon emissions — to become GHG
neutral.

To date, the members of the exchange have traded more than
1 million tons of CCX Allowances (see table and figure). It is paradoxical that the first multisector, multinational market has emerged
in the United States where there is no legislative imperative. This is
the story of how it all happened.

Table. Trading statistics in the Chicago Climate Exchange
12 December 2003–12 September 2004

	Prices ($/tonne)			Volumes (tonnes)	
Vintage	High	Low	Close	Traded volume	Total volume*
2003	1.00	0.73	0.96	103,600	203,600
2004	1.05	0.77	0.96	436,700	436,700
2005	1.00	0.71	0.96	412,900	437,900
2006	0.99	0.80	0.96	245,300	245,300
Total				1,198,500	1,323,500

* Total volume includes traded volume and auction transferred allowances

It all began in Ipanema. It was the week of the Earth Summit
held in Rio de Janeiro in 1992. I presented a paper at a side-event
sponsored by the UN Conference on Trade and Development. It
was a lively setting that reminded me of my teaching days at Berkeley
in the 1960s. There was more tie-dye than a grateful dead concert.
It felt like a movement.

Following the side-event, I made another more formal presentation to the Rio de Janeiro Chamber of Commerce. It had been an
exhausting flight and both presentations had taken their toll. It was
time to sit on the beach, eat some barbecued shrimp and drink a
caipirinha. I felt that sense of calmness that comes to me only after

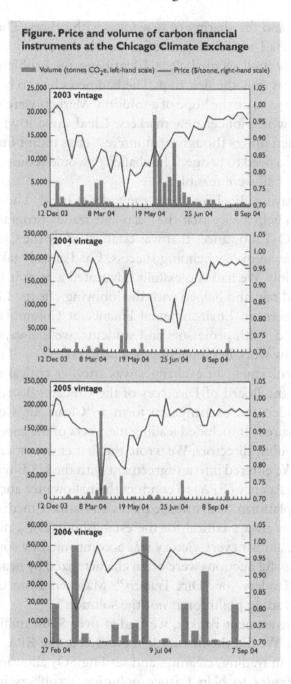

Figure. Price and volume of carbon financial instruments at the Chicago Climate Exchange

hard work and the sharing of new ideas with others. The guilt that I normally had when being inactive wasn't there.

Suddenly it all seemed clear. Identifying the problem of global warming was only the first step. The bad news had to be delivered. But there had to be the hope of a solution. Markets were the answer. I knew how to pioneer new markets. I had done it with financial futures when others thought that interest rates didn't fluctuate and there was no need to hedge. The challenge would require thousands of tasks, but all were feasible.

After leaving Rio I set about the tasks at hand. The first objective was to help assure that the "cap-and-trade" program in sulfur dioxide (SO_2) allowances that was established by the Clean Air Act of 1990 was an over-whelming success. I had already taken steps in that direction. We had successfully advocated a market-based solution to acid rain and helped with the lobbying efforts. I had taught the first course in Environmental Finance at Columbia. The academic world, both professors and students, were always the foundation of my work in pioneering new markets.

The involvement of exchanges was another critical step. I had served on the Board of Directors of the Chicago Board of Trade. We persuaded the exchange to form a "Clean Air Committee", which I chaired. It included leading members of the capital markets as well as public directors. We wrote the first environmental futures contract. We entered into an agreement with the US Environmental Protection Agency (EPA) to conduct their allowance auctions. This gave us a platform to distribute prices and attract media coverage. The latter is always critical for the establishment of a new market. Of course, almost every victory was accompanied by some frustration. Successful auctions were often characterized by headlines such as "Smut Traders" or "Dirt Traders". Marchers from Greenpeace chanted "trading pollution is not the solution".

As an investment banker, we traded over $100 million of SO_2 allowances. We did the first trade registered at the EPA. We gained experience in trading, clearing, and settling SO_2 allowances trades. We used trades to help finance pollution scrubbers installed by municipal power plants to reduce emissions. When it appeared that we had done all that was possible intellectually and commercially we left that business. All of those experiences would prove invaluable in developing a GHG emissions market.

Fueled by the success of the Acid Rain Program, I then began focusing on weather derivatives. We developed markets for catastrophic insurance. Weather futures that facilitated hedging of hurricanes and tornadoes were developed. We also invented earthquake futures. Once again, we had to deal with failure. Although these new instruments succeeded in the day-to-day business of insurance companies, they failed on the Chicago Board of Trade. Nevertheless, the invention of these new financial instruments led to the development of key relationships within the insurance sector. This was critical because they would be the biggest losers in any global warming scenario.

I continued to write and lecture on market-based solutions to climate change. We took every opportunity to present our ideas. At that time, there was no commercial logic to much of our work. It was a series of frenetic activities. I was the environmental supplicant at industry meetings and seminars, but it wasn't easy. The right wing objected to our vision because they thought we were environmentalists. The left wing objected because they thought we were capitalists.

This actually gave us some comfort. I was always taught that in chess, politics, and football the game is controlled from the center. Nevertheless, progress was extraordinarily slow. I always had a sense of anxiety and there were many sleepless nights. Despite these setbacks, I continued to be excited about the work. It was one big chess game.

Then our first moment of fortuity occurred. You must understand luck is very important in any endeavor. But you should also strongly believe in Louis Pasteur's comment that "chance favours the prepared mind".

The previous five years had prepared us. In 1995, we made a presentation to a UN conference in Glen Cove, New York. That conference was the beginning of a turning point in my work. I met Paula DiPerna, who then was a vice president for the Cousteau Society. She would subsequently become president of the Joyce Foundation, which financed the vision that I outlined at that conference.

New scientific and anecdotal evidence of global warming attracted a growing interest in our work in subsequent years. We were invited to the White House, testified before various Senate Committees and made presentations to industry groups in the United States and around the world. We attended Kyoto and gave our input to a variety of government officials and business leaders. As the years passed, we continued to attend virtually any event to which we were invited. It was a constant struggle but we would go anywhere at any time. The continuous exposure to industry of financial innovations is critical to the inventive process. I finally knew what it was like to be a lounge act.

Subsequently, in 2000, the Joyce Foundation funded a feasibility study into a voluntary, pilot program to trade GHGs in advance of US participation in Kyoto. We engaged experts from all fields — attorneys, accountants, scientists, foresters, and so on — and studied issues of monitoring and verification of emissions. We concluded it could work: we could start a self-governed exchange that would issue the allowances directly — without the government. We included emissions offsets to issue credits based on the capture of carbon in soil and trees. We thought the concept of financing ongoing environmental services might someday be a valuable tool in helping avoid the destruction of the world's rainforests.

In the middle of these intellectual challenges being met, the world as we knew it began to change. The United States turned its back on Kyoto. Our efforts seemed dead, but the Joyce Foundation remained undeterred in its support and gave us another grant to implement the idea. We asked 30 companies to help build a consensus on the specifics of a market. We sought opinions from more than 100 experts. Each triumph was matched by some sobering event. After 11 September 2001, our efforts properly seemed to take a back seat to terrorism. That tragedy was important, but I knew that global warming was potentially another future tragedy. We just kept pushing. The war in Afghanistan, the burst in the dot.com bubble, the crash in the stock market and the decline in the economy all posed a succession of body blows. Our financing ran out. I had to spend personal savings and seek financial help from that oldest funding source: friends and family.

We had stopped all other commercial activity, so there was no alternative but to move forward. We completed the implementation study, which included a plan to arrange additional funding and turn our research into a sustainable business. The economy was still weak and firms were reluctant to commit to emission reductions, which would be costly. We had bloody knees from begging and a braided stomach from crawling. In the months that followed, we finally got 14 heroes to join the exchange, including some of the major companies in the United States as well as the City of Chicago. Mayor Richard Daley — a visionary who is dedicated to making Chicago the greenest city in America — agreed to become honorary CCX chairman. We continued to recruit, and hired an investment banker to raise financing. The economy stayed in a recession and the second Iraq war started. Once again our resolve was tested.

But another critically important individual had the vision. Neil Eckert, chairman and CEO of Brit Insurance, was a hero. Indefatigable in his efforts, he helped us raise capital. He introduced us to creative investment bankers in the United Kingdom who came up with a very original form of financing. We formed a closed-end investment company — Chicago Environmental — that would be listed on the London Stock Exchange. This allowed institutional investors to make an investment in a private nonlisted company. We completed an $18 million round of financing one week before the CCX opened.

While we were creating a carbon market in North America from scratch, the United Kingdom started a pilot GHG emissions market in 2002. Their incentives to participate cost the government $300 million. There are no such incentives at the CCX, and our total costs of research and implementation barely totaled $5 million. We should not underestimate the benefits of a free-market economy.

Our challenges continue to be enormous. In spite of our good beginning, we are still a start-up company. We have proven somethings but still have a long way to go. A significant milestone occurred just one month ago. We signed a memorandum of understanding with the London-based International Petroleum Exchange to license them our intellectual property. We are now forming a venture to help develop the EU's Emission Trading Scheme. This is the beginning of the European Climate Exchange.

The world faces some massive environmental problems that will take decades for us to learn how to manage. Rainforest destruction, globally-spread pollutants, and expansion of deserts in northern Africa and China pose serious problems to local populations. Desertification may be an even more pressing problem than global warming. We are looking into establishing water markets both domestically and internationally. We hope to expand into the use of markets to preserve biodiversity and endangered species. Market failures also occur in medicine. We also hope to make a contribution in this area.

So what's the point of this story? The point is that a sound concept is not enough to win the day. Hope, perseverance, and vitality are even more important.

The planet is a small piece of real estate that is running out of resources. New ideas, the creative use of old concepts and international cooperation will all be needed to solve the complex problems of the 21st century. It has taken and will continue to take our best and brightest to mitigate the threat of global climate change. We need to spend our resources — time and money — to address this and other potential environmental and social disasters. What else are we saving it for? We need to put our idealism to work for the good of society.

Idealism and adrenaline can't keep one going forever, though. When I am exhausted and the world seems at its bleakest, I stop and watch a movie.

A song in Frank Capra's 1959 film *A Hole in the Head* sums up the spirit that I hope you will have. The song is "High Hopes". It's about an ant that tried to move a rubber tree plant.

> *Anyone knows an ant can't*
> *Move a rubber tree plant*
> *But he's got high hopes, he's got high hopes*
> *He's got high apple pie in the sky hopes*
> *So, any time you're getting low,*
> *'stead of lettin' go,*
> *just remember that ant.*
> *Oops there goes another rubber tree plant*

I would like to thank Dr. Murali Kanakasabai for his help with the preparation of last month's article.

Chapter 52

The Benefits of Corporate Sustainability

November 2004

The trend remains unmistakable. This time of the year, we take the opportunity to update readers on the status of the Dow Jones Sustainability World Index (DJSI World). Sustainable investing continues to make an impact in the halls of the business community. The United Nation Global Compact Summit held in June saw major investment companies endorsing the integration of environmental, social, and governance criteria as standard components in judging corporate performance and investment decision-making.

The DJSI World offers a consistent, flexible, and investable index for global sustainability portfolios and provides investors with an independent benchmark based on economic, environmental, and social criteria. For those unfamiliar with these indexes, the DJSI tracks the performance of companies that lead their fields in terms of corporate sustainability — a business approach that creates long-term shareholder value by embracing opportunities and managing risks derived from economic, environmental, and social developments.

Since its launch five years ago, the DJSI World has grown to include more than 300 companies from 60 industry groups in 34 countries, with a market capitalization of more than $6.2 trillion. This is a good indicator of the growing importance of corporate sustainability in the business community and the increasing

Largest 20 components of DJSI World at 31 March 2004

Name	Economic sector	Weight (%)
Pfizer	Healthcare	4.06
Citigroup	Financial	4.05
BP	Energy	2.81
Intel	Technology	2.68
HSBC Holdings	Financial	2.48
Vodafone Group	Telecommunications	2.45
Johnson & Johnson	Healthcare	2.28
Procter & Gamble	Consumer non-cyclical	2.06
GlaxoSmithKline	Healthcare	1.77
Toyota	Consumer cyclical	1.67
Novartis	Healthcare	1.63
Nestlé	Consumer non-cyclical	1.56
Royal Dutch Petroleum	Energy	1.50
Nokia	Technology	1.49
Royal Bank of Scotland Group	Financial	1.30
Home Depot	Consumer cyclical	1.29
UBS	Financial	1.21
Dell	Technology	1.15
Amgen	Healthcare	1.14
AstraZeneca	Healthcare	1.13

Source: Dow Jones Sustainability Indexes

awareness that companies' environmental and social strategies are linked to their market and financial strategies.

The methodology for calculating, reviewing, and publishing the DJSI mirrors that for the Dow Jones Global Indexes. The DJSI World captures the leading 10%, in terms of sustainability, of the biggest 2500 companies in the Dow Jones Global Index. The constituents are selected according to a systematic corporate sustainability assessment that identifies the leading sustainability-driven companies in each industry group. The table presents the 20 largest components of the DJSI World index as of 31 March 2004.

In addition to a composite DJSI World index there are also specialized indexes that exclude certain activities or commodities such as alcohol, gambling, tobacco, armaments, and firearms. There is also a European index, the Europe-Dow Jones STOXX sustainability Index, whose benchmark includes 167 companies from 12 countries. The assets managed by the DJSI licensees now total close to €3 billion in DJSI-based funds and structured products, as well as exchange-traded funds listed on Euronext. These numbers represent an increase of almost 30% from last year, according to Alex Barkawi, managing director of Sustainable Asset Management (SAM) indexes.

As indicated by Figures 1 and 2, the DJSI World would have outperformed the DJGI index over the past 10 years and compares well with other global indexes in the year to September 2004. This is a good indicator that issues of corporate sustainability are moving out of the academic arena and into the mainstream corporate world.

The annual review of the DJSI indexes indicates promising developments for corporate sustainability. It shows that sustainability strategies are continuing to be integrated into companies' core business. This is indicated by an increasing number of corporates integrating sustainability reporting with their annual reports. In addition, external verification and internal assurance systems are

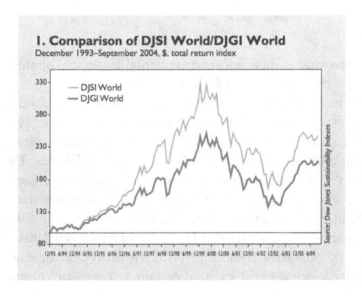

I. Comparison of DJSI World/DJGI World
December 1993–September 2004, $, total return index

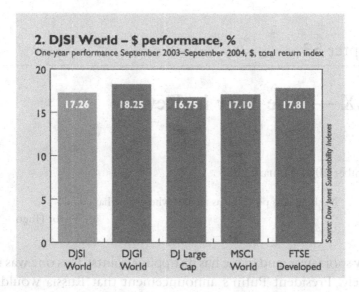

2. DJSI World – $ performance, %
One-year performance September 2003–September 2004, $, total return index

DJSI World	DJGI World	DJ Large Cap	MSCI World	FTSE Developed
17.26	18.25	16.75	17.10	17.81

Source: Dow Jones Sustainability Indexes

on the increase. Recent developments in the Kyoto framework and the increasing importance of environmental capital all point in one direction. For example, with Russian ratification of the Kyoto Protocol and the impending European Union's Emissions Trading Scheme, companies are seeing financial benefits from sustainable action. We see a bright future for those corporates that engage in environmentally sustainable actions. The narrowing of boundaries between financial and sustainable strategies points to a win-win for society.

I would like to thank Murali Kanakasabai for his assistance in the preparation of this chapter.

Chapter 53

CCX — The Year in Review

December 2004–January 2005

> "Nothing is as powerful as an idea whose time has come"
> — Victor Hugo

Every sport, war, and game has its tipping points. This one was really unlikely. President Putin's announcement that Russia would sign the Kyoto treaty heralded a whole new era for the Chicago Climate Exchange (CCX). On 23 September, the price of the exchange's "carbon financial instruments" was $0.96 and total volume was 1,315,100. Since that eventful moment, prices have doubled and volume has increased to 2.3 million tons of carbon dioxide (CO_2).

Exactly a year ago, we began active trading at the CCX. The baby is now 1-year-old and growing fast. In this chapter, I will present some of the lessons learned from implementing the world's first multinational and multisector marketplace for reducing and trading greenhouse gas (GHG) emissions.

CCX was formally established in September 2000, helped by a Joyce Foundation grant to study the feasibility of a voluntary carbon market in North America. The design phase participants developed a market architecture that calls for reduction of overall emissions by 1% per year relative to a 1998–2001 baseline. The programme, now in its first phase, extends from 2003 through 2006 and has an emission reduction target of 4% below baseline in 2006. The overall CCX baseline is approximately 230 million tons of CO_2, which equals the United Kingdom's annual allowance allocation in the European Union (EU) Emissions Trading Scheme. Participants can reach their legally binding reduction objectives through on-site emission reductions, allowance trading, and use of a limited range of offset projects, including projects in Brazil.

CCX has clearly demonstrated that a multisector voluntary GHG reduction market is viable. We established a comprehensive market architecture with rules addressing issues such as baselines, emission ownership, offset project eligibility and quantification, emissions monitoring and reporting, included facilities and opt-in provisions, participation by energy end-users, project verification, market constraints, and other technical provisions. Combined with emission audits, an electronic trading platform and its self-governance system, the CCX has established an end-to-end carbon market infrastructure.

The environmental and market outcomes of these efforts signal a promising start to the program. Over the past year, CCX members have traded 2.3 million tons of CO_2 across the four allowance vintages in which trading is offered (see Figure 1 and Table 1). CCX members now number more than 70 and include a diverse range of participants. Importantly, there has also been active participation by the trading and financial community which will be critical to the long-run success of these markets.

However, the true indicator of environmental success is the level of compliance achieved by the participants. In addition to achieving the environmental objective, comprehensive compliance is indicative of the successful linkage between the environmental, legal, and financial experts within the members. We are happy to report that all CCX members have achieved final compliance for 2003. In fact, members have collectively reduced emissions 8% beyond the first-year reduction requirement.

CCX has also taken steps to advance its goal of harmonizing and integrating with other international and regional trading regimes. We recently signed a cross-recognition agreement with the World Economic Forum that will allow CCX members' emissions data

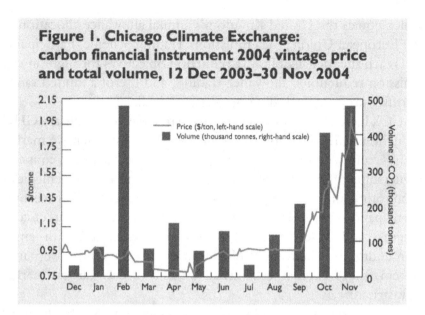

Figure 1. Chicago Climate Exchange: carbon financial instrument 2004 vintage price and total volume, 12 Dec 2003–30 Nov 2004

Table 1. Chicago Climate Exchange: trading statistics, 12 Dec 2003–2 Dec 2004

	Prices ($/tonne)			Volume (tonnes)	
Vintage	High	Low	Close	Traded	Total *
2003	1.80	0.73	1.68	227,600	327,600
2004	2.03	0.77	1.68	623,800	623,800
2005	2.06	0.71	1.68	795,000	820,000
2006	2.04	0.80	1.68	629,900	629,900
Total				2,276,300	2,401,300

Includes trade volume and auction transferred allowances

to be included in the Global GHG register without further verification. In a similar agreement, CCX and the California Climate Action Registry signed an agreement intended to make it easier for companies to participate in both programs by undergoing a single certification audit, while also creating a potential vehicle for trading forestry offset projects registered with the registry.[1] CCX is also

---

[1] Subject to approval by the CCX Forestry Committee.

involved in the emerging EU Emissions Trading Scheme through the opening of its subsidiary, the European Climate Exchange, which will allow for exchange-based trading of CO_2 spot and futures contracts.

This first year has also been a period of tremendous learning for us. Here are some of the lessons:

- The importance of getting started. Both the private sector and policy professionals need to experience firsthand the many intricacies of market-based carbon management in order for these mechanisms to succeed and evolve in a positive direction.
- The importance of a comprehensive system that covers everything from baseline definition, target setting, measurement, auditing, auctions, and trading. There is no better way for industry to be prepared for a world where carbon has monetary value than to engage a full range of corporate talent in understanding and efficiently managing both commitments and the associated commercial opportunities.
- The importance of simplicity in objectives and design. The administration of program rules — which govern emission ownership, offset projects, and trading mechanisms — quickly gets complicated as one moves from theory to practice.
- The amazing depth of both goodwill and intellectual talent in the private sector. The CCX was built on the premise that the private sector would respond positively to the opportunity to act, before required by law, to begin managing GHGs. The positive response has been evidenced all the way from the CEO level through to the professional staff that administer each CCX member's participation.

CCX and its members continue to refine the North American GHG programme, and to extend the concept of allowance trading to other environmental commodities and into other geographical regions. This month CCX started a new subsidiary called the Chicago Climate Futures Exchange with an initial offering of futures contracts on US sulfur dioxide emission allowances. We look to the future with optimism and enthusiasm.

Special thanks to Murali Kanakasabai, Michael J Walsh, and Claire M Jahns for their assistance in the preparation of this chapter.

Chapter 54

Here Come the States III

January 2005

> "Those who cannot remember the past are condemned to repeat it"
> —George Santayana, *The Life of Reason*

Approximately a century ago, the US Congress was debating product standards for traded commodities. In Historical Review of the US Grades and Standards for Grain, Hoffman and Hill noted that: "Congress finally took action in 1906 ... ten more years went by before any legislation adopting uniform standards was passed". They added that, "In place of research, trade practices and public hearings were used to identify acceptable grades". Is history repeating itself in the current US debate on climate change? Is it possible that federal law on greenhouse gas (GHG) emissions will be driven by state and local governments as well as private sector activity?

The successful launch of the European Union (EU) Emissions Trading Scheme in January has infused new energy into the international agenda on climate change. In addition, Russian ratification of the Kyoto Protocol in November 2004 has solidified participating nations' mandatory emission reduction targets. Yet, despite these developments, the United States remains on the sidelines of the debate, still lacking a comprehensive national agenda for addressing climate change. State and local governments, however, have used their jurisdiction over transportation, taxation, land use, and building codes to play a highly active role in developing the US climate change agenda, while the private sector continues to inform the debate.

According to the Pew Center on Global Climate Change, 28 US states have developed programs for reducing GHG emissions. Such strategies range from direct measures targeting emissions to less direct policies targeting energy efficiency and renewables. Oregon established a law in 1997 requiring utilities to offset 17% of new plants' GHG emissions through projects with the Climate Trust. In 2001, Massachusetts capped various emissions, including carbon dioxide (CO_2), from its six largest power plants and plans to reduce these emissions by 10%. New Hampshire passed legislation on electric power plant emissions, including CO_2 which must be reduced to 1990 levels by 2006. Many states have passed legislation that aims indirectly to mitigate climate change. For example, California has passed energy efficiency legislation, West Virginia has introduced tax incentives for renewable energy, and many states, such as Texas, have established renewable energy portfolio standards.

In addition, as many as 39 states have established inventory processes for their GHG emissions. Beyond one-time assessments, Wisconsin requires large emitters to report their GHG emissions. New Jersey requires any facility that reports any type of emissions to report CO_2 emissions as well. New Hampshire, California, and Wisconsin have also established voluntary GHG emissions and reductions registries.

The state of California has used its authority to formulate its own air quality standards to tackle GHG emissions generated by the transportation sector. In September 2003, California regulators approved the first law mandating cuts in GHG emissions from vehicles. It requires automakers to reduce GHG emissions from passenger and light-duty vehicles sold in the state by 30%, phasing in from 2009 through 2016. Connecticut, Massachusetts, and New York have said they intend to follow California's standard.

At the regional level, several northeastern states and eastern Canadian provinces, led by New York governor George Pataki, have established an accord to limit the region's CO_2 emissions to 1990 levels by 2010 and then to further reduce them by an additional 10% by 2020. To achieve these goals, New York, New Hampshire, Vermont, Maine, Massachusetts, Rhode Island, Delaware, Connecticut, and New Jersey have formed the Regional Greenhouse Gas Initiative (RGGI) with the intent of establishing a cap-and-trade mechanism. Initially, this trading scheme will cover only CO_2 and will regulate emissions from regional power plants of over 25 MW. The door will be left open to include other sectors of the economy later. Among the issues still to be finalized are:

- the size of the aggregate regional emissions cap;
- how the cap will be apportioned among individual states;
- whether the cap will be instituted at once or phased in;
- the possibility of admitting offset projects and, if so, what types;
- whether banking or borrowing of allowances will be allowed; and
- the possibility of interaction with other GHG trading systems.

The RGGI intends, by April 2005, to articulate its standards for the base year, its reduction targets and procedures for the allocation, and auctioning of emission allowances.

Municipalities have also been exploring and establishing policies to mitigate their carbon footprint. Nearly 150 local governments are participating in the Cities for Climate Protection Campaign which includes setting a baseline period for emissions analysis and an emissions reduction target. One of the more ambitious announcements came in November last year with San Francisco's decision to reduce emissions by 20% relative to a 1990 baseline by 2012. Portland has set a reduction target of 10% below 1990 levels by 2010 and Austin is aiming for a 20% reduction relative to a 1990 baseline by 2010. The city of Chicago, as a founding member of the Chicago Climate Exchange (CCX), has committed to a 4% reduction below a 1998–2001 baseline by 2006.

These state and local initiatives represent a broad spectrum of policy tools, from voluntary measures to command-and-control to market-based programs. They serve the important task of informing the public and advancing policy learning, but they also represent a highly fragmented and uncertain policy format. Against the backdrop of these initiatives, the CCX has created and launched a multisector emissions trading scheme that includes 76 member companies with GHG emissions equal to that of a G7 country.

Arnold Schwarzenegger, the charismatic governor of California, has been particularly effective because of his ability to make his case to the people. Suppose he and the other west coast governors successfully implement a cap-and-trade system that is currently being examined. Let's further suppose that governor Pataki's leadership provides the impetus for a successful eastern state cap-and-trade system. What would be the reaction of industrial America to differential regulation and fragmented markets? Would an army of attorneys costing millions of dollars have to be dispatched from Sacramento in the west to Albany in the east? Would reductions made in California be counted in New York and vice versa? Is it possible that this might either evolve into harmonized regional systems (a quasi national market) or a legislated federal cap-and-trade system? Perhaps it is worthwhile reconsidering the admonitions of George Santayana.

I would like to thank Natalie Ratajczak, Mike Walsh, Murali Kanakasabai, Nathan Clark, and Claire Jahns for their assistance in the preparation of this chapter.

Chapter 55

Talking about the Weather

March 2005

It seems to be front-page news on a regular basis. This year it's the cool weather and excessive rains in California. Last year it was hot weather and droughts in the southwest.

Weather continues to have a profound effect in different regions of the United States. The US Department of Commerce estimates that nearly one-third of the US economy, or $3.5 trillion a year, is affected to some degree by the weather.

Weather risk markets continue to grow apace. Weather derivatives are used to manage risk as a consequence of weather-related events and, as financial instruments, they are on a sure road to maturity. Businesses that face increased costs or decreased revenues as a result of fluctuations in weather events stand to benefit from hedging in the weather markets.

Although power and gas companies maybe obvious users of the product — given the close correlations between temperatures and the use of their products — there are a wide variety of industries that could stand to benefit from minimizing their exposure to the weather. Agriculture, tourism, travel, construction, project finance, transportation, entertainment — all depend directly or indirectly on the weather and could find participation in this market a useful means of managing cash flows.

These instruments can be based on a variety of statistics such as temperature, precipitation, or wind speed, and are critical for businesses that face increased costs or decreased revenues as a consequence of fluctuations in these indicators. The Weather Risk Management Association (WRMA), the international trade organization of the weather risk management industry, calculates that the notional value of weather risk management contracts transacted from April 2003 through March 2004 reached a value of $4.6 billion, representing a 10% increase over the previous year.

At this point in time, the class of weather financial products can be divided into two subsets — insurance and derivatives — although there is a blurring of the line between the categories. Here, we focus on derivative products, which can again be separated into those listed on exchanges, and the over-the-counter (OTC) market. In the former, the Chicago Mercantile Exchange (CME) has offered weather futures contracts since 1999 and has, over time, broadened its product suite. Currently, both monthly and seasonal exchange-traded weather products are available for American, European, and Japanese cities.

At the CME, 125,775 contracts were traded in the 5-month period from September 2004 to the end of January 2005. When we last wrote an article on the weather markets in 1999, the CME had just launched its first weather futures contract and 341 contracts had traded in the same 5-month period. In 2004, the notional value of exchange-traded weather contracts was $2.2 billion. A key component that has contributed to growth is the existence of lead market makers, who make it easy for users to enter and exit the market.

In addition to listed markets, OTC markets in weather risk have also grown. Because the OTC contracts are privately negotiated, hard data are difficult to come by. However, after a difficult couple of years after the collapse of Enron, and the retrenchment of many of the energy companies active in weather derivatives, the market is growing again, with hedge funds recently joining the reinsurers, investment and commercial banks, and energy and utility firms already active.

It's also happening in Europe. Euronext Paris and Météo France, the French weather bureau, have joined forces to grow the European market in weather derivatives. They are creating weather indexes to act as underlying values for derivatives, to be followed by weather derivatives for trading on the regulated market.

Expect to see continued growth in this market as managing weather risk attracts new economic interests and new geographic locations. After all, developing countries such as China and India have a need to hedge weather events as well. At the same time, growth in markets related to weather, such as emissions, and new markets in natural resources such as water, will continue to be launched — promising to offer synergies with existing weather markets.

I would like to thank Kellee James, Murali Kanakasabai, Andy Ertel, Jeff Bortniker, and Coi Dangand Jon Davis for their assistance in the preparation of this chapter.

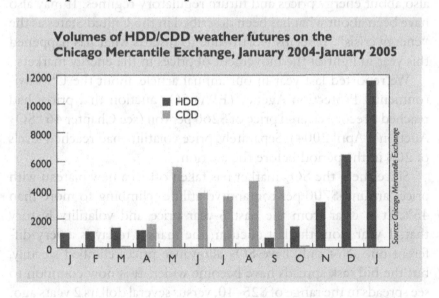

Volumes of HDD/CDD weather futures on the Chicago Mercantile Exchange, January 2004–January 2005

Source: Chicago Mercantile Exchange

Chapter 56

SO$_2$ Prices — Where Do We Go from Here?

April 2005

Last year's battle over United States, sulfur dioxide (SO$_2$) allowance prices was once again about direct supply and demand, but it was also about energy prices and future regulatory regimes. It may also have been about what has been described in the United States as the "energy crisis". It seems worthwhile to discuss what has happened this year in light of the movement of prices in the energy markets.

We reported last year in our annual article about the US Environmental Protection Agency (EPA) SO$_2$ auction that prices had reached a record cleared price of $260 per ton (see Chapter 46 "SO$_2$ Auction", April 2004). Separately, price volatility had reached levels of 20% in the period before the auction.

Since then, the SO$_2$ market has taken off to a new plateau with prices around $700 per ton and volatilities climbing to more than 45%. It is clear from the past 5-year price and volatility history that, 1 year from the last auction, the market today is a very different one. Not only have SO$_2$ allowance prices climbed steadily, but the bid/ask spreads have become wider. It is now common to see spreads in the range of $25–40, versus several dollars 2 years ago. In light of significant changes in the market dynamics, our objective for this chapter is to present an economist's view of the emissions marketplace.

While in the past, we have presented an overview of results from the SO$_2$ auction — due this year on March 29, just after *Environmental Finance* went to press — the market function has matured considerably, reducing the importance of the price discovery role of the annual auction. As with any mature market, today's SO$_2$ market has grown to respond to more fundamental drivers. Here we present some explanation for recent market dynamics and share our thoughts on what needs to happen to reach the next level in the environmental marketplace. These are not predictions or forecasts, but merely observations from students of this fascinating and evolving market.

So why are prices so high now? One fundamental fact that will increasingly play a role in the future is that the amount of 'banked' SO$_2$ allowances is drying up. A bank of more than 11 million allowances in 2000 had decreased to around 8.63 million in 2003, a decrease of more than 20%. This compels regulated entities to depend increasingly on the marketplace to meet their compliance targets. Moreover, this reduction of allowance banks coincides with increased environmental regulation. With the new Clean Air Interstate Rule taking the place of President Bush's stalled Clear Skies Initiative, new EPA regulations demand that affected entities reduce SO$_2$ emissions in the eastern United States by more than 70% from 2003 levels. This means an increase in uncertainty as several points of the initiative will be dealt with via litigation in the court system rather than through legislation.

Short-term shocks have also been responsible for the recent price dynamics. Here, some analysts have implicated higher natural gas prices in the increase in SO$_2$ allowance prices. From a utility operator's standpoint, rising natural gas prices mean as witch to cheaper substitute fuels, mostly more polluting coal.

Price movements and volatility should also be examined in the context of market size. While the annual volume of SO$_2$ allowance transactions between economically distinct players has been stable at around 8 million allowances, the dollar value of the SO$_2$ allowance market has been steadily increasing (see the figure). The market

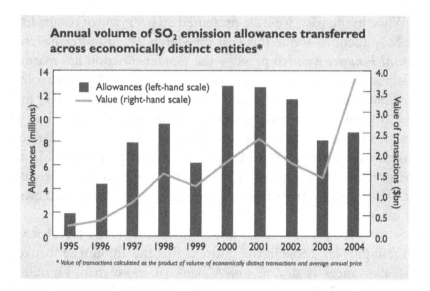

Annual volume of SO₂ emission allowances transferred across economically distinct entities*

* Value of transactions calculated as the product of volume of economically distinct transactions and average annual price

value of economically distinct transactions in 2004 was close to $4 billion, a 97% increase from 2003 numbers. Adding this year's allocation, and at current market prices, would take the value of potential transactions to over $6 billion.

The market has also become more diverse in terms of its participants. No longer is the SO_2 allowance market simply a market for the "polluters". Today, participants range from the obvious power utilities to major financial players, brokers, and educational and environmental organizations, as well as other participants with purely speculative interest. This is an important shift and a lesson for other comparable environmental markets. The beauty of free markets is to create real monetary and trading value, attracting participants from all sectors of the economy. These dynamics will in turn help determine the true societal price for the emissions of a ton of SO_2.

One set of participants in the SO_2 market whose participation we believe is important to future growth is the financial players. Already, several financial institutions are active in the market, including Barclays Capital and Courage Capital Management. Several other banks and financial institutions including Citibank, Bank of New York, and Fifth Third Bank have EPA SO_2 allowance accounts. Considering

SO$_2$ allowances as an asset class that is not correlated to other financial assets might make them attractive to many financial institutions. Hedge funds, in particular, should take a good look at SO$_2$ derivatives products.

The SO$_2$ allowance market has paved the way for emissions markets becoming accepted by the mainstream. The time is now ripe for the next big leap for environmental markets — that is, environmental futures and options trading. The risk and uncertainties in the marketplace dictate that this will be the new direction. The structure of the SO$_2$ allowance market, ensuring transparency, monitoring and verification and ease of trade execution, provide the ideal framework for this next big step. Time will certainly tell, but we don't think it is going to be a long wait.

Murali Kanakasabai is a research economist at the Chicago Climate Exchange. Murali and I would like to thank Kellee James for her assistance in the preparation of this chapter. We would also like to thank Amerex for providing SO$_2$ allowance price data.

Chapter 57

Weathering the Crude Oil Crisis

May 2005

Everybody seems to be talking about it. From corporate board rooms to policy desks to the average Joe filling up his gas tank, our oil-hungry economy is looking for ways to cope with fluctuating crude prices. Worldwide oil demand in 2005 is expected to be about 84.3 million barrels a day,[1] an increase of 2.1% from last year.

Americans account for about 25% of global consumption and, to add to our woes, a quarter of our supply comes from unstable regions in aging[2] tankers into refineries that are working above capacity.[3] And all this at a time when the value of the dollar is falling. Some analysts predict crude oil prices of over $50/barrel for a considerable time and we seem to have quietly accepted the inevitability of having to live with the consequences.

Here, we consider two fundamental questions. What are the economic costs of crude oil dependency? and Are the markets signaling a shift in direction from our current dependence on crude oil? From an economist's perspective, these costs can be thought to include two components. First, shocks associated with oil price volatility and second, costs arising from permanent increases in oil prices.

---

[1] International Energy Agency.
[2] Most investment in crude oil tankers was made during the 1970s in the US.
[3] EIA estimates oil refineries in the United States are working to 75% to 95% of their capacity.

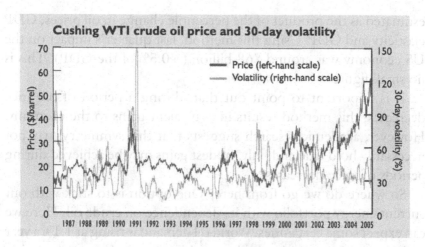

We addressed the first component in a previous issue of this column.[4] The idea was that one could theoretically hedge the risk in crude oil price volatility in the futures market. Using forward option pricing analysis, we estimated the annual cost to hedge the US economy's consumption of crude oil that is subject to price risk to be around $7 billion/year. We indicated that this figure was relatively insignificant when compared to US real GDP.

Here, we address the second component: the impact of a permanent rise in oil prices. The negative effect of a permanent rise in crude oil prices on GDP has been well documented in academic literature. Shocks from crude oil price increases and price volatility have been implicated in depressing economic growth, raising inflation and unemployment as well as dampening the value of asset holdings. One estimate relates a permanent $10 increase in crude oil prices to a 0.5% decrease in global GDP.[5] We estimate the potential losses to the US economy from a permanent increase in crude oil prices using a fairly simple formulation. Here, GDP losses are

---

[4] *Environmental Finance*, September 2004.

[5] J. D. Hamilton, "Oil and the Macroeconomy since World War II", *Journal of Political Economy*, 91, no. (2) (1983): 228–248.

estimated as the product of the percentile change in oil prices, GDP elasticity and GDP. Using this method, last quarter's impact on the US economy was around $68 billion (~0.5% of the GDP). This is no small figure.

It is important to point out that, during a period of oil price decreases, this method results in equivalent gains to the economy. However, academic research suggests that this symmetry may not necessarily hold true and only modest gains may be achieved during periods of price decreases.

So where do we go from here? One option is to stick with our current energy portfolio with its dependence on crude oil. Here we can expect some certainties. World oil demand is rising at 1.1% a year and demand from the developing world is expected to put increasing pressure on existing supplies. The imported fraction of US crude oil is projected to increase to about 70% in 2025, with imports from OPEC projected to double. Some analysts have suggested that inadequate investment is what is sustaining these high oil prices, thereby calling for greater investment in refining capacity, tankers, and other infrastructure. But it takes around 7 years to build and operate a new oil refinery.

The second option is to introduce some diversity into our energy portfolio. With our high dependence on foreign oil, diversification might help combat some issues of security. Here, a cleaner and greener alternative is the greater use of renewables. US renewable energy consumption grew 3% in 2003, accounting for 6.1 quadrillion British thermal units. However, only a small portion of a huge renewable resource has so far been tapped. For example, in some regions wind energy is fast becoming competitive with other sources of electric generation.

In addition, other co-benefits can be reaped from using renewable energy. The most obvious are the environmental benefits from using clean sources of energy. States also find the renewable energy sector helps boost local economic development and job creation. One study estimates that wind and solar energy generate 40% more jobs when compared to coal mining.[6] In the US alone, tripling the use of biomass energy is expected to produce $20billion in new income for farmers and rural landowners.[7] The most important reason for considering a switch to renewables might be the fact that it secures the energy future for our children and their children.

Another policy that cannot go wrong is that of energy efficiency. The United States experienced success with this during the 1979 oil shocks when better vehicle fuel efficiency was a key strategy in tackling the crisis.

Technological innovation, creativity and the willingness to think unconventionally have been the greatest strengths of mankind. Continual high prices of crude may be the market signal that triggers such innovation. To those naysayers who believe such a transition will take too long or be too expensive, we will let the history of crude oil tell its own story. It took a mere 15 years for crude oil to displace the predominant energy source of its time — sperm whale oil — as the primary cheap source of illumination. I think in 2005 there is no dearth of commonsense solutions or innovation that did not exist in the 1800s.

Nobel Prize–winner Andre Gide once remarked, "One doesn't discover new lands without consenting to lose sight of the shore for a very long time". We all know the new direction we must sail for a cleaner and more secure energy policy in this nation. Let us agree to lose sight of these old shores and a new future awaits us.

Special thanks to Murali Kanakasabai and Michael Walsh for their assistance in the preparation of this chapter.

---

[6]Virinder Singh, BBC Research and Consulting, and Jeffrey Fehrs, "The Work That Goes into Renewable Energy," *Renewable Energy Policy Project*, November 2001, 8.

[7]Hopkins, TrendsAlert: *Renewable Energy*, 13.

Chapter 58

Trading Away Conflict

June 2005

> "The difference between what we do and what we are capable of doing would suffice to solve most of the world's problems"
>
> — Mahatma Gandhi

There are no heads of governments peaking or even attending. There are no vistas of mountains with snow-covered trees. Why should we even compare it to the beautiful Swiss city of Davos and the annual meeting of the World Economic Forum (WEF) that takes place there? The Milken Institute Global Conference takes place in the fashionable community of Beverly Hills, California, but it does have some important similarities to the WEF meeting. This year it attracted more than 2,300 people. Panelists included seven Nobel Prize winners, as well as such notable individuals as former US vice president Al Gore, General Wesley Clark, and News Corp CEO Rupert Murdoch. It appeared to me that institutional investors controlling at least $2 trillion were there.

This year's conference focused on improvements in health care, improvement of education from early childhood to retirement, and increasing productivity through more widespread use of financial tools and technologies. Environmental issues such as climate change were also addressed. Simply put, it is a group of intellectuals who hammer down on world issues, trying to provide solutions with common sense and logic.

I've had the privilege in the past few years of being on a financial innovation panel. This year, I was invited to sit on an unusual panel titled "Privatising the peace process: Market solutions to the Middle East Conflict". It inspired us to turn our attention to the role of markets in conflict resolution.

The remarkable economic growth seen by Northern Ireland, after the Good Friday agreement of 1994, is testimony to the economic benefits of peace. This "peace dividend" resulted in tourism in Northern Ireland rising 20% within a year, a drop in unemployment to the lowest levels in 14 years and £48 million in new investment ventures in the 6 months following the agreement. All parties have benefited, although there is still some way to go. Is it possible for markets to play a similar role as political agreement?

The peace privatization approach was extended by the panel to address decades of strife between the Palestinians and Israelis. Some might argue that the Israeli-Palestinian conflict is purely a political issue but the panel described the role for markets quite succinctly. By using financial resources, structures and technical knowledge to align the interests of the parties, resolve conflicts, and create jobs, the private sector has the capacity to bring peace and prosperity to the region. Glenn Yago, director of capital studies at the Milken Institute has made the point eloquently: "Increasingly, the stable engine of growth and peace will be entrepreneurs and managers in the new Middle East. Markets don't forgive political vanities of any extremist persuasion. Markets can mitigate the sharper edges of regional conflicts and discipline the peace process better than governments. Economic sovereignty and peace will ultimately be determined by economic growth and capital access, not real estate".[1]

We would like to take this one step further. The chances of economic prosperity in the region without environmental sustainability are remote. The region is characterized by high population density, severe constraints on arable land and depletion of freshwater resources. Furthermore, groundwater pollution from industrial and domestic waste, and chemicals from intensified agriculture, are major causes of concern.

---

[1] Glenn Yago. "Trade Jobs for Peace in the Middle East." *The Los Angeles Times*, 7 December 1998.

Bickering over scarce water resources is already a source of tension in the region. Consider this: the Yarqon River that meanders through the densely populated Dan region of Israel has its origins in Palestinian areas. This river is a source of recreation to the 1.5 million people who live close to it, and a source of economic activity. However, major stretches of the Yarqon are severely polluted. While there is a sewage treatment plant in the Palestinian town of Qalqilyah, it requires a major upgrade. While the Palestinians have no interest in investing in what could be essentially flushed out into the Mediterranean, the Israelis, concerned about effluents flowing through Tel-Aviv, have essentially blocked up the water flow. To add to the problem, Palestinian snipers during the Intifada shot at Israeli guards who visit the area to spray mosquito repellents.

Sadly, this situation is not an isolated one.

The Milken panel began with the Israelis and Palestinians each presenting their case for peace. But, in spite of its amicable nature, the political process seemed to be stalled. It now became clear why I had been invited to participate. It seemed obvious to me that one solution could be the creation of a regional water rights market in the Yarqon. We made the following case: Developing a market-based trading system for water rights can democratize the resource, creating consumer sovereignty through a system of individual bilateral trades. As with any other environmental market, such flexible mechanisms would reward water conservation efforts and foster innovation, while improving water quality.

A basic structure for the market is laid out below:

- Establish a neutral, transparent and publicly accountable body, possibly in the form of a special purpose company, to administer the trading programme.
- Establish a mutually acceptable cap on total water usage, perhaps by sector, and define an acceptable quality of water.
- Build fairness, with assurances that the water needs of families are addressed.
- Establish tools for monitoring and verification of water usage.

- Delineate individual water rights to the Palestinian people who live upstream.
- Make investments in effluent water treatment in Palestine to ensure the delivery of required water quality to buyers downstream.
- Create a system by which Israeli water users who live downstream can buy water rights that allow them to use a specific quantity of water of a defined quality, at a market determined price.

While the above structure provides the skeleton for a market-based system in Yarqon, several features need to be modified or added to fit the unique reality of the region. We have some ideas about how to solve many of the technical problems. This broad approach provides a framework in which the Palestinians and Israelis have an economic incentive to work together in their own self-interest. It provides an economic rationale for people torn apart to cooperate in a meaningful way to help preserve their common resources. The hope is that development of such markets, and the economic dividends they offer, will not just bean outcome of peace, but a precursor to peace. The political roadmap provides hope. The economic and environmental roadmap will help ensure this hope turns into reality on the ground.

This year's conference provided for many thought leaders to provide similar insights into problems that concern the entire world. A very special thank you goes to Michael Milken for orchestrating this brilliant conference, and to Mike Klowden for his leadership in organizing and implementing the event. The Milken Institute Global Conference is well on its way to becoming the North American equivalent of the WEF meetings held in Davos.

Authorship of this article is shared with Murali Kanakasabai, economist at the Chicago Climate Exchange. Special thanks go to Dr Glenn Yago of the Milken Institute for his helpful comments and suggestions. The authors wish to thank Michael Walsh for his assistance in preparation of this chapter.

Chapter 59

Verifying Emissions — Lessons from the CCX

July–August 2005

Any emissions trading system relies on three pillars: overall targets, registries to allow the transfer of allowances, and a process to verify participants' emissions. Now that the European Union (EU) Emissions Trading Scheme (ETS) has completed the allocation of allowances, and with progress under way on its registry systems, we felt it would be timely to share some of the lessons learnt in developing the verification process at the Chicago Climate Exchange (CCX).

The CCX is a voluntary exchange, which began trading in 2003. Its 33 full members have taken a legally binding commitment to reduce their greenhouse gas (GHG) emissions to 4% below the 1998–2001 average by 2006.

The verification process was designed around CCX rules for gathering and reporting emissions data. It is important to emphasize that the verification process must not only ensure accuracy, but also minimize both out-of-pocket costs and the cost of management time. Lack of attention to this point could impose significant and unnecessary costs on regulated entities.

The National Association of Securities Dealers (NASD) has been given the responsibility of receiving and verifying the emission reports of all CCX members for accuracy and completeness — for the 1998–2001 baseline period through the end of the pilot program in 2006. NASD is the world's leading private sector provider of financial regulatory services, and its involvement lends transparency and rigor to CCX members' emissions verification.

CCX and NASD completed the first annual "'true-up" of members' annual emissions and the reduction targets in November 2004, for calendar year 2003, and announced the results of the Conditional Compliance True-up for calendar year 2004 in June of this year. What follows is a description of the CCX-NASD verification process.

The NASD performs an analysis of each CCX member's GHG emissions data for the period 1998–2001 to verify the reported baseline, and verifies each member's subsequent emission reports to ensure compliance with the CCX Emission Reduction Schedule. This process is designed to determine whether data submitted are consistent with actual emissions claimed by the member, based on a review of actual proofs of energy usage or purchase.

CCX members must submit baseline and annual emission report data to NASD for verification according to the following procedures.

Each member must:

- Complete a baseline initiation questionnaire, which will assist the member in summarizing its emissions profile;
- Apply appropriate emission factors, derived from CCX rules, to quantify emissions;
- Use the standard Emission Reporting Form to document total emissions, broken down by emission source, location and year; and
- Provide internally generated worksheets and/or spreadsheets that highlight fuel consumption or other data used in calculating emissions, broken down by location, division, year and source in terms of its raw unit of measure. A corporate officer of the firm must attest to the content of the full report.

The NASD then conducts an initial review. NASD staff will contact the member to discuss the full report and the nature of its components (i.e., number of energy sources per facility) and will seek to determine the types of external data available to substantiate the emissions claims. Once the initial review is complete, the NASD determines a sample size from among the submissions to be analyzed for compliance with CCX rules. The NASD will then issue a request, in writing, to the member, for third-party proofs to support the sampled elements.

The member provides the data for the sample. The NASD compares the sample data and supporting worksheets against the proofs.

An NASD proprietary sampling tool is used to draw a representative test sample from the overall population. This tool creates a review sample of size and distribution necessary to generate projections about the accuracy of the data in the total detection population at a 95% confidence level. These projections and the staff's ability to identify and isolate the root causes of the noted discrepancies provide the basis for generalizations about the accuracy of the member's emission reports.

Upon completion of the emissions verification, NASD provides feedback to the member identifying specific discrepancies or errors in the original report. This communication allows the member to address areas of concern identified by NASD staff and, where appropriate, amend the emission statements. Based on the findings of the NASD's written report, the CCX Environmental Compliance Committee, composed of CCX member representatives, makes the final determination regarding the accuracy and the registration of the emissions claim. If a member's actual emissions have not fallen annually by 1% below the baseline, that member must purchase "Carbon Financial Instruments" on the CCX trading platform.

As a result of completing the first annual true-up and beginning the second, the CCX members and NASD have improved the efficiency of verification while reducing costs to members, and the rigorous review is viewed by many as a highlight of the CCX pilot program. The first annual true-up highlighted strengths and weaknesses in the design of the verification process resulting from efforts to maintain a high level of verification accuracy while reducing costs. Exchange participants have modified internal procedures to improve performance and reporting and verification efficiency since then. The procedure has by no means been perfected, but it has been improved through practical experience. Some of the lessons learned include:

- Make the process transparent — all stakeholders must have a thorough understanding of the requirements and methodologies for reporting and verification;
- Prepare the back office — regulated entities should coordinate internal finance, trading, accounting, tax, and legal departments to ensure the reporting requirements are met;
- Energy and emissions data management is performed most efficiently when it is centralized;
- Reliance on third-party support data is not always practical — internal records will need sufficient detail to establish source credibility;
- Participants need to be conscious of maintaining adequate records to support baseline and annual calculations, including third-party records to support annual emissions;
- Participants need to review and familiarize themselves with the data they send to verifiers before it is sent; and
- Start as soon as possible.

CCX members have noticed significant improvements in their internal reporting procedures this year, and NASD has observed major improvements in the verification functions. Members' energy use and purchase tracking systems are now in place, and the verifier is familiar with the clients and their data sets.

A fragmented and opaque verifier approval process, in which each EU member state has to examine and approve the acceptable emissions verifiers, will only amplify the difficulties that will be encountered by regulated entities. The ETS dwarfs the CCX — involving the verification of more than 12,000 sites as opposed to approximately 460 in the CCX — but we believe some of the lessons learned from our experience have relevance for the EU. The cost-minimizing procedural improvements we've realized as a result of experience should serve to support the suggestion that participants in the EU ETS begin to go through the motions of reporting and verification in practice as soon as possible.

This article was coauthored by Claire M Jahns. We would like to thank Dr. Murali Kanakasabai for his assistance in the preparation of this article.

Chapter 60

Beyond Kyoto: Some Thoughts on the Past, Present, and Future

September 2005

> "A thousand-mile journey always starts with the first step".
> —Lao Tse, Chinese Philosopher, 6th century BC

> "We cannot cross the sea merely by staring at the water".
> —Rabindranath Tagore, Indian thinker and Nobel Prize winner

It's been a long journey, spanning more than a dozen years and four continents. The first steps were taken in Rio de Janeiro. Five years later, an international treaty emerged in Kyoto. Six years later, the first rules-based, multisectoral marketplace began in Chicago and a mere two years later the European Union (EU) Emissions Trading System (ETS) got started. This pilot has been extraordinarily successful in a short time but the future task of successfully implementing the Kyoto Protocol is formidable. The post-Kyoto period presents an even greater set of challenges. But all of these hurdles look less daunting in view of our experiences over the past 13 years.

In 1992, during the Earth Summit, we presented a paper on a framework for a global emission trading system at a "side show" in a tent overlooking the beautiful beaches of Rio; the idea was received with great skepticism. Concern over climate change was limited to a few scientists and environmentalists. The concept of emissions trading was but a theoretical chapter in economics textbooks.

Fifteen years later, the situation is quite different. From corporate leaders to academicians to the common person, we seem to be taking a more serious look at global warming. Market-based mechanisms such as emissions trading have become widely accepted as a cost-effective method for addressing climate change and other environmental concerns. Environmental issues are fast moving out of the confines of corporate EH&S departments into the realm of corporate financial strategy.

The pace of this transformation has left few unaffected: cities managing their greenhouse gas (GHG) emissions; equity and debt analysts paying close attention to climate liability; peasants in Cambodia exploring the possibility of linking to the global GHG marketplace.

However, the skeptics are still around. They question the effectiveness of climate action without the big three: the United States, China, and India. They question the survival of Kyoto after 2012. They cite lack of harmonization in international climate action and argue that there is little direction and much uncertainty on a post-2012 framework. They complain about too many "hot air" reductions and a lack of infrastructure for the Clean Development Mechanism (CDM) to be able to take off.

In this article, we would like to address some of these concerns by attempting to look at what lies ahead. By no means is this a prediction of future events or a market forecast. We, like everyone else, have no crystal ball to predict the future. This is merely a vision statement that this student of markets would like to share with you. We begin by looking at our journey thus far.

The Road So Far

The short history of global climate efforts paints a positive picture of things to come. Last February, the Kyoto Protocol entered into force, signaling that the international community was serious about climate change. In Europe, the start of the EU ETS has given a boost to the global efforts to manage climate change.

Australia, Japan, and Canada also seem to be aware of the need for action. The Australian states are looking into setting up trading schemes, without federal support. Canada recently released a proposal for honoring its Kyoto targets that include provisions for offsets projects. Japan has plans to first reduce emissions domestically, then invest in sinks through CDM and Joint Implementation (JI).

In the United States, a wide variety of policy initiatives are evolving. The Regional Greenhouse Gas Initiative (RGGI), organized by nine northeastern states, and climate proposals by Washington, Oregon, and California, are good examples. At the federal level, congressional interest in climate change action has been on the rise, as indicated by a significant increase in the number of climate related legislative bills over the years in Congress. The US private sector is also showing greater sensitivity to climate change. Major corporations, including recently General Electric, have announced intentions to manage their GHG emissions.

The CDM process, though painfully slow and plagued by bureaucratic hurdles, is making progress. Only 15 projects have been so far registered, mostly confined to landfill gas, renewable energy, and small-scale hydroelectric projects. However, the CDM Executive Board seems to have made progress in other areas. Notably, the first version of the CDM registry is now operational and progress is being made on linking this with the International Transaction Log.

Private interest in the marketplace has also been tremendous. The Chicago Climate Exchange (CCX), a voluntary program for GHG reduction and trading in North America, has seen membership rise from 16 founding members to more than 100 in less than two years. Recently, two big Brazilian corporations, which are nonbinding members under Kyoto, have signed up to take on the binding CCX emissions reduction commitment. This is one case that demonstrates that private action against climate change knows no geographic or regulatory boundaries.

Our analysis of the story up to this point has been one of cautious optimism. The market is surely still in its evolutionary stages but the "baby" is growing fast and healthy.

The Road Ahead

So where do we go from here? We think the future state of climate action will be based on a well-integrated plurilateral system. The major components will likely be:

- regional trading systems;
- the CDM; and
- voluntary markets.

Adding to these important variables in the form of participation from China, India, and the United States; the potential role of carbon sinks, especially from forestry and agriculture, and we may have the essential components for our analysis.

It is inevitable that the numerous regional trading initiatives will move towards some form of harmonization and uniformity to reap the full benefits of a globalized environmental market. This is necessary for the success of the carbon market — both from a financial viewpoint and as an environmental policy. We are already seeing early signs of harmonization in, for example, procedures and quantification methods, as indicated by the GHG Protocol. The RGGI system will potentially be open to EU ETS and Kyoto allowances. Many corporations, which are increasingly members of multiple climate initiatives, will serve as catalysts to this convergence.

The CDM has tremendous potential, but there is need to simplify the process. The mechanism is an important vehicle for forging political consensus between the industrialized and developing countries, thereby expanding the comprehensiveness of the Kyoto Protocol. As early as 1998, we shared with the public our suggestions for a "simplified" CDM at the annual UN climate change meeting, in Buenos Aires.

In that paper, we discussed the need for standardization and the development of a rules-based CDM system. This would help reduce transaction costs associated with establishing emission baselines and project additionality on a nonstandardized, project-by-project basis, thereby promoting sustainable development.

Here it is important to note that the pace of CDM reform has huge implications for the cost of compliance. In fact, a failure to address this could undermine the EU ETS and the Protocol itself by sending a signal that compliance costs will be too high to be practical. Eventually, the CDM process will have to respond to market demand, and standardization and simplification is expected to occur.

Meanwhile, the voluntary markets provide opportunities to link regulated and unregulated sectors of the global carbon marketplace. There is a growing interest among entities unregulated by Kyoto to participate in some form of climate action. These constituents, including numerous cities, office-based organizations and universities, are redefining their roles by taking a proactive stance with respect to climate change. A global trading regime among such voluntary entities has tremendous potential to be viable on its own.

China, India, and the United States

There is also a great deal of debate about the United States, China, and India participating in a binding form of emissions reductions. The United States has rejected entry into any agreement that excludes China and India. However, despite the fact that these latter face significant risks from climate change, they have argued on moral and ethical grounds against taking reduction targets. China and India base their exclusion on the carefully developed principle of common but differentiated responsibility included in the UN Framework Convention on Climate Change (which spawned Kyoto) and the reality that per capita emissions are far below those in the developed world.

Sadly, the fact remains that the sheer size of US emissions (accounting for about 23% of the global total) and tremendous economic growth in China and India, fueled by coal, will undermine any efforts by the rest of the world. The uncertainty of United States, Chinese, and Indian participation in global climate action is imposing considerable costs to the shape of future climate policy.

Assuming that the trigger point for US participation is entry by China and India, we focus our attention on the latter two. The principles of equity and fairness are useful guideposts. Economic and environmental indicators in these two nations provide a good starting point. The facts speak for themselves. China and India account for 14% and 5.6% of global GHG emissions respectively. Rapid increases in electrification, burgeoning transportation sectors and rising industrial production, primarily based upon fossil fuels, all point to higher GHG emissions from emerging Asia.

China and India are also the fastest growing economies in the world today. The figure below indicates China will surpass the United States as the world's largest emitter in 2014. India, on the other hand, having surpassed Germany's emissions in 1998, is expected to account for 6.8% of global emissions in 2014. China's and India's shares of world GDP in 2014 are expected to be 17% and 9%, respectively. The issue of equity and fairness post-2012 may dictate that these countries take some responsibility for their emissions.

Finally, we turn to the inclusion of a broad-based set of carbon sinks, especially from forest and agricultural sectors. There has been a quiet transformation in these sectors over recent decades. From being just providers of food, fiber, and wood, parts of agriculture and forestry have redefined their roles as providers of environmental goods and other multifunctional benefits. Parallel developments in international trade agreements such as those in the World Trade Organization necessitate reductions in domestic commodity price support policies. The desire to provide income support and meet environmental goals is likely to increase the level of coordination between these two societal objectives.

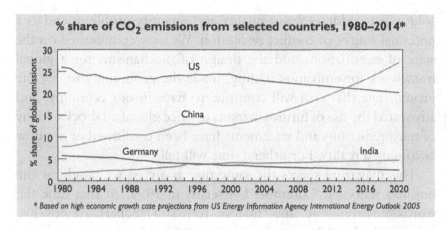

% share of CO$_2$ emissions from selected countries, 1980–2014*

* Based on high economic growth case projections from US Energy Information Agency International Energy Outlook 2005

This opens great opportunities for agriculture and forestry to participate in carbon trading. For example, the total carbon sequestration from US crop land alone is estimated to be around 75 million–208 million tons of carbon annually, valued at $1 billion–3 billion at current carbon prices. On the other hand, total commodity subsidies in 2003 were in the order of $11.5 billion. An agricultural carbon sequestration program could therefore provide for 10%–27% of all expenditures on commodity subsidies. The vision is clear. The challenge of global warming dictates a new direction to the way farming has been practiced.

Conclusion

Many analysts feel that the current GHG market is merely at the beginning of what could be the biggest financial market in the world. I am as excited about this development as I was when I was involved with the birth of financial futures in the 1970s. There is no doubt that the idea is still new and the challenges immense. But I believe we know our destination and this will lead to continued growth in the environmental marketplace.

It is hard to believe it has been 6 years since we started to write this column. In these pages we have covered topics ranging from the rise of sustainability indexes to the potential use of market-based solutions to address water quality and quantity problems and as a potential source of conflict resolution. We have commented on the state of negotiations and the design of mechanisms for a global framework for emissions trading; made the economic case for the prominence that coal will continue to have in our economy; and advocated the use of futures markets to price global oil shocks. Many of our predictions and statements have been confirmed or are now becoming a reality. For others, time will tell.

This magazine shares the same title as a class we taught at the business school at Columbia University in 1991. At that time the words "environment" and "finance' were still far apart. We now live in a world where they are forever intertwined."

Thank you to Murali Kanakasabai, Claire Jahns, and Rafael Marques for their assistance in the preparation of this article. I would like to thank the staff of the CCX for their intellectual input and support over the past six years and all the individuals from business and academia who have provided their expertise in our articles. Many thanks to Graham Cooper for the invitation to share our thoughts with the readers. Special thanks to my wife Ellen, my children, and grandchildren for their support throughout this journey. To all of the readers of Environmental Finance *who have supported us over the past six years, "au revoir mes amis" and "hasta luego".*

Chapter 61

What a Difference 10 Years Make

October 2009

> For 5 years, from 1999 to 2004, Richard Sandor wrote a monthly
> column in *Environmental Finance* — while spending his spare time
> building the world's predominant environmental exchange com-
> pany. Here, he reviews its development and looks forward to the
> future of — environmental markets

It started 10 years ago, with a grant to develop a pilot program
that would apply financial innovation to advance environmental and
economic goals. It has resulted today in a cap-and-trade system in
the United States with an annual baseline of 600 million tons of
carbon dioxide and cumulative cuts of more than 400 million tons.
This market — created by the Chicago Climate Exchange (CCX) —
compares with a 2 billion ton baseline in the European Union's
(EU) Emissions Trading Scheme.

The road from there to here is one that has been paved by the
early actions of forward-thinking businesses; a rules-based, transparent, and regulated market; and innovation.

Along the way, everything that could have gone wrong sure
enough did: the United States pulled out of the Kyoto Protocol, the tech bubble burst, September 11 changed the world,
Enron wreaked havoc on energy markets and a recession hit the
United States.

But what we thought we knew and set out to show in 1999 was
that if you could monitor and verify emissions, you could establish a
voluntary market, and you could reduce greenhouse gases in a cost-
effective way. We brought together 30 companies from the power

industry, forestry, and agriculture and we dared them to set legally binding and ambitious emission reduction goals. We took on the technical infrastructure challenges and our staff and our visionary members built a market.

Fast forward to 2009: CCX membership now includes 11% of the Fortune 100 companies, and 22% of the public power sector of the United States. We also have two US states, eight cities, and numerous banks and liquidity providers on board.

Following the launch of the CCX in 2003, we launched the Chicago Climate Futures Exchange (CCFE) in 2004. The CCFE is regulated by the Commodity Futures Trading Commission, and offers standardized, cleared futures and options contracts for more than 20 environmental products. In the United States, a robust voluntary market — with an industrial emissions baseline larger than the entire emissions of Germany — has now been joined by regionally mandated markets. The Regional Greenhouse Gas Initiative (RGGI) is a group of 10 states in the northeast that banded together to establish a CO_2 cap-and-trade system for electricity companies. Since the RGGI market launched in January of this year, open interest is up 275% on CCFE.

In a real world example of how carbon may trade under a federal mandate in the United States, CCFE also lists a contract called the CFI-US which requires, starting in 2011, delivery of mandatory federal CO_2 emissions allowances. In the event that legislation has not yet passed, the contract would require delivery of another mandated allowance, such as a RGGI allowance. Open interest in CCFE's CFI-US futures contract has now surpassed 1 million tons.

The 21st Century Will be Driven by the Commoditization of Air and Water

Globally, we have expanded over the past 10 years under the umbrella of Climate Exchange Plc, a publicly traded company on the London stock market. In 2004, we launched the European Climate Exchange which is now the leading exchange in the EU

Emission Trading Scheme. Last year, we entered into a joint venture with China National Petroleum Corporation (CNPC) and the City of Tianjin to establish the Tianjin Climate Exchange — the first emissions trading system in China. We recently partnered with People's Bank of China and CNPC to establish a new center — the China-US Low Carbon Finance and Development Research Center — that will conduct research on financing of low-carbon initiatives, including large-scale demonstrations of market-based methods for addressing environmental challenges in China.

So, what of the next decade? In the United States, the national discussion on how to confront climate change, and the recognition that a market mechanism and a price signal will play an integral part in that solution, continues at full throttle. The Senate is taking up consideration of a bill this autumn following passage of the American Clean Energy and Security Act by the House of Representatives this summer. Where this process ends up will have great implications for the market going forward.

But what's also clear is that there is an inexorable trend here. Interest is growing globally in carbon markets as a way to achieve better strategic management of energy costs, new products and new sources of revenue and create jobs and alleviate poverty. Going forward, I see this developing on what I call a "pluri-lateral" basis. There will be markets in different pockets of the world linked by similar contracts — much as with crude oil today or as we saw with cotton in the 19th century.

There is an interesting story to be told looking back through the 20th century at the drivers of wealth creation. We saw manufacturing in the 1970s as well as inflationary pressures that led to financial innovation with interest rate hedging products and mortgage instruments. In the 1980s, there was commoditization of interest rates and asset liability management. In the 1990s, it was the commoditization of information.

Looking forward, I think the 21st century will be driven by the commoditization of the two most important resources on the planet: air and water.

We've seen a strong, growing market in carbon. In addition, as water shortages — both in quality and quantity — grow around the world, new solutions will increasingly be needed to meet demand and curtail waste. The opportunities for using market innovations to address other resource scarcity also continue to develop.

While each country has unique characteristics that come with different demands and needs, what seems to be clear across the board is the importance market mechanisms will play in meeting those demands. The results — cleaner air and water, more abundant resources, the creation of "green" jobs — are all things that will continue to provide opportunities and benefits around the world.

Listing of Articles by Subject

EU Emissions Trading Scheme